# Interlibrary Loan

# Interlibrary Loan
## Theory and Management

**Lois C. Gilmer**

1994
LIBRARIES UNLIMITED, INC.
Englewood, Colorado

*For my husband, Marshall, who helped me prove*
*the interlibrary loan statement:*
*Shared poverty does not produce wealth.*

LIBRARIES UNLIMITED, INC.
P.O. Box 6633
Englewood, CO 80155-6633
1-800-237-6124


Louisa M. Griffin, Project Editor
Pamela J. Getchell, Design and Layout
Diane Hess, Copy Editor
Laura Taylor, Proofreader

---

**Library of Congress Cataloging-in-Publication Data**

Gilmer, Lois C.
    Interlibrary loan : theory and management / Lois C. Gilmer.
    xviii, 264 p. 17x25 cm.
    Includes bibliographical references and index.
    ISBN 0-87287-947-X
    1. Interlibrary loans--United States. I. Title.
Z713.5.U6G55    1994
025.6'2'0973--dc20                                          93-35855
                                                            CIP

# Contents

# List of Acronyms

| | |
|---|---|
| AAP | Association of American Publishers |
| ACRL | Association of College and Research Libraries |
| AIM | Automation of Interlending by Microcomputer |
| ALA | American Library Association |
| AMIGOS | (a multistate regional auxiliary enterprise network) |
| ARL | Association of Research Libraries |
| ARLCAUSE | (the professional association for the management of information technology in higher education) |
| ARPANET | Advanced Research Projects Agency Network (also called DARPA) |
| BACS | Bibliographic Access and Control System (of Washington University) |
| BALLOTS | Bibliographic Automation of Large Library Operations Using a Time-Sharing System |
| BITNET | Because It's Time NETwork |
| BLDSC | British Library Document Supply Centre |
| BNB | British National Bibliography |
| CAPCON | Capitol Consortium |
| CARL | Colorado Alliance of Research Libraries |
| CCC | Copyright Clearance Center |
| CLASS | Cooperative Library Authority for Systems and Services |
| COM | computer output microfilm |
| CONSER | the CONservation of SERials project |
| CONTU | National Commission on New Technological Uses of Copyrighted Works |
| CRL | Center for Research Libraries |
| DARPA | Defense Advanced Research Projects Agency (also called ARPANET) |
| DOCLINE | (National Library of Medicine's ILL software) |
| DTW | document-transmission workstation |
| EDDS | Electronic Document Delivery Service |

| | |
|---|---|
| EDUCOM | (a nonprofit consortium of colleges, universities, and other institutions involved with campus information networking) |
| E-mail | electronic mail |
| EPIC | (online service used by OCLC) |
| ERIC | Educational Resources Information Center |
| ESTC | Eighteenth Century Short Title Catalog |
| FAUL | Five Associated University Libraries |
| FEDLINK | Federal Library Network |
| FETCH | (the LC on-line system of transmission) |
| F.I.L.L.S. | Fast Interlibrary Loans and Statistics |
| FLAN | floppy disk local-area network |
| FLIN | Florida Library Information Network |
| GTEL | Georgia Tech Electronic Library |
| IDS | Interlibrary Delivery Service |
| IFLA | International Federation of Library Associations |
| I-LITE | Iowa Library Information Teletype Exchange |
| ILL | interlibrary loan |
| ILLINET | Illinois Library and Information Network |
| ILLRKS | Interlibrary Loan Record Keeping System |
| InCOLSA | Indiana Cooperative Library Services Authority |
| ISDN | Integrated Services Digital Network |
| ISN | Information Systems Network |
| ITPS | Integrated Technical Processing System |
| KIC | Kansas Information Circuit |
| LANs | local-area networks |
| LASER | London and South Eastern Library Region |
| LC | Library of Congress |
| LCPC | *Library of Congress Catalog of Printed Cards* |
| LOCIS | Library of Congress Information System |
| LSCA | Library Services and Construction Act |
| LSP | Linked Systems Project |
| MARC | machine-readable cataloging |

| | |
|---|---|
| MDS | Medical Documentation Service |
| METRO | New York Metropolitan Reference and Research Library Agency |
| MIDLNET | Midwest Region Library Network |
| MILNET | (military-use component of ARPANET) |
| MINITEX | Minnesota Interlibrary Telecommunications Exchange |
| MUMS | Multiple Use MARC System |
| NAC | Network Advisory Committee |
| NCLIS | National Commission on Libraries and Information Sciences |
| NCR | no carbon required |
| NELINET | New England Library Information Network |
| NOTIS | (a Northwestern University software program) |
| NREN | National Research and Education Network |
| NSFNET | National Science Foundation Network |
| NST | *New Serials Titles* |
| NTIS | National Technical Information Service |
| NUC | *National Union Catalog* |
| NYSILL | New York State Inter-library Loan Network |
| OCLC | Online Computer Library Center |
| OCTANET | (a regional ILL loan system) |
| OhioLINK | Ohio Library and Information Network |
| OHIONET | Ohio Network |
| OPAC | online public-access catalog |
| OSI | Open Systems Interconnection |
| PALINET | Pennsylvania Area Library Network |
| PHILNET | (a combination of PHILSOM and OCTANET) |
| PHILSOM | Periodical Holdings in Libraries of Schools of Medicine |
| RARE | Rochester Area Resource Exchange |
| RBBS | Remote Bulletin Board System |
| RLG | Research Library Group |
| RLIN | Research Libraries Information Network |

| | |
|---|---|
| SCIPIO | Sales Catalog Index Project Input On-Line |
| SCORPIO | Subject-Content-Oriented Retriever for Processing Information On-Line |
| SEFLIN | Southeast Florida Library Information Network |
| SLA | Special Libraries Association |
| SOLINET | Southeastern Library Network |
| SULAN | State University Library Automation Network |
| SULAN/LINKWAY | (a SULAN hypermedia software product) |
| TALINET | Telefax Library Information Network |
| telex | Teleprinter Exchange Service |
| TIE | Texas Information Exchange |
| TOM | Text on Microfiche |
| TWX | Teletypewriter Exchange Service |
| UCI | University of California at Irvine |
| ULS | *Union List of Serials* |
| UTLAS | University of Toronto Library Automation Center |
| WATS | Wide Area Telecommunications Service |
| WILS | Wisconsin Interlibrary Loan Service |
| WIPO | World Intellectual Property Organization |
| WLN | Western Library Network (formerly Washington Library Network) |

# List of Illustrations

# Acknowledgments

The author is indebted beyond repayment to Jane Maddan, who typed the manuscript for this book and who kept insisting, "Yes, we will meet our deadline." Joy Lawson, Kelly Nabors, and Mike Thomas assisted with various aspects of the work. Without their assistance and support, the project would have surely faltered.

James D. Smith added the author's stack of interlibrary loans to his work load, as did the circulation and interlibrary loan staff members at the University of West Florida in Pensacola. Their help, and the assistance rendered by Dr. Mike Bundrick of the Mathematics and Statistics Institute at the university for programming the data from the interlibrary loan survey, are very much appreciated.

Interlibrary loan librarians everywhere deserve much of the credit for this book. They inspired it and, indeed, helped write it through their own contributions to the professional literature, through their participation in the author's survey, and through their willingness to share their library materials. Special permission to use various forms, statements, and contracts has been granted by individual librarians, networks, and by the American Library Association and the International Federation of Library Associations and Institutions.

# Introduction

As purchasing power in libraries declines, cooperative resource sharing receives increased attention. Resource sharing has at least three aspects—interlibrary loans (ILLs), intralibrary loans between a library and its branches, and reciprocal borrowing.

Interlibrary loan is the primary focus of this book. Interlibrary loan means one library lending its materials to another library—not the traditional patron/library relationship, but transactions between libraries. A library may loan the material itself, or it may send copies.

A long history, both nationally and internationally, precedes our present-day routine of borrowing back and forth made possible by modern technology. Even though interlibrary loan activity entered the library picture early, it was hampered by lack of holdings information, lack of standardized codes, demand spread over a small number of large libraries, and sometimes a reluctance to share. Standardization, along with the ability to share holdings information and to speed up the delivery of interlibrary loan materials, has revolutionized the process.

Yet, interlibrary loan volume is, for most libraries, very small in comparison to total circulation. Interlibrary loan is very labor intensive, and it is costly as well. Its original intent was to provide specialized materials to those in pursuit of scholarly research; interlibrary loan service has since become a service to the general populace.

In no other area of the library has automation had an influence more than on the interlibrary loan unit, although usually its effect on interlibrary loan has been the by-product of some other library service. Development of the MARC (machine-readable cataloging) by the Library of Congress was intended to standardize and share cataloging data, but it also allowed libraries to produce machine-readable bibliographic databases. Then computer networks allowed libraries to share their databases, making available not only cataloging data but holdings data, too.

Automation of other library operations—acquisitions, circulation, and interlibrary loan—followed and has changed organizational and staffing patterns in libraries. On-line public catalogs and local area networks (LANs) provide quick access to bibliographic information not only in the library, but at home, too.

In order to portray as accurate a picture of interlibrary loan as possible, the author conducted a nationwide survey of multitype libraries (academic, public, special, school district). A stratified random sample was chosen from listings in the *American Library Directory*. Simple frequencies were compiled, and the results have been reported throughout the body of this work.

Many other surveys and practical experiences of interlibrary loan librarians appear in the professional literature. Some of them have been documented in this work to try to present a balance of theory and practical management techniques. It is believed that such a work is needed to help train librarians for the very special job of interlibrary loan librarian. Even though interlibrary loan is considered a vital link in sharing resources between libraries, it is more often learned through conversation, trial and error, reading, on-the-job training, or workshops, rather than through instruction in library school. Perhaps this work will not only be a part of the professional library of interlibrary loan librarians, but also make the suggested reading list of library schools.

# chapter 1
# Historical Overview

Interlibrary loan (ILL) activity in the Western world can be traced to the eighth century.[1] In the seventeenth century Nicolas Claude Fabri de Pieresc tried to establish an international system of lending by arranging loan transactions between the Royal Library in Paris and the Vatican and Barberini libraries in Rome.[2] Gabriel Naude wrote about the principle of interlibrary cooperation in his book, *Avis pour Dresser une Bibliothèque*, first published in 1627: "By this means [a catalog] one may sometimes serve and please a friend, when one cannot provide him the book he requires, by directing him to the place where he may find a copy, as may easily be done with the assistance of these catalogues."[3]

To fully appreciate the development of interlibrary loan activity, one needs to have some knowledge of the history of library development itself, because the idea of sharing threads its way throughout. Quite naturally, borrowing from library to library began with some of the oldest libraries and filtered downward from the largest libraries.

In all library matters, not just in interlibrary loan, Italy stood in the front rank, along with France and England, until after the middle of the seventeenth century, when it slipped into the background. The Vatican Library, the library of the Roman Catholic church, founded in 1447, houses one of the world's most important collections of early manuscripts and books. The Bibliothèque Nationale, located in Paris, is the national library of France. In 1536, the king ordered that one copy of every book printed in France be deposited there.

The British Museum was opened in 1759. It was meant to provide free access, but that access was made difficult by all sorts of formalities. Its natural history collection formed the most important part of its holdings, so it was, indeed, more of a museum than a library. The Department of Printed Books served as the national library of Great Britain.

Other national libraries were also formed. Our own Library of Congress (LC) was established by the U.S. Congress in 1800. The Swiss National Library at Bern was founded in 1895. The National Central Library in Great Britain was active in the ILL movement. The Leningrad Public Library has made tremendous strides since the revolution.[4]

The United States participated in international interlibrary loan very early in the ILL movement in the United States. In 1906, the German government made overtures to the government of the United States concerning international loans of manuscript and printed material. The Library of Congress volunteered to cooperate with national libraries of other countries.[5]

1

## Library Development in the United States

In her *Introduction to Librarianship*, Jean Key Gates devotes several excellent chapters to the development of libraries in the United States. She writes that among the valued possessions brought by the early American settlers were libraries, and although the libraries were private, they were often shared with friends and neighbors. The size of the libraries varied from the two books said to be owned by Captain John Smith to the 1,000+ volumes owned by John Winthrop, Jr., governor of Connecticut. Even though a printing press began operating in Massachusetts in 1639, books continued to be imported for many generations. The importance of learning to the colonists can be further documented by their early efforts to establish colleges, all containing books and libraries. Provisions for what is called the first public library in the colonies were made by Captain Robert Keayne in his will of 1655 or 1656. The resulting building served the people of Boston for almost a century. During prerevolutionary times, the social library, which grew out of the social club idea, flourished, but because of the war, the libraries suffered; some were lost, and others were forced to suspend operations during the war.

After the American Revolution, the growth of the social library was greatly accelerated, and new forms appeared. Some were organized for a particular purpose, such as the athenaeum (reading room); others were designed to meet the special needs or reading interests of a particular clientele, such as mechanics' apprentices, mercantile clerks, factory and mill workers, and members of the Young Men's Christian Association.

The first attempts to open circulating libraries in the colonies—in 1762 and in 1765—did not meet with much success. Following the Revolution, however, the circulating libraries, designed to provide popular reading materials, operated successfully in connection with bookshops, general stores, and other kinds of shops, as business enterprises.

A developing sense of nationalism followed the Revolution. That, along with the building of towns and cities, interest in education, and the accumulation of great wealth, was accompanied by the establishment of many libraries. Even though the nation's library, the Library of Congress, was authorized in 1800, it was not until 1876 that every state and territory had a governmental library. Meanwhile, in 1827, Governor De Witt Clinton of New York recommended the formation of school-district libraries.

Free town libraries date from Captain Robert Keayne's gift to Boston in the mid-seventeenth century. Three endowed libraries—the Astor, the Lenox, and the Tilden Trust—were consolidated in 1895 to form the New York Public Library. Other endowed libraries were the Peabody Institute of Baltimore; the Newberry Library and the John Crerar Library, both in Chicago; the Huntington Library in San Marino, California; and the Pierpont Morgan Library in New York City. City libraries, during the latter part of the nineteenth century, were funded throughout the country by Andrew Carnegie.[6]

## Interlibrary Loan in the United States

The idea of positive extension of loans outside libraries and among libraries did not blossom, because books were scarce; but the idea persisted and took firm root in our country and elsewhere as soon as the times were right. In 1849, in response to a questionnaire from Charles C. Jewett, librarian of the Smithsonian Institution, 14 libraries reported loans to "persons at a distance."[7]

Based on Naude's ideas for interlibrary cooperation, Jewett had by 1850 formulated a plan for a universal catalog.[8] In 1853 he and a group of 82 delegates met to discuss common library problems at a conference in New York.

It was not until 1876, however, that the idea of lending books between libraries in the United States was suggested by Samuel S. Green, director of the Worcester Free Public Library. He has been called the professional forefather of interlibrary loan in this country, even though the idea, he freely admitted, was transplanted. In the very first number of the *Library Journal* appears a letter from him titled "The Lending of Books to One Another by Libraries." He says, "I am informed that a plan of this kind is in operation in Europe and that in many places it is easy to get through the local library books belonging to libraries in distant countries." Then, "Perhaps the matter is worthy of the consideration of the Conference of Libraries in Philadelphia."[9] This willingness on the part of Green, William Poole, author of *Poole's Index to Periodical Literature*, Jewett, and others to work together was very evident at the first conference of the American Library Association (ALA), which was held in 1876. Only the idea of a universal catalog was addressed at the meeting, however.

In 1891, when Green became president of the ALA, he again referred to the question of interlibrary loan, naming some of the libraries in the country that had adopted his idea.[10] At the ALA Conference in 1898, a paper by Green was read in which he presented his experiences of 20 years in borrowing from and lending books to other libraries. He suggested that interlibrary loan should be expanded, with small libraries lending to one another and small libraries borrowing from large libraries.[11]

A proposal that libraries enter into agreement to furnish books to each other was advanced in 1892 by Bunford Samuel of the Ridgway Library in Philadelphia. The editors of the *Library Journal*, commenting on this proposal, remarked that such interlibrary lending was not "unexampled" and cited frequent lendings of this kind between Harvard College and the Boston Athenaeum.[12]

Ernest C. Richardson, librarian of Princeton University, suggested, in 1899, a national lending library.[13] That same year, as chairman of the College and Reference Section of the ALA, he delivered a paper in which he pointed out three impediments to research in America: 1) many works were not in North American libraries (3,160 of the 8,600 titles listed in *Catalogue of Scientific Periodicals*, for example), 2) there were difficulties in locating titles held in libraries, and 3) traveling to libraries was expensive. He called for the development of union catalogs, rationalization of collections, and interlibrary loan, all ideally served by a national lending library.

He concluded his paper by bringing up two new issues. They were sending books by mail and quieting fears of book dealers who might feel threatened by an increasing volume of ILLs.[14]

In his presidential address of 1905, Richardson again urged cooperation.[15] He was concerned about the unnecessary duplication of periodicals. He also visualized a central national library in Washington, with branches in New Orleans, San Francisco, Chicago, and New York. He predicted that with the principle of lending well established, cooperation in specialization and cataloging would receive new impetus.[16]

By 1915 interlendings had increased to the point that the ALA found it necessary to begin work on the first of its codes of regulations. The cooperative movement among libraries, however, was seen in different ways in the nineteenth and twentieth centuries. Pioneers were, for the most part, interested in bibliographic description. Resource sharing became a by-product, as it was assumed that once material was described and made widely available, delivery would not be much of a problem. After 1876, with the establishment of the ALA and the introduction on a wide scale of Melvil Dewey's classification scheme, cooperative efforts abounded.[17] Dewey himself was involved in interlibrary lending as evidenced in his writings in the *Library Journal*. He said, "The last few years have witnessed a great change in the rules of many of our best libraries. Interlibrary loans which were a little while ago almost unknown are now of daily occurrence." He warned against abuse of the system and mentioned the disadvantages: the extra trouble involved in processing requests, exposure of the book to injury, and that a book borrowed is apt to be wanted at the lending library. He felt that these disadvantages were not of great weight if the borrowing library was sure of the need for the request and if packing was careful. "As yet I have had to recall but one book needed locally while on loan and that was when I had yielded to an unreasonable request for a very recent periodical."[18]

The first list of indexed periodical articles, which grew into the famous *Poole's Index to Periodical Literature*, was published in 1847. When the Library of Congress began printing library catalog cards in 1901, the mechanism for interlibrary cooperation was set in place, for this resulted in the *National Union Catalog* (NUC).

In 1899 E. C. Richardson of Princeton wrote that some method for locating books in libraries should be found.[19] Other prominent librarians interested in the formation of union catalogs were Charles C. Williamson, dean of the School of Library Service and director of libraries of Columbia University; H. M. Lydenberg, librarian of the New York Public Library, and Herbert Putnam, Librarian of Congress.

Two ideas central to interlibrary loan were advanced in 1908. Charles H. Gould, librarian of McGill University, proposed the establishment of regional libraries. In an article in the *Library Journal*, he wrote, "The library world has hitherto been occupied with the evolution of single libraries. Is not the twentieth century to see the welding of all these separate entities into one complete system?"[20]

Gould hadn't used the word, but he was talking about a network. He disagreed with Richardson and others on the subject of a single national lending library. Also in 1908, W. C. Lane of Harvard suggested the production of union lists and a lending bureau.[21]

In 1909 Gould made cooperation the theme of his presidency of the ALA.[22] R. R. Bowker called it the subject of the century.[23] Bowker distributed the first questionnaire on ILLs, the results of which were published in the March and May 1910 issues of *Library Journal* in summary form, as follows:

> Inter-library loan ... represents a decided economic advantage in library administration. It is evident that the demand of inter-library loans is and should be confined to a few classes of books or to individual books so rare that only a few libraries have or can have them.
>
> The trend of library opinion ... is evidently toward the development of the interlibrary loan system by the Library of Congress and other existing libraries, rather than in the establishment of a reservoir or other new forms of libraries for the special purpose.
>
> The limitations to library-loan developments are practically those of dollars and cents, both to the library loaning and to the user borrowing.... The larger libraries, supplying wider demands, will have to meet the question of cost.... Of course this question may be partly met by a fee charged to the individual borrower, but the use of the library loan system is unduly limited now because of the considerable cost of transportation which the individual borrower must pay.[24]

The library center idea proposed by Richardson and Lane was discussed by the ALA Committee on Coordination in 1910, but because cooperation existed, the idea was dropped. Suggestions were made that the ALA should be a clearinghouse, that libraries send statistics to the headquarters, and that the borrowing libraries be levied accordingly. Even though there was sustained interest and the practice of lending books to each other was practiced, at least among the larger libraries, the ILL movement developed slowly.

At the 50th-anniversary conference of the ALA in October 1926, the two sessions of the College and Reference Section were devoted to a discussion of interlibrary loan. This subject was presented in all of its phases by speakers from abroad, as well as from our own country. Representatives from the following libraries gave presentations: the Great Britain Library, the Birmingham Public Library Commission, the Library of Congress, the Harvard College Library, and the University of Illinois. It was hoped that the volume that resulted—the proceedings of the conference—titled *Selected Articles on Interlibrary Loans*, compiled by James A. McMillan and published in New York by H. W. Wilson Company in 1928, would serve as an ILL manual.

# International Interlibrary Loan

Despite the well-meant efforts of numerous librarians all over the world, international interlibrary loan did not develop very systematically. Two hundred years after Pieresc's efforts to develop an international system failed, the practice of interlibrary loan had grown in Europe to the point where legal recognition and regularization seemed necessary. By a decree in 1883, the Austrian government allowed libraries to lend to foreign libraries without specific ministerial permission and by post rather than through diplomatic channels. Before 1900 almost a dozen European countries were doing the same thing, and before the First World War destroyed the spirit of international cooperation, the practice of interlibrary loan was apparently adopted by every country in Europe.

After the war, two organizations took the lead in promoting interlibrary loan—the International Institute of Bibliography and the Institute for Intellectual Cooperation. The greatest impetus to the development of an international loan system was, however, due to the efforts of the Germans and English in developing highly centralized interlibrary-lending systems for domestic libraries and in extending these systems to international lending.

Both Germany and England had a national clearinghouse with a union catalog through which all requests for loans were made. In Britain it was the National Central Library and in Germany, the Auskunfstbureau of the Prussian State Library in Berlin.

In 1934 the libraries of 30 countries lent 11,450 volumes to libraries in 38 countries. Of this number, German libraries lent 5,359 volumes. Ranked by volumes lent, the other countries in the top 10 were Austria, Switzerland, Sweden, the United States, Denmark, England, France, The Netherlands, and Belgium.[25]

It was proposed in 1935 by the librarian of the Swiss National Library that the supervision of international lending should be established through an organization sponsored by the International Federation of Library Associations (IFLA) and a few simple rules were adopted the following year. The rules, which were very similar to American ILL rules, recommended but did not require that requests to foreign countries be sent to the national ILL centers. To belong to the organization a library needed only to be willing to lend to foreign libraries and to send in an annual report on ILL activity.[26]

All that had been accomplished was wiped out by World War II. Following the war, Archibald MacLeish recommended an expanded system of international loans to try to undo what the war had done, but the ALA recommended "that international interlibrary loans should be encouraged, but because of the hazards of transportation, should be largely in the form of photographic reproductions."[27] This stand by the ALA was disappointing, and it was not until the first postwar meeting of the IFLA in 1947 that serious discussion was held on restoring the ILL system that had existed before the war.

New international rules were developed in 1954. The new rules caused not only a rapid growth in ILL activity but also a better distribution of the work load among libraries. Eastern European countries were allowed to reenter the system.[28]

American libraries continued to be reluctant to participate in international lending on a large scale. Major obstacles were said to be distances involved, no national clearinghouse, and currency restrictions.

Following ratification of the *International Interlibrary Loan Procedure for United States Libraries* by the ALA in 1959, more American libraries were willing to participate in international lending. Generally, the American procedure follows the IFLA rules but differs in that it applies to loans outside the North American continent, and postage must be paid in advance.

Maurice Line, director of the IFLA Office for International Lending and director general of the British Library Lending Division, summarized a 1977 study carried out by IFLA from which broad generalizations about international interlending practice could be made. Union catalogs were almost universally found, with union lists of serials being the most common. Union catalogs were often unpublished, and the coverage varied considerably. Libraries requested from one library to another without going through a center, even though some degree of centralization was found in many countries.

A detailed description of the interlending situation in most countries would present a very complex, and possibly confused, picture, according to Line. It was not clear in most countries, he said, where responsibility for interlending—planning, supervision, and monitoring—lay. Almost no information on the performance of interlending systems, such as satisfaction rates, speed of supply, and cost, existed at that time. Data available suggested satisfaction rates did not exceed 70 percent, supply times of three weeks or more were the norm, and costs could only be guessed.[29]

## Bibliographic Compilations Fostering Interlibrary Cooperation

Mobilization of library resources could become a reality only after bibliographic notation became standardized and some method of locating materials in other libraries was devised. Lists and bibliographies indicating subject specialization, book catalogs for individual libraries, union lists, and union catalogs were developed to meet the need.

### Resource Lists

The earliest national resource list, indexed by subject and describing library collections and catalogs, is William C. Lane and Charles K. Bolton's 1892 *Notes on Special Collections in American Libraries*. This was followed by a large number of similar directories.

The systematic analyses of regional and national libraries and resources such as R. B. Downs' three volumes—*American Library Resources, Resources of New York City Libraries*, and *Resources of Southern Libraries*—and

*Resources of Pacific Northwest Libraries* are among the useful tools outlining the nature and location of the library wealth of the country. Additional guides to subject holdings and the location of special strength are the *Directory of Special Libraries* and the *American Library Directory*.[30]

Specialization was forced upon all institutions because competition among libraries made it a financial impossibility for all libraries of higher learning to obtain sets of the rarer journals especially. Division of the field of knowledge into particular sections or localities was almost necessary if that region was to have at its disposal the research materials it needed. One of the earliest general agreements about subject specialization was drawn up by the Chicago Public Library, the Crerar Library, and the Newberry Library in 1896. Although brief and stated in general terms with no formal procedures established for its implementation, the agreement was doubtless effective in determining the characteristics of these collections and helped to give Chicago stronger resources than it would have had without it.[31]

## Union Catalogs

The union catalog idea has been traced to the fifteenth century. At least four European catalogs were begun in the 1880s and 1890s. Germany was ahead of other nations in the production of a national union catalog. The *German Union Catalogue* (*Deutscher Gesamtkatalog*) was followed by the *Bibliothèque Nationale Catalogue* and the *British Museum Catalogue*.

The *National Union Catalog* was produced by offset printing of catalog cards printed by the Library of Congress for all imprints dated 1956 and later. A large number of American libraries submitted titles they owned. The purpose of the *National Union Catalog* was to disseminate information about the holdings of large American libraries and perhaps redistribute the load of interlibrary lending. Prior to that time, one could write to the Library of Congress for a search to be made. The choice had to be made whether that should be done first or whether it would be more prudent to write to other libraries that might be closer. The publication *A Catalog of Books Represented by LC Printed Cards Issued to July 31, 1942*, and its supplements, provided bibliographical aids to verification as well as helped to standardize cataloging practices. The Library of Congress also published a large number of bibliographies; especially important among them was the monthly checklist of state documents.[32]

Even as the *National Union Catalog* was being perfected, libraries were calling for the building of regional and municipal union catalogs. Despite the availability of millions of volumes in large libraries, smaller libraries sought to borrow more among themselves. Union catalogs were thus established by cities, counties, states, and regions, as well as by nations. It was expected that the libraries in the locality covered by the union catalog would borrow from each other before sending requests elsewhere.

Prior to 1930, the California State Library had compiled the only regional union catalog. A great impetus for founding union catalogs in the United States was the sudden availability of free labor from federal relief agencies.

A variety of city, county, state, regional, exchange, and subject union catalogs spread throughout the country.

A survey of union catalogs, originated by the American Council of Learned Societies and the Social Science Research Council, was begun in 1938. Its purpose was to provide data for coordinating regional union catalogs with each other and with the *National Union Catalog*, and to advise whether a union catalog should be established in one or another region. Conclusions drawn from the survey were that, for the most part, union catalog sponsors had not been particularly concerned with the problem of fitting their catalogs into any kind of national plan; consequently, some duplication of effort, questionable regional divisions, and other lack of integration was evident. The catalogs also suffered from financial instability. A directory of 117 union catalogs in existence by the early 1940s was published in *Union Catalogs in the United States*, which appeared as a result of the survey.[33]

A file of 14 million cards located in the Wisconsin State Historical Society was used as a location device for early-American books needed for research. Winchell's *Locating Books for Interlibrary Loans*, published in 1930, indexed many library catalogs by author and subject. The professional literature of the 1930s and 1940s abounds with articles on union catalogs.

In later years, librarians exchanged copies of their catalogs by converting to the COM (computer output microfilm) catalog and other computer catalogs in networks to replace the book catalog. Bro-Dart COM catalogs, for example, have been used in the Black Gold Co-op in California, the Woodlands Library Cooperative in Michigan, the Hidalgo County Library System in Texas, and many other library systems. The Illinois Public Library service, which consists of a network of 18 public library systems, including 97 percent of all local libraries and 4 research and reference centers (the Chicago Public Library, Southern Illinois University, the University of Illinois, and the Illinois State Library), put its entire catalog on microfilm.[34] The New Jersey State Library developed the automated microfilm catalog.[35]

More recently, electronic developments have impacted heavily on library cooperation. Many libraries have placed their catalogs on CD-ROM, a plastic disk on which data are encoded and read with the use of a computer, a special keyboard, a CD-ROM drive, a floppy disk, and a printer. The CD-ROM disks may be union catalogs or single catalogs to be shared.

Since the mid-1970s many large libraries have automated their public catalogs. They have also formed networks so that the holdings of more than one library, or more than one state, region, or nation could be represented in one on-line union catalog.

## Cooperative Bibliographies

Of equal value to the *National Union Catalog* is the publication of several special cooperative bibliographies. Before World War I, the *International Catalogue of Scientific Literature* was published by the Royal Society. The *Union List of Serials*, a cooperative project of American and Canadian libraries, was published in 1927. *New Serials Titles*, published in 1953, continued the *Union List of Serials*. The *Union Catalogue of Incunabula* was published in 1925. The second volume of the *World List of Serials* for the location of sets of journals in British libraries appeared in 1927. A similar compilation in Germany in 1914 was *Gesamt-Zeitschriften* (1914-1924) and (1927+). The comprehensive *British National Bibliography* (BNB), established in 1950, is a product of cooperation among the British Museum, The Library Association, the Publishers' Association, and seven other bodies.

## American Librarians Active in Interlibrary Cooperation

Innovative librarians recognized the need for cooperation, and the names of the librarians associated with the ILL movement read like a who's who of the library profession. That these librarians were able to succeed depended largely on their positions in the profession and their ability to win the cooperation of others in this country, as well as in foreign countries. Following are brief biographical sketches of librarians identified as the most active in the history of the ILL movement.[36]

### William Warner Bishop

The groundwork for the organization of the IFLA was laid by Bishop in 1924, when he was sent by the ALA and the Carnegie Endowment for International Peace to extend invitations to European librarians to attend the 50th-anniversary meeting of the ALA. In 1931, he was elected president of the IFLA and in that capacity served for five years. He was particularly concerned with the formation of ILL agreements and the exchange of librarians. He also helped arrange for the attendance of foreign librarians at the ALA meeting in Chicago in 1933. Through frequent visits to Europe, Bishop maintained contact with the commission charged with the erection of the League of Nations Library. He was librarian at the University of Michigan from 1915 to 1941.

### Richard Rogers Bowker

Bowker was literary editor for the *New York Evening Mail*. In 1876 he helped found the *Library Journal* and arranged the meeting that year at which the ALA was organized. He was the owner and editor of *Publishers' Weekly*. Other periodicals and books were published under the R. R. Bowker Company imprint.

## Melvil Dewey

Librarian at Amherst, Dewey developed his classification system in 1876. He was librarian at Columbia University when he became the head of the first library school in the United States in 1887 (moved to the New York State Library, 1889). Dewey was the most active of the founding fathers of the ALA. He became the first editor of *Library Journal*.

## Charles H. Gould

The establishment of regional libraries was proposed by Gould while he was librarian of McGill University. He was president of the ALA in 1909.

## Samuel S. Green

As librarian, Green made the Free Library in Worcester, Massachusetts, one of the most progressive in the world. He has also been called the librarian most responsible for interlibrary loan development in this country. He was one of the founders of the ALA, serving as its president in 1891. One of his publications is *The Public Library Movement in the United States*.

## C. C. Jewett

Establishment of a union catalog, cooperative cataloging, and building up the Smithsonian Institution Library—which he served as librarian—as the national library of the United States were all proposed by Jewett. His ideas were not well received, however. He later became librarian of the Boston Public Library.

## William C. Lane

Lane was librarian at Harvard. In 1892 he contributed *Notes on Special Collections in American Libraries*. He suggested both union lists and a lending bureau to assist with the ILL process.

## H. M. Lydenberg

Librarian of the New York Public Library, Lydenberg assisted in the completion of Sabin's *Dictionary of Books Relating to America*, the publication of various union lists, and the study of union catalogs.

## William F. Poole

While attending college at Yale, Poole began to compile an index to material in current periodicals. Published in 1848 as *An Alphabetical Index to Subjects Treated in the Reviews and Other Periodicals*, it was later called *Poole's Index to Periodical Literature*. He was librarian at the Boston Athenaeum, public libraries in Cincinnati and Chicago, and the Newberry Library, which he also organized. He worked for the ILL cause at the very first conference of the ALA.

## Herbert Putnam

Putnam was the Librarian of Congress. His direction of the war service of the ALA in 1917-1919 and his assistance to other libraries—through the printing of catalog cards and the publication of classification schedules, the provision of depository catalogs, the development of the *National Union Catalog*, the provision of consultant and bibliographical service for scholars, and his participation in the conferences of a national and international nature—were characteristic of his administration.

## Ernest Cushing Richardson

During the time Richardson, Princeton University librarian, was an honorary consultant in bibliography at the Library of Congress, he directed the NUC project that he had suggested earlier. He was also president of the ALA and the American Library Institute.

## Bunford Samuel

Samuel was librarian of the Ridgway Library in Philadelphia. He presented a proposal in 1892 that libraries enter into ILL agreements with each other.

## Charles C. Williamson

Williamson was dean of the School of Library Service of Columbia University and director of libraries of Columbia from 1926 to 1943. He was instrumental in speeding up the publication of the catalog of Bibliothèque Nationale and in securing a Rockefeller Foundation grant for funding for the project.

## Justin Winsor

Winsor was president of the ALA (1876-1885), one of the founders of the *Library Journal* (1876), a member of the Board of Trustees of the Boston Public Library (1866), and librarian in 1868. In 1877 be became librarian of Harvard University. During his second presidency of the ALA, he was asked to represent it at an international conference of librarians in England and to expand relations between American and European libraries.

# Roles Played by Professional Organizations

Cooperation has been fostered by the professional associations—the ALA, the Special Libraries Association (SLA), the Association of Research Libraries (ARL), and the IFLA. American library associations have played an important role in international library cooperation since 1877, when several librarians who had attended the first ALA convention went to London to attend the founding conference of the Library Association. It is impossible to study the ILL movement without realizing that it flourished because of the support it gained from the professional associations of the day.[37]

## American Library Association

The ALA was founded in 1876 for libraries, librarians, library trustees, and others interested in libraries. Its membership is composed of representatives from all parts of the world. Its goals are to make libraries accessible to all, to establish professional standards of librarianship, and to publish materials useful to the profession.

Librarians prominent in the history of American libraries have also played prominent roles in the ALA. The names of a number of prominent American librarians appear in the professional literature as representatives of the ALA extending relations into foreign countries. Among them are Justin Winsor, who was also one of the founders of the *Library Journal,* and William Warner Bishop, active in the formation of the IFLA.

In its role of raising standards of library service, the ALA has issued standards for public libraries, college and research libraries, and school libraries. Interest in library cooperation really developed with the founding of the ALA and the subsequent development of standardization of bibliographic entries, codes, and practices and procedures.

## Association of Research Libraries

The ARL was founded in 1932. Its membership now totals over 100 large university, public, private, and governmental research libraries. Its purpose is to serve the research needs of students, faculty, and the research community and to strengthen the member libraries. Member libraries provided the bulk of interlibrary loans in the developmental stages of the movement.

*International Federation of Library Associations (IFLA)*

This organization promotes library cooperation among the nations of the world and studies problems of international relations among libraries, library associations, bibliographers, and others in library work. William Warner Bishop, librarian of the University of Michigan and a representative of the ALA, was instrumental in the organization of the IFLA in 1927 and later served as its president.

The IFLA was responsible for achieving such international cooperation as the agreement on international interlibrary loan in 1954 and, with the help of UNESCO, the International Conference of Cataloging Principles held in Paris in 1961.[38]

*Special Libraries Association*

The SLA, founded in 1909 with 26 members, is an international group of professionals in libraries serving business, government, and other specialized groups. The loan of specialized materials was part of the history of the ILL movement. The SLA presently has members in excess of 12,000. It addresses problems such as library automation, legislative issues, networking, and library instruction. In addition to publishing its official organ, *Special Libraries*, it publishes bibliographies, sourcebooks, and directories.

# Federal Legislation

Federal funds were made available through the Works Progress Administration agency, formed by executive order in 1935, to establish libraries to be supervised by workers on the federal relief rolls. By 1941, 5,800 mobile libraries had been built. Although these libraries were established to provide employment, some of them were later absorbed into county libraries. Unemployed workers were also given clerical library jobs in book binding and repair and other nonprofessional activities.

One special program provided at the agency was the Federal Writer's Project. Participants prepared state and regional guidebooks, organized archives, indexed newspapers, and so on. Some of these resources, coupled with union catalogs that were compiled as a result of free labor, proved to be a great boon to interlibrary loan.

Through the State Technical Services Act of 1965, the federal government has encouraged cooperation of special libraries. The act contributed matching federal funds to state programs to make scientific and technical information available to business. Much earlier, large corporations had set up a system whereby branch libraries could borrow from each other.

Interlibrary loan activity at the state level was sparked by the Library Services Act of 1956 (later named the Library Services and Construction Act), sponsored by the ALA and passed by Congress. Legislation included the construction of buildings, the experimentation with cooperative arrangements, the establishment of the National Commission on Libraries, and the passage of library components in the Elementary and Secondary Education Act and the Higher Education Act, both passed in 1965. Other areas of contribution were programs for the handicapped, strengthening of major urban libraries, and the vitalization of state library agencies as the focal points of coordinated library development.

One requirement for receiving aid through the Library Services Act was that a state plan be developed to serve rural areas. Growth was stimulated to a higher degree when the act was amended in 1966 to include the Title III on Interlibrary Cooperation and Resource Sharing. It promotes cooperative networks of libraries that provide for systematic and effective coordination of the resources of school, public, academic, and special libraries and information centers and encourages preservation and development of library technology for resource sharing. Hawaii, Pennsylvania, and New York were pioneers in developing strong, comprehensive statewide systems with ILL activity.

Nationwide cooperation has been stimulated by centralized services in the national libraries funded by federal legislation and aimed at coordinating the efforts of libraries. The Library of Congress maintains a large ILL program, made possible by the compiling of the *National Union Catalog*. Another national library is the National Library of Medicine, which mechanized its indexing services in 1960. It also produces a book catalog. The library has a massive ILL program of photocopied articles. The Department of Agriculture was designated a national library in 1962. In 1967, the *Dictionary Catalog of the National Agricultural Library, 1862-1965* was published. One other type of governmental library found in the United States is the international library: The United Nations headquarters library in New York City, the Dag Hammarskjöld Library, was founded in 1947.[39]

## Interlibrary Loan Activity

National ILL activity has shown an ever-increasing growth. In 1911, for example, the John Crerar Library approved 184 ILL requests; in 1931, it approved 2,406 requests. In the year ending June 30, 1914, the University of Illinois lent 124 volumes; in 1932, it lent 1,427 volumes. The Library of Congress lent for the year ending June 30, 1909, 1,023 volumes and for the year ending June 30, 1926, over 20,000 volumes. The Library of Congress lent to 682 other libraries in the United States, Canada, Italy, Germany, and Norway. The increase in ILL transactions led the librarian to suggest that the ALA provide a bibliographic embassy to work in the Library of Congress with interlibrary loan if American libraries insisted on borrowing in such large numbers. The Library of Congress expressed a preference for lending books to those libraries whose catalog cards were on file there.[40]

No class of books seemed to be excluded from ILL activity, and publications were borrowed for undergraduates as well as for more serious scholars. Librarians complained that as high as 60 percent of the requests received were incomplete or inaccurate.

Charles Brown of Iowa State College suggested that a revision of the 1917 code might help but would not solve the problems being encountered. He suggested that it might be more appropriate for each library to restrict its own loans, perhaps imposing a small charge to cover part of the cost, or even to deter the borrowing of items not absolutely necessary. At Iowa State the charging of transportation costs to instructors caused the number of books borrowed to drop from 489 to 206 during the year the regulation went into effect. Additional suggestions were made for those libraries not wishing to charge. He and others urged that the advantages of the system be preserved and that the disadvantages, or problems, be solved.[41]

The problems did not go away, however. Of special interest was the cost, both direct and indirect, of making loans. There was agreement on both sides of the question regarding charging patrons for shipping. Holske believed that free circulation of books—including interlibrary loans—was an important expression of American civilization and should be an American policy everywhere. To defray the cost of interlibrary loans, he suggested charging loan costs to research.[42]

Karl Koopman disagreed. Only in a utopia, he said, would such a policy work. He pointed out that sometimes it is the professor, and not the college, who benefits from research, and the beneficiary should pay the cost.[43]

In 1949 a survey of the practices and experiences of 48 college and university libraries that carry on considerable interlibrary loans was conducted. Conclusions reached following the survey were as follows: 1) it would help if colleges would adopt a standard citation form; and 2) because ILL service is essentially part of the national research program, libraries should be granted franking privileges in mailing such materials.[44]

The idea of franking privileges had been previously suggested, in 1945, in the report of the John Crerar Library. It is interesting to learn also from this report that interlibrary loan made its way into the Chicago John Crerar Library before circulation to patrons did. The librarian wrote in his historical report of the library that

> inter-library loans developed out of a necessity arising from the growing need of research material in all parts of the country. Individuals in need of material not locally available may borrow what they urgently need at some library center by application to their local library, public or institution. The general spread of this system is largely a 20th century development. Here, too, we at first responded reluctantly, especially because we as a library had little need for this service. The demand has grown out of all reasonable proportions and during the second World War, reached proportions of which we never dreamed in times past. We do not think inter-library loan is troublesome, but do believe that inter-library loans ought to receive free franking privileges or all inter-library loan should be taken over by the Library of Congress.[45]

In a study of interlibrary loan service in 20 university libraries, White found that 59 percent more loans were made through other libraries in 1952-1953 than in 1947-1948, and 22 percent more were borrowed during that same time. He concluded that although photocopying may have prevented a greater increase, such factors as enriched collections, gaps caused by the war, increased graduate study and postdoctoral research, and new programs and an expanding clientele might have caused the increase in ILL activity.[46]

Perhaps the most comprehensive investigation of ILL activity in academic libraries was the study initiated in 1971 by the Interlibrary Loan Study Committee of the ARL. Results of the study, conducted by Westat, were compiled by Vernon Palmour and others in a book published in 1972 by Greenwood Press. The most important objective of this study was to make available data on the costs of interlibrary loans by academic libraries. Previous studies on the characteristics of interlibrary loans had focused on special classes of materials such as serial publications, scientific and medical publications, or loans within a certain geographical area.[47, 48, 49, 50]

It was found that the average lending cost per request for large academic libraries, based on direct costs and a 50 percent overhead rate, was $2.12 for an unfilled loan request and $4.67 for a filled loan request, with a wide range of costs within the sample. No consistent relationship was found between lending cost per transaction and collection size. Lending cost per transaction seemed to be related to the geographical location of the library.

Variations in lending costs may result from physical conditions within the library, of professional staff, and in the efficiency of the units. About 60 percent of loan requests received originated in other academic libraries, and about 71 percent of loan requests received were filled. Fifty-four percent were for originals, and 43 percent were for photocopies. About 54 percent of loan requests not filled were reported not owned, so evidently there was a problem with lack of verification.

The study concluded that then-current trends indicated that by 1975, interlibrary loan borrowing by academic libraries might increase to about 2 million volumes per year. Requests for loans processed by academic libraries might represent in excess of 3 million volumes.[51]

A study of interlibrary loan at the Library of Congress in 1976 showed that academic libraries were the most frequent borrowers and that requests were most often for materials in the humanities. The Library of Congress received proportionally more requests for old items than academic libraries did, and it filled 54 percent of all requests it received. Distributions of language and place of publication of requested items, as well as time required for handling requests, were also investigated. Three reasons were given for unfilled requests: 1) noncirculating (35 percent), 2) material not on shelf or charged out (32 percent), and 3) not owned (24 percent). Great variations were shown in the time required to process requests—from 6 to 27 days.[52]

National studies of interlibrary loan have focused on the academic library because academic libraries have been major participants in the activity. Ideally, however, studies done on ILL activity should include all types of libraries. Dianna Lynne Smith studied libraries of different types in her thesis written at the University of Illinois in 1976, but in order to keep the study manageable, she restricted it to libraries in Tennessee. The main purpose of the questionnaire she devised was to secure data on the volume of interlibrary loan and the types of libraries most frequently involved.

Smith found that public libraries may be the heaviest users of interlibrary loan. Smaller college libraries in Tennessee sent out a low volume of requests. Public libraries concentrated their borrowing within the state, whereas the opposite was true for academic and special libraries. As might be expected, the larger libraries, including public, academic, and special, were called upon most, even though each type of library borrowed and lent mostly with the same kind of library as itself.

Eighty-five percent of Tennessee requests were filled through photocopy or loan. Public libraries overwhelmingly requested books; special libraries requested articles in almost the same proportion. Academic libraries borrowed more specialized things. Overall, books constituted one-half of the materials requested. Serials met with the highest success rate (90 percent).[53] Interlibrary loan at the Tennessee-state level was also reported by Stevens and Smith in 1977.[54] Linsley and Goldhor studied Florida and Illinois, respectively.

Goldhor reported that 3,979 ILL requests were initiated by all types of libraries in the Illinois Library and Information Network (ILLINET)—60 percent public, 26 percent academic, 9 percent special, and 5 percent correctional—during the month of February 1975. Over two-thirds of all requests were for adults, a quarter were for college students, 8 percent were for high school students, and 2 percent were for elementary school students. 84 percent of all requests were filled.[55]

A survey conducted by Laurie Linsley in 1982 examined ILL activity among participants in the Florida Library Information Network (FLIN). It revealed that the largest amount of borrowing was done by college and university libraries and public libraries. College and university libraries and some of the special libraries (corporate and government) borrow more articles than books. Community colleges, public libraries, and school libraries, and some of the special libraries (military, state institution, and other), borrowed almost twice as many books as photocopies. The fill rate for both books and photocopies for these libraries was more than 80 percent. The fill rate for college and university libraries was 74 percent. Linsley explained that this was probably because public library patrons are willing to wait longer for materials. Almost half of the requests were filled by academic libraries.[56]

McDonald and Bush estimated the total volume of interlibrary loan borrowing in the United States in 1981 as part of a report they prepared for the U.S. Copyright Office. A sample of 149 libraries composed of public, academic, federal, and special libraries was studied and the results projected to the total population.

Interlibrary loan borrowing for public libraries was estimated at 14,344,000 (57.7 percent), academic libraries at 5,255,000 (21 percent), federal libraries at 1,986,000 (8 percent), and special libraries at 3,262,000 (13.1 percent). Total interlibrary loan borrowing was estimated at 24,858,000 in 1981.[57]

Waldhart compared activities of the 88 libraries that were members of ARL in 1974-1975 with those same libraries through 1982-1983. ARL university libraries represent about 3 percent of all college and university libraries in the United States, yet they accounted for 27.5 percent of all borrowing transactions and 49.1 percent of all lending transactions. In recent years, concern has been expressed in ARL libraries about their ability to continue lending as well as borrowing for their own patrons. Waldhart found that ILL activity, even though stabilized for a time, continued to increase. The average annual growth rate for photocopies lent was +1.5 percent. The most important finding of the study was that the ARL libraries increased borrowing activities for their own patrons, and because the cost of borrowing is greater than it is for lending, ILL activity is becoming an increasing burden.[58]

A number of developments occurred during the 1970s that should have caused a negative growth of ILL activities—the introduction of fees by many net-lending libraries (libraries that lend more books than they borrow), new copyright legislation, and on-line document ordering. At about the same time, however, developments occurred that should have caused libraries to rely more heavily on resource sharing—a liberalized interlibrary loan code, on-line ILL systems, on-line search services, and state and federal support of library networks.

Under an increasing load of research, ILL activity has increased with no end in sight. Many also believe that the scope of interlibrary loan must be expanded to serve general information, teaching and learning, and recreational-avocational interests. This expanded service is reflected in the creation of state systems and in the drafting of more liberal codes for states, regions, and groups.

# Notes

[1]Lester Condit, "Bibliography in Its Pre-natal Existence," *Library Quarterly* 7 (October 1937):567.

[2]Francis W. Gravit, "A Proposed Interlibrary Loan System in the Seventeenth Century," *Library Quarterly* 16 (October 1946):331-34.

[3]Gabriel Naude, *Advice on Establishing a Library* (Los Angeles: University of California Press, 1950), 12.

[4]Alfred Hessel, *A History of Libraries*. Translated with supplementary material by Reuben Peiss. (New Brunswick, N.J.: Scarecrow Press, 1955), 109.

[5]James A. McMillan, *Selected Articles on Interlibrary Loans* (New York: Wilson, 1928), 14-16.

[6]Jean Key Gates, *Introduction to Librarianship*, 2d ed. (New York: McGraw-Hill, 1976), 53-71.

[7]William Carlson, "Mobilization of Existing Library Resources," *Library Quarterly* 16 (October 1946):284.

[8]Charles C. Jewett, *Report of the Assistant Secretary in Charge of the Smithsonian Institution for the Year 1850.* Senate Miscellaneous Documents no. 1, Special Session (March 1850), 28-41.

[9]Samuel Green, "The Lending of Books to One Another by Libraries," *Library Journal* 1 (September 1876):15-16.

[10]Samuel Green, "Address of the President of the American Library Association at the San Francisco Conference," *Library Journal* 16 (1891):C5-6.

[11]Samuel Green, "Inter-Library Loans in Reference Work," *Library Journal* 23 (October 1898):567-68.

[12]Carlson, "Mobilization of Existing Library Resources," 287.

[13]McMillan, *Selected Articles on Interlibrary Loans,* 15.

[14]Ernest C. Richardson, "Co-operation in Lending Among College and Reference Libraries," *Library Journal* 24 (1899):C32-36.

[15]Ernest C. Richardson, "Presidential Address," *Library Journal* 30 (1905):C6.

[16]Ibid.

[17]Joel S. Rutstein, "National and Local Resource Sharing: Issues in Cooperative Collection Development," *Collection Management* 7(2) (Summer 1985):1-16.

[18]McMillan, *Selected Articles on Interlibrary Loans,* 14.

[19]Richardson, "Co-operation in Lending," C32-36.

[20]Charles H. Gould, "Regional Libraries," *Library Journal* 33 (June 1908):219.

[21]William C. Lane, "A Central Bureau of Information and Loan Collection for College Libraries," *Library Journal* 33 (November 1908):429-33.

[22]Charles H. Gould, "Coordination, or Method in Cooperation," *ALA Bulletin* 3 (September 1909):122-28.

[23]"Discussion on Library Coordination," *ALA Bulletin* 3 (September 1909):156.

[24]Richard R. Bowker, "Editorial," *Library Journal* 35 (March 1910):101.

[25]John C. Colson, "International Interlibrary Loans Since World War II," *Library Quarterly* 32 (October 1962):259-69.

[26]"International Interlibrary Loan," *ALA Bulletin* 34 (February 1940):99-100, 112.

[27]Edwin E. Williams and Ruth V. Noble, *Preliminary Memoranda: Conference on International Cultural, Educational, and Scientific Exchanges, Princeton University, November 25-26, 1946* (Chicago: ALA, 1947): xvii.

[28]"New Rules for International Loan," *UNESCO Bulletin for Libraries* 14 (January 1955):5-6.

[29]Maurice B. Line, "National Interlending Systems: Existing Systems and Possible Models," *Interlending Review* 7(2) (1979):42-46.

[30]Carlson, "Mobilization of Existing Library Resources," 284.

[31]Robert T. Grazier, "Cooperation Among Libraries of Different Types," *Library Quarterly* 16 (October 1946):335.

[32]Hessel, *History of Libraries*, 121.

[33]Robert B. Downs, ed. *Union Catalogs in the United States* (Chicago: ALA, 1942), xxi.

[34]Anthony W. Miele, "The Illinois State Library Microfilm Automated Catalogs (IMAC)," in *Microforms and Library Catalogs: A Reader*, ed. Albert J. Diaz (Westport, Conn.: Microform Review, 1977), 89.

[35]Oliver P. Gillock, Jr. and Roger H. McDonough, "Spreading State Library Riches for Peanuts," *Wilson Library Bulletin* (December 1970):354-57.

[36]Louis Round Wilson and Maurice F. Tauber, *The University Library* (New York and London: Columbia University Press, 1956), 531-47.

[37]Curt D. Wormann, "Aspects of International Library Cooperation—Historical and Contemporary," *Library Quarterly* 38 (October 1968):347.

[38]Ibid.

[39]David C. Weber and Frederick C. Lynden, "Survey of Interlibrary Cooperation," in *Proceedings of the Conference on Interlibrary Communications and Information Networks*, ed. Joseph Becker (Chicago: ALA, 1971), 72.

[40]F. W. Ashley, "Interlibrary Loan from the Viewpoint of the Lending Library," in *Selected Articles on Interlibrary Loans*, ed. James A. McMillan (New York: Wilson, 1928), 55.

[41]Charles H. Brown, "Interlibrary Loans: An Unsolved Problem," *Library Journal* 57 (November 1932):887-89.

[42]Alan Holske, "On Meeting Interlibrary Loan Costs," *College and Research Libraries* 7 (January 1946):74-77.

[43]Karl H. Koopman, "Thoughts on Interlibrary Loan," *College and Research Libraries* 8 (April 1947):157-60.

[44]R. Harry and H. Astvold. "Interlibrary Loan Service and National Research," *College and Research Libraries* 10 (April 1949):145-50.

[45]John Crerar Library, *1895-1944; An Historical Report Prepared Under the Authority of the Board of Directors by the Librarians* (J. Christian Bay) (Chicago, 1945), 15.

[46]Carl M. White, "Services to Scholars," *Library Trends* 3 (1954):151.

[47]Sarah Katherine Thomson, *General Interlibrary Loan Services in Major Academic Libraries in the United States* (New York: Columbia University, 1967).

[48]James L. Wood, *A Review of the Availability of Primary Scientific and Technical Documents Within the United States* (Washington, D.C.: Chemical Abstracts Service, 1969).

[49]Charles W. Schilling, *A Study of the Interlibrary Loan Activity of the National Library of Medicine for the Fiscal Year 1967* (Washington, D.C.: National Library of Medicine, 1968).

[50]Nelson Associates, *Interlibrary Loan in New York State* (New York: Nelson, 1969).

[51]Vernon E. Palmour, et al., *A Study of the Characteristics, Costs, and Magnitude of Interlibrary Loans in Academic Libraries* (Westport, Conn.: Greenwood Press, 1972), 4.

[52]Melissa D. Trevvett, "Characteristics of Interlibrary Loan Requests at the Library of Congress," *College and Research Libraries* 40 (January 1979):36-42.

[53]Dianna Lynne Smith, *The Magnitude and Characteristics of Interlibrary Loan Involving Public, Academic, and Special Libraries in Tennessee* (Urbana: University of Illinois, 1976), 64-68.

[54]R. E. Stevens and D. L. Smith, "Interlibrary Loan in Tennessee," *Southeastern Librarian* 27 (1977):175-80.

[55]H. Goldhor, "An Evaluation of the Illinois Interlibrary Loan Network (ILLINET)," *Illinois Libraries* 61 (1979):14.

[56]L. S. Linsley, "Academic Libraries in an Interlibrary Loan Network," *College and Research Libraries* 43 (1982):292-99.

[57]D. D. McDonald and C. G. Bush, *Libraries, Publishers, and Photocopying: Final Report of Surveys Conducted for the United States Copyright Office* (Rockville, Md.: King Research, 1982).

[58]Thomas J. Waldhart, "The Growth of Interlibrary Loan Among ARL University Libraries," *Journal of Academic Librarianship* 10 (September 1984):204-6.

# chapter 2

# Standardization

As has been noted in chapter 1, interest in borrowing from one library to another has prevailed through much of library history. Development of the concept lagged, however, due to lack of information about holdings and lack of standardization among libraries.

Bibliographies, union lists, and shared machine-readable cataloging (MARC) provided the desired information about holdings. As libraries became more standardized in their cataloging (to which their holdings records were attached), it became easier to standardize in other areas.

The ALA led the way in developing codes outlining in some detail the policies and procedures to which libraries wishing to borrow from each other agreed to adhere. To enhance the codes, ALA also devised a common request form. Forms used within the various interlibrary loan offices also took on a standarized look as time went by.

## Interlibrary Loan Codes

The Boston Public Library loaned books to other libraries in New England during the 1890s. A special form was printed and made available to borrowing libraries, the conditions of which became part of future codes. The form specified the following:

1. The book asked for must be one out of the ordinary course—not such as it is the ordinary duty of the applicant library to supply.

2. It must be required for purposes of serious research.

3. It must be a book which may, without injury, be sent by express.

4. It must be a book which may be spared, for the time being, without inconvenience to our local readers.[1]

At about the same time, Joseph Rowell, librarian at the University of California, called for a closer relationship among the nation's larger libraries, offering to enter into a reciprocal agreement with any library willing to lend to the University of California. He issued primarily the same requirements as did the Boston Public Library, with the additional statement that receipt of a book should be acknowledged by borrower and lender.[2]

## Code of 1917

The first official code establishing interlibrary loan procedures was the ALA Interlibrary Loan Code of 1917. The code has been modified several times. It is being revised even as this book goes to press.

The code stresses serving the graduate and research needs of university scholars. It further points out that borrowing from one library to another is a privilege, that lending is not an obligation.

Even after the Interlibrary Loan Code of 1917 had been approved, larger lending libraries established their own unwritten code, allowing greater flexibility in borrowing. In a questionnaire survey conducted in college and university libraries and published in 1932, K. J. Boyer found that 53.7 percent of the institutions loaned to undergraduates, that 71 percent loaned periodicals, that 31.5 percent of the institutions loaned to individuals as well as to libraries, and 58.1 percent did not require materials to be used within the library building.[3]

Harold Russell, librarian for the University of Minnesota and chairman of an interlibrary loan committee of the Association of College and Reference Libraries that was working on revision of the 1917 code, maintained in an article in the 1939 *ALA Bulletin* that the code should be reaffirmed, updated, and made available to all in the library field. He wrote that a generation before, research workers (ILL borrowers) had been far fewer in number and that the rise in their numbers had been caused primarily by the proliferation of indexes and abstracting services. Furthermore, he said that increases in interlibrary loans had made inroads into library staffing and should be kept within reasonable limits.

Russell's article discussed the 1917 code section by section, reaffirming the old code or suggesting changes that should go into a new code. It is, therefore, an interesting study of both codes. Russell's views of the 1917 code were as follows.

He felt that the preamble should remain unchanged except for perhaps more emphasis on the statement "No library can be expected to send its books a thousand miles for a reader whom it would not feel called upon to serve at its own door."

Article 1 indicates that the purpose of interlibrary loan service is 1) to aid research and 2) to augment the supply of the average book to the average reader and to aid the graduate student. He found that not all libraries were willing to borrow for anyone who had not yet received the master's degree.

Article 2 states that the lender must decide whether a particular loan should be made and also suggests photographic reproduction. Russell felt that photographic reproduction, especially since cheap films had appeared, could lead to wholesale discontinuance of periodical subscriptions and undue reliance upon films.

He reaffirmed Article 3, which mentions materials that ought not to be borrowed—books and periodicals that may be readily purchased.

Article 4, which covers materials that can be lent only under unusual circumstances, was also reaffirmed. It includes whatever is not physically suited for lending and books that should be used within the library that owns them.

Article 5 provides that music may be lent the same as books but calls attention to copyright provisions. Russell maintained that theses should also receive special copyright attention.

Article 6 emphasizes borrowing from the closest library and calls for the necessary bibliographical information. Russell noted that author, title of article, and source of verification should be added.

Article 7 indicates that the number of volumes borrowed at a time should be left to discretion. Russell agreed.

Article 8 calls for a four-week loan period. Russell thought the loan period should be shortened to two weeks, except in special cases.

Article 9, which deals with notices of receipt and return, is still as important as it was in 1917. Russell felt it was no longer necessary, however, to give call numbers or to indicate an express company for shipping. He said that labels should contain the full address and that materials should be returned the same way they were sent.

Article 10 states that shipping both ways, and insurance, if used, must be paid by the borrowing library. The author insisted that a package should always be insured.

Article 11 deals with safeguards. He felt that this article should not be changed.

Article 12, which outlines the responsibility of the borrower, was reaffirmed.

Article 13, which provides that ILL privileges may be withdrawn from institutions that abuse them, was reaffirmed.

Russell suggested that several statements about borrowers should be added to the code. He stated that every request should mention the name and status of the person for whose use a book is borrowed so that the lender can decide if the loan should be made, that libraries should borrow only for the use of their own patrons, and that the lending library should not send loans for patrons at libraries that did not initiate the request.[4]

## Code of 1940

The code for interlibrary loans, which was approved in 1940 by the ALA Council, was written by and for college, university, and research librarians. It was also followed by librarians from other types of libraries when requesting from college, university, and research libraries, although all sections of the code did not apply.

Lyle suggested that library policies could prevail if the borrowing library recognized its responsibility in requesting loans by 1) locating the most likely source from which material could be borrowed; 2) verifying the title of the publication; 3) substituting photostat and film purchase for interlibrary book loans; and 4) assuming the routine responsibilities of transportation costs, observing rules of lending libraries, returning books promptly and safely, maintaining the proper forms and records, filing regulations of libraries from which loans are frequently made, and making available the college's own policy on borrowing.[5]

In his article "Remarks upon Interlibrary Loans Mid-20th Century Style," Charles David, director of libraries, University of Pennsylvania, recommended ways to cut down on the cost of an interlibrary loan and suggested less formality in notifying of items shipped and received except for expensive or fragile items. Items could be loaned directly to individuals, or items could be requested by a library yet shipped direct.[6]

## Code of 1952

The 1952 code represented a liberalization of ILL rules of the past and widened the scope of lending from "unusual books" to materials for "serious study." For the first time, the code honored loans for undergraduates.

The code was further liberalized by making provision for other codes entered into by states or other geographical regions that might supersede the national code. If the liberal policies were to prevail, the borrowing library had to recognize its responsibility for locating the library the material might be borrowed from, for scattering requests to even the load, for verifying the title requested before requesting, and for supplying complete bibliographical information in accordance with the standard ALA interlibrary loan request form.

The proliferation of material in photocopy form brought a new tool to supplement and extend interlibrary loan, and special provision for borrowing of such material was provided in the 1952 code. In order to help solve some of the problems that arise in ILL service, the code also suggested that "payment of transportation costs both ways, including insurance is to be met by the borrowing library except where agreements to the contrary exist."

## Code of 1968

The general Interlibrary Loan Code of 1952, which was revised in 1956, was entirely superseded by the National Interlibrary Loan Code of 1968. The text of the code was approved by the ALA Reference Services Division, which merged with the Adult Services Division in 1972 to become the Reference and Adult Services Division. The new code called for the use of the revised ILL form, a four-part form with the same colors as before. The format was spaced to accommodate typewritten entries. NCR (no carbon required) paper was used.

Appended to the code was a model code that might be used by regional, state, local, or other special groups of libraries. It was recommended as a more liberal code. It was believed that a model code was timely because all states had money available under the Library Services and Construction Act Title III, to be used to enhance ILL cooperation. A review of the professional literature reveals an abundance of state codes drawn up during the 1960s and 1970s.[7, 8, 9, 10, 11, 12]

David Taylor from the University of Rhode Island was concerned that the following statement from the 1968 code could cause an ethical problem for the ILL department constantly bombarded by a particular professor doing research in a very specific area of study. The statement reads, "It is assumed that each library will provide the resources to meet the study, instructional, informational, and normal research needs of its users.... If an individual needs to use a large number of items located in another library, he should make arrangements to use them at that library."[13]

## Code of 1980

The latest revision of the ILL code occurred in 1980. Like all of the other codes before it, this national code contains general guidelines for borrowing and lending. The code, at first glance, closely resembles the original code and its many revisions. It is divided into eight sections labeled "Definition," "Purpose," "Scope," "Responsibilities of Borrowing Libraries," "Responsibilities of Lending Libraries," "Expenses," "Duration of Loan," and "Violation of Code." Earlier versions of the code contained many more sections, but as standardization was achieved through ILL manuals and forms, either some of the earlier concerns vanished or it became possible to lump several early sections into a single section.

In this version of the code, much deference is given to codes that have been developed by libraries organized geographically, by subject interest, or by some other specific agreement. Many such codes existed at that time, or they were written shortly thereafter.[14, 15, 16, 17] The introduction to the code indicates that it was designed primarily to regulate lending relations between research libraries and between libraries operating outside networks or consortia.

"Responsibilities of Borrowing Libraries" is the largest section of the code, placing the largest burden of responsibility on the borrowing library. The instructions are quite specific as to what the borrowing library must do to follow the code. Users must be informed of the ILL policies, and all requests should be screened and verified using standard bibliographic tools.

Changes that have occurred in the ILL process due to technological developments are taken into account in this latest revision of the code. It is stated, for example, that standard ILL formats should be used for all requests, regardless of the means of transmission. (See appendix A for various interlibrary loan codes.)

## Policies and Procedures

The different codes provided guidelines for lending, but something further needed to be done to establish the procedures by which the code was administered. Following the earliest code, James McMillan's book *Selected Articles on Interlibrary Loans* served the purpose of supplying various librarians' versions of how the code would work. In McMillan's book, M. O. Young, reference librarian, Princeton University, outlined policies and procedures quite specifically, as summarized here.

1. All possible information should be obtained from the requester. The librarian should make sure the request is necessary and that there is not a copy in the library.

2. Availability of the publication is then checked according to union lists or catalogs, subject bibliographies, or knowledge about library collections. The request is sent to the nearest place. Past experience, likelihood of response to the request, and other indefinite factors determine the choice. Duplicate inquiries can be sent provided a statement is made that the book need not be sent until requested.

3. A card record file (or some other separate record) must be kept for interlibrary loans. At the top of the card, author and title should be written. Below that, divisions should be set up for date sent, returned, for whom, date of acknowledgment of return, and so on, as desired. The card can be used for borrowing or lending, although the use of different colors is advisable.

4. When the book arrives, acknowledgment and postage should be immediately sent, the person requesting it should be notified as to its receipt and its date of return, and the card should be placed in the received file.

5. The requester should be reminded before or at the time of the due date, and, if necessary, a renewal should be requested.

6. When the publication is returned to the lending institution, notification of shipment should be made and the card record placed in the "Returned" file or kept in a separate file until the lending library acknowledges return of the book.

7. There is variation in libraries as to methods of notification of postage due. Some suggest that notification should be sent yearly. Young suggested that notification be made loan by loan. When the loan is made, a form telling of its shipment, method of shipment, time limit, and financial obligation should be sent. If a book is requested and the library either doesn't own it or is unable to send it, that fact should be forwarded.

8. Shipment may be made, depending on size and distance, by express mail (collect, if being loaned; prepaid, if being returned), registered mail, insured parcel post with special handling, or even by messenger.

9. To whom should a library lend? Distance makes little difference.

10. How long should the publication be kept? Young prefers no time limit but suggests a month, just to keep things from being lost. Libraries should retain the right to recall a loan. The librarian should ask for renewals, assuming renewal is granted, unless otherwise notified.

11. What should be done with the publication? Should it be for library use only?

12. Who may request? Anybody should be able to borrow. The lending library should decide if the material requested can be lent.

13. What can be lent? Young suggests no limitations, except for periodicals. Expensive and foreign titles should be lent.[18]

In 1949 Carl Melinet from Syracuse University published a thesis based on his research into the question of the administration of interlibrary loans in American libraries. Librarians, he said, had voiced a desire to know what other librarians were doing, and he believed that students needed an overall survey of practices and procedures. A questionnaire was designed to determine at which points practice varied from library to library and at which points it was uniform. Actual practice was then compared with the 1940 code. The questionnaire was sent to 55 university and special libraries, 32 college libraries, and 26 public libraries.

Great variation was shown in the responses to the 35 questions (15 for borrowing; 20 for lending). The majority of libraries responded that they used the ALA code for both borrowing and lending. Sixty percent indicated they used the code plus their own regulations for borrowing, and 65 percent used the code plus their own regulations for lending. Thirty-four percent of the libraries handled all ILL work in the reference department; 31 percent handled it in the circulation department; 13 percent had reference handle borrowing and circulation handle lending. Twenty-two percent of the libraries handled ILL work in various other ways.

Only 28 percent indicated they did not provide photocopies or lend microfilm. With so much use of film and copies, however, only 15 percent indicated that policy materially reduced the number of periodicals sent out. Seventy-seven percent reported asking for photographic reproduction only if the actual publications could not be borrowed. There was a great variety in the types of materials both borrowed and lent—even reference and rare books. Uncopyrighted theses were also borrowed and lent—with 34 percent of libraries placing no special restrictions on them. Thirteen percent required users of theses to sign a statement of use.

Verification of requests was attempted by 87 percent, only 41 percent reported receiving requests that had been verified. Sixty percent gave name and status of user. Lenders indicated that status of the user was more important (55 percent) than name (31 percent) or purpose (38 percent). Thirty-seven percent, however, indicated that none of the above was important. Seventy-six percent did not set limits on the number of items borrowed for faculty members, and 74 percent set no limit for other patrons. Eighty-four percent did not set limits on the number of items lent. The most popular loan period was two weeks (55 percent), followed by one month (34 percent). Even periodicals were lent for two weeks (57 percent), followed by one week (15 percent). Only 14 percent would not grant renewals on periodicals, and 4 percent would not grant renewals on books. Fifty-seven percent suspended borrowing, and 55 percent suspended loans during the Christmas season.

Materials were sent book rate or parcel post (49 percent), or some variation according to distance, type, and value of materials (41 percent).

Forty-eight percent did not instruct the borrowing library on how to return the material. Only 30 percent did in all cases. Ninety-eight percent charged no fees, with 45 percent of the libraries paying all ILL costs. Some collected shipment costs (24 percent), photostat or film costs (3 percent), or any fee that the lending library charged faculty members (16 percent). Figures were slightly higher for other patrons such as graduate students, undergraduate students, and nonuniversity patrons (49 percent for cost of shipment both ways, 44 percent for cost of photostat or film, and 24 percent for any fee charged by the lending library).

Requiring that borrowed material be used in the borrowing library varied; most patrons complied with such requests. Patrons who abused ILL privileges were told that their actions could cause the library to be denied borrowing privileges (56 percent) or that they themselves would be denied privileges (27 percent). Thirty-three percent indicated that no sanctions seemed to be necessary. Sixty-six percent never needed to apply sanctions for material kept overtime.

The greatest problems identified by libraries in connection with borrowing were difficulty of finding out what library might have the material (46 percent), difficulty of getting patrons to observe due dates and other rules (21 percent), amount of time and money spent on interlibrary loan not being proportional to results obtained (17 percent), and reluctance of libraries to lend certain types of materials (12 percent). The greatest problems identified with lending were unverified citations (55 percent), unreasonable amounts of material requested (29 percent), unreasonable kinds of material requested (16 percent), and heavy drain of this type of service on the library budget (15 percent).[19]

In later years, following the 1968 code revision, policies and procedures for handling interlibrary loan activity were described in considerable detail by Sarah Katherine Thomson in her *Interlibrary Loan Manual*, published by the ALA. Her work has been continued by Virginia Boucher of the University of Colorado, Boulder.

Boucher's *Interlibrary Loan Practices Handbook*, which describes the procedures outlined in interlibrary loan codes, includes chapters on borrowing and lending and copyright concerns as they relate to photocopying of journal articles and the use of dissertations and theses. Managing the ILL office and international interlibrary loan are also covered.

## Forms

Interlibrary loan administration involves many details, many of which are handled by the use of forms. The early forms were devised by individual librarians to meet their own needs, but they were shared and librarians copied each others' work. Printed blanks were used by the Boston Public Library as early as 1896.[20] Other public libraries used them as well.

In 1909 William Warner Bishop reported that LC printed blank forms were used by the Cincinnati Public Library, Harvard University, Johns Hopkins University, Princeton University, the University of Chicago, the

University of Virginia, Yale University, the Boston Public Library, and Clark University. These request forms represented less than 10 percent of the total, however. Other libraries requested through letters from the librarian.[21]

During the 1930s, the use of letters was promoted by Constance Winchell. The most common forms used during the 1930s were request slips filled out by patrons, request letters, acknowledgments, notices to patrons that material had arrived, and return notices. For outgoing loans, shipping notices and notices that the volume requested could not be lent were the prevailing forms.

In the 1949 Melinet study, libraries responded that they used at least 1 form card. Some used as many as 20; the average was about 12. The forms showed great variation in size and shape—3"-x-5" cards, 4"-x-6" cards, or a full 8½"-x-11" page.

The major ILL routines at that time were divided into borrowing and lending with the following types of action called for:

### BORROWING

1. The application is received from the patron.

2. The request is transferred to the record card.

3. A search is conducted for location of the item. This may involve sending the form to the LC to be checked against the *National Union Catalog* or to some other bibliographic center.

4. A request letter is sent to the lending library.

5. Receipt of the item is acknowledged.

6. A book slip is placed in the book for the patron's information.

7. The patron is sent a notice of arrival.

8. An overdue notice may have to be sent to the patron.

9. A renewal request may be sent to the lending library

10. Notice of return of the item is sent to the lending library.

### LENDING

1. The request is received and recorded.

2. A notice of inability to lend the item may be sent.

3. An application for photographic reproduction may be sent if the item cannot be lent.

4. A "sending" notice is mailed.

5. The item is sent.

6. An overdue notice may be sent.

7. A renewing notice may be sent.

8. Return of the item is acknowledged.

9. If the item is not returned, the patron may be sent a suspension-of-service notification.

10. Statistics are kept on loans. [22]

In 1950, Elizabeth Chamberlin, medical librarian at the College of Medicine, University of Vermont, promoted the use of a 3"-x-5" slip for ILL transactions. The triplicate request form incorporated the forms of the Veterans' Administration Library Service and other library forms.[23]

## ALA Order Forms

A four-part multiple-carbon ILL form was developed, also in 1950, for use among the eight campuses of the University of California. The following year an Association of College and Research Libraries (ACRL) committee recommended at the ALA conference that all libraries use the new California form.[24]

There were numerous advantages to having a uniform form. Having only one title request per form was one advantage. In addition, spaces for entering brief information or simply adding a check mark were provided on the form, eliminating the necessity of sending a cover letter. All retyping was avoided because of the carbons and window envelopes that were used with the form.

Five years after the form came into general use, a survey was conducted by an ILL committee to find out if changes were needed. The survey disclosed a deep gulf between a number of 3"-x-5" form users (mostly state and government libraries handling a large volume of loans) and those who advocated the newer 5"-x-8" form.

Even though more librarians preferred the 5"-x-8" form, a number of suggestions for improvement were offered. These concerned the carbons and the white space on the form. The carbons were deliberately made not to go completely to the right edge so that all three carbons could be removed at once by pulling the stub at the left. Some thought the carbons should continue to the edge to capture information that might be written there. The committee called the manufacturers' attention to the carbon problem. It was solved by the use of NCR paper.

The securing of additional space required in-depth study by the committee, however. Space for remarks at the top of the form was found, as was a little additional space in the center for author and periodical title. Two items were combined into a "verified in" statement, with "cannot verify" being removed. "Any edition" was added to the form in response to demand. The wording concerning microfilm or photocopies was changed to "If non-circulating, please send cost estimate for microfilm (or) photoprint."

Several changes were made in the right-hand portion of the form. Spaces were provided for microfilm or photoprint estimates. Lending libraries were given an option to check "hold placed" and "request again."

Around the edges of the form, librarians were reminded to enclose shipping labels and to send stamps to cover transportation costs. "Notice of return" was underlined as a reminder. "Mail Separately, Do Not Return With Book" was added to the top of sheet D. "Checked by" was replaced by "Authorized by."

The usefulness of the C sheet was called into question. It was used for holds and renewals and as a packing slip. It was also recommended that lending libraries that modified shipping addresses send two addressed return labels with a note asking that one be placed on the D form to replace the original address. The revised form was adopted along with the revised Interlibrary Loan Code in 1968.[25]

A standardized photoduplication order form was developed by the ALA Resources and Technical Service Division in 1962-1963 and revised in 1974. It is similar to the form used for loan requests. Sarah Katherine Thomson reported from her 1967 doctoral study of interlibrary loans that 31 of the 203 forms used for ordering photocopies were the photoduplication order form, so use of it apparently developed slowly.[26]

With the implementation of the Copyright Revision Law of 1976, modification of the order form became necessary to provide space for copyright information. An ALA subcommittee on interlibrary loan solicited suggestions and comments from librarians concerning their perceptions of other needed revisions and set about to revise the ILL form. This resulted in the following changes and reasons for change:

1. "Requests for loan or photocopy." Title of the form was changed because it was often used for photoduplications. Boxes were included to make it easier for the receiving library to sort requests.

2. "Requests of" was added so that an alternate source could be suggested.

3. "No renewals" was added for those who do not renew.

4. "Note: the receiving library assumes responsibility for notification of non-receipt" was displaced by the copyright statement.

5. The lower-left corner contained language enabling a supplier to be assured the requester was in compliance with the law.

6. "If non-circulating ..." The language was changed for clarification.

7. "ISBN, or ISSN, or LC card, or OCLC, or other number, if known" was added to speed delivery.

8. The revised language, "Verified in: OR item cited in:" attempted to clarify what information was sought.

9. Lines for author and title were changed to clarify language. Parentheses were removed because they tend to suggest secondary information. The word "year" was substituted for "date." The word "series" was included.

10. "Not needed after" was added for guidance.

11. "Requestor's Order No." was deemed necessary for billing.[27]

The ALA interlibrary loan form is, and has been since 1951, considered the standard ILL form (see fig. 2.1). The second paper form, the photographic order form, is also still used (see fig. 2.2, on page 36). When teletype, or TWX (Teletypewriter Exchange Service), machines became popular for transmitting requests in the mid-1960s, formats were abbreviated and changed to meet network requirements (see fig. 2.3, on page 37). Additional ILL formats were developed in the later 1970s by the bibliographic utilities, which introduced automated ILL subsystems. Herbert Goldhor stated in his 1977 report of the evaluation of the Illinois Interlibrary Loan Network (ILLINET) that 81 percent of the requests were on system library forms, 10 percent were on ALA forms (used about equally by academic and special libraries), and 9 percent were on other forms.[28]

## International Interlibrary Loan Form

The IFLA adopted an ILL form in 1936 (see fig. 2.3). As early as 1947, objections to it had been raised. The objections were very similar to those raised about the form adopted for American libraries by the ALA. It was considered too small to include all pertinent bibliographical information. It also made no provision for securing information about photocopies, causing unnecessary correspondence.[29]

When the international rules, or code, were changed in 1954, a new request form was devised. It measured 11 inches by 4 inches. Information is provided on both sides of the form—bibliographic data concerning the request on the front and verification information and instructions for forwarding the form if material requested is unavailable on the reverse. The form is written in French, English, and German. It may be obtained from J. Jorgensen and Company in Copenhagen, Denmark.

**A REQUEST**

Request for ☐ LOAN or ☐ PHOTOCOPY
According to the A.L.A. Interlibrary Loan Code

**REPORTS:** Checked by
SENT BY: ☐ Library rate ☐
Charges $_____ Insured for $_____
Date sent _____
DUE _____

**RESTRICTIONS:** ☐ For use in library only
☐ Copying not permitted ☐

**NOT SENT BECAUSE:** ☐ In use
☐ Not Owned
☐ Non Circulating
☐ Request of _____

Estimated Cost of: ☐ Microfilm _____
☐ Hard copy _____

**BORROWING LIBRARY RECORD:**

Date received _____
Date returned _____
By ☐ Library rate ☐
Postage
enclosed $_____ Insured for $_____

**RENEWALS:** ☐ No renewals
Requested on _____
Renewed to _____ (or period of renewal)

Note: the receiving library assumes responsibility for notification of non receipt

DEMCO
Madison, Wis.
Fresno, Calif.
NO. 65-250

Date of request: _____ Not needed after: _____ Requester's order no.

CALL NO.

BORROWING
LIBRARY

FILL IN LEFT
HALF OF FORM
INCLUDING
BOTH LIBRARY
ADDRESSES
IN FULL

For use of _____ Status _____ Dept.

Book author: OR periodical title, vol. and date

FOLD
HERE

Book Title, edition, place, year series: OR periodical article author, title, pages. ☐ This edition only

SEND SHEETS
A, B AND C
TO LENDING
LIBRARY, AND
ENCLOSE
SHIPPING
LABEL

Verified in: OR: item cited in

ISBN, OR ISSN, or LC card, or OCLC, or other number if known _____
If non-circulating, & cost does not exceed $_____ , please supply ☐ Microfilm ☐ Hard copy

LENDING
LIBRARY

FILL IN PER-
TINENT ITEMS
UNDER
REPORTS,
RETURN SHEETS
B AND C TO
BORROWING
LIBRARY

AUTHORIZED BY: (full name) _____
TITLE _____

Request complies with
☐ 108(g)(2) Guidelines (CCG)
☐ other provisions of copyright law (CCL)

REV 6/77

Fig. 2.1. ALA interlibrary loan form.

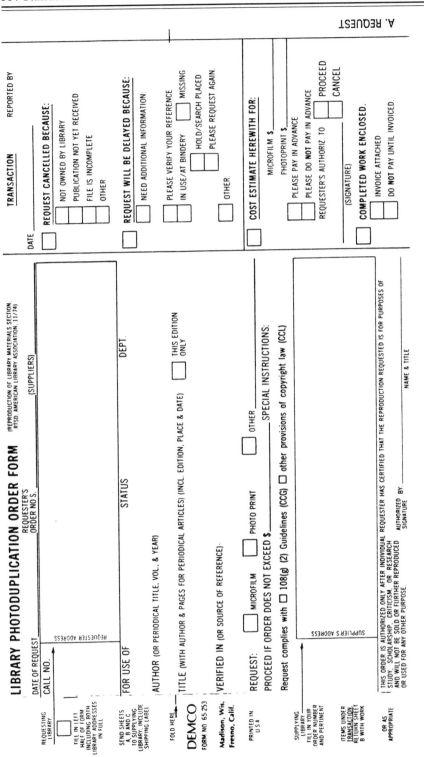

Fig. 2.2. ALA photo duplication order form.

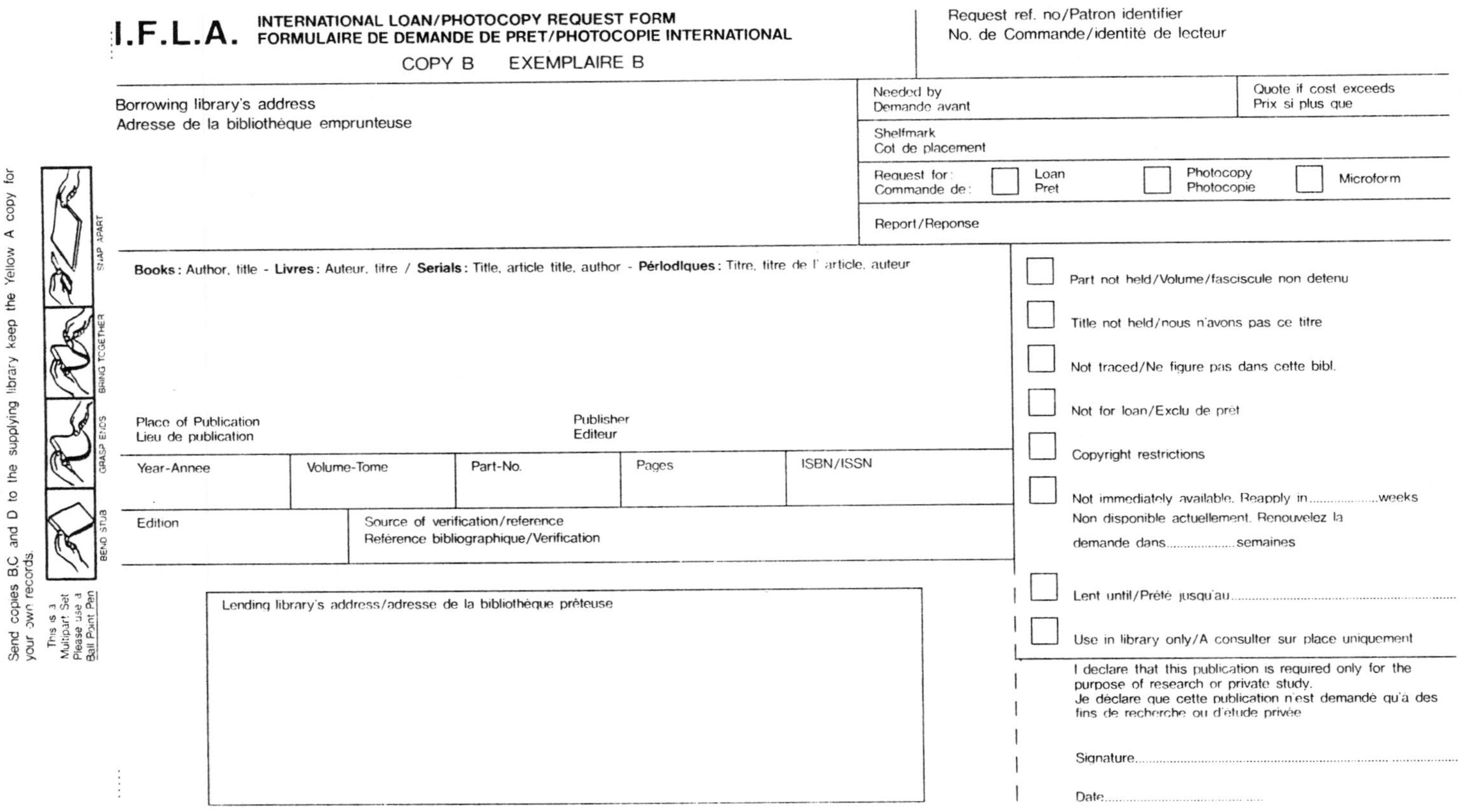

**I.F.L.A.** INTERNATIONAL LOAN/PHOTOCOPY REQUEST FORM
FORMULAIRE DE DEMANDE DE PRET/PHOTOCOPIE INTERNATIONAL

COPY B EXEMPLAIRE B

Request ref. no/Patron identifier
No. de Commande/identité de lecteur

Borrowing library's address
Adresse de la bibliothèque emprunteuse

Needed by
Demande avant

Quote if cost exceeds
Prix si plus que

Shelfmark
Cot de placement

Request for: / Commande de: ☐ Loan / Pret ☐ Photocopy / Photocopie ☐ Microform

Report/Reponse

**Books:** Author, title - **Livres:** Auteur, titre / **Serials:** Title, article title, author - **Périodiques:** Titre, titre de l' article, auteur

Place of Publication
Lieu de publication

Publisher
Editeur

| Year-Annee | Volume-Tome | Part-No. | Pages | ISBN/ISSN |
|---|---|---|---|---|

Edition

Source of verification/reference
Reférence bibliographique/Verification

Lending library's address/adresse de la bibliothèque prêteuse

☐ Part not held/Volume/fasciscule non detenu

☐ Title not held/nous n'avons pas ce titre

☐ Not traced/Ne figure pas dans cette bibl.

☐ Not for loan/Exclu de prêt

☐ Copyright restrictions

☐ Not immediately available. Reapply in ..................weeks
Non disponible actuellement. Renouvelez la demande dans..................semaines

☐ Lent until/Prêté jusqu'au..................

☐ Use in library only/A consulter sur place uniquement

I declare that this publication is required only for the purpose of research or private study.
Je déclare que cette publication n'est demandé qu'à des fins de recherche ou d'etude privée

Signature..................

Date..................

Send copies B,C and D to the supplying library keep the Yellow A copy for your own records.

This is a Multipart Set Please use a Ball Point Pen

SNAP APART
BRING TOGETHER
GRASP ENDS
BEND STUB

Fig. 2.3. International interlibrary loan form.

# Notes

[1]"Inter-library Loans," *Library Journal* (February 1893):61.

[2]"Inter-library Loans," *Library Journal* (March 1898):104.

[3]K. J. Boyer, "Inter-library Loans in College and University Libraries," *Library Quarterly* 2 (April 1932):113-34.

[4]Harold Russell, "The Interlibrary Loan Code," *ALA Bulletin* 33 (1939):321-25.

[5]Guy R. Lyle, *The Administration of the College Library*, 3d ed. (New York: Wilson, 1961), 141.

[6]Charles W. David, "Remarks upon Interlibrary Loans Mid-20th Century Style," *College and Research Libraries* 10 (October 1949):429-33.

[7]E. P. Watson, "Interlibrary Loan Code for Louisiana College and University Libraries," *Louisiana Library Association Bulletin* 26 (Summer 1963):69-70.

[8]R. J. Beck, "Interlibrary Loan Code for Idaho," *Idaho Librarian* 20 (July 1968):98-102.

[9]"Interlibrary Loan Code for New Mexico and the Channels for Interlibrary Lending in New Mexico," *New Mexico Libraries* 2 (Spring 1969):21-30.

[10]Oklahoma Library Association, "Interlibrary Loan Code for the State of Oklahoma," *Oklahoma Librarian* 26 (July 1976):19-21.

[11]Wyoming Library Association, "State Interlibrary Loan Code," *Wyoming Library Roundup* 29 (March 1974):12-15.

[12]Arkansas Library Association, "Interlibrary Loan Code for the State of Arkansas," *Arkansas Librarian* 23 (1976):23-26.

[13]David C. Taylor, "Concerning the 1968 Interlibrary Loan Code," *RQ* 8 (Spring 1969):195-96.

[14]"Interlibrary Loan Code for Georgia Libraries, 1981," *Georgia Librarian* 18 (November-December 1981):16-17.

[15]"Interlibrary Loan Code for the Libraries of Mississippi, a Draft," *Mississippi Libraries* 14 (Winter 1980):178-82.

[16]"Interlibrary Loan Guidelines: Results of a Study of Wisconsin Referral Patterns," *Wisconsin Library Bulletin* 76 (July-August 1980):147-52, 189.

[17]"Liberal Interloan Code Adopted by AMIGOS," *Library Journal* 105 (November 1980):2256-57.

[18]James A. McMillan, *Selected Articles on Interlibrary Loans* (New York: Wilson, 1928), 17-22.

[19]Carl H. Melinet, *The Administration of Interlibrary Loans in American Libraries* (Syracuse, N.Y.: Syracuse University, 1949), 84-88.

[20]Constance M. Winchell, *Locating Books for Interlibrary Loans* (New York: Wilson, 1930), 12.

[21]William Warner Bishop, "Interlibrary Loans," in *The Library Without the Walls*, ed. Laura M. Janzow (New York: Wilson, 1927):409.

[22]Melinet, *Administration of Interlibrary Loans*, 7-8.

[23]Elizabeth G. Chamberlin, "An Interlibrary Loan Form for Small Libraries," *Library Journal* 75 (December 1950):2131.

[24]Margaret D. Uridge, "Labor Saving Form Aids Interlibrary Loan," *Library Journal* 76 (June 1951):1010-11.

[25]Foster M. Palmer, "Interlibrary Loan Form—A Five Year Report," *Library Journal* 81 (October 1956):2167-69.

[26]Sarah Katherine Thomson, *General Interlibrary Loan Services in Major Academic Libraries in the United States* (New York: Columbia University, 1967), 49.

[27]Nancy H. Marshall and Ronald P. Naylar. "Interlibrary Loan Issues," *RQ* 17 (Fall 1977):59-64.

[28]Herbert Goldhor, "An Evaluation of the Illinois Interlibrary Loan Network (ILLINET)," *Illinois Libraries* 61 (1979):14.

[29]"Projet de Révision du Règlement du Prèt International," *Libri* 4 (1954):167-70.

chapter 3

# Networking

A network is a system or pattern made up of interconnecting parts, according to the dictionary. A network is also described as two or more organizations engaged in a common pattern of information exchange through telecommunication links, for some objectives that the organizations share in common.[1] In the library field, a network is a system made up of libraries for the purpose of providing access to shared resources. Even though the word *network* often brings to mind a computerized system, that is not necessarily the case. Linking must include a communications mechanism of some sort, however.

In the past, the library community and the academic computing community have used the word *network* to describe two different phenomena. To the computing community, a network is a general-purpose structure that links computers and supports a wide range of activities. It is like a highway system, providing a basic facility, a means to get from one place to another. Library networks, however, are organizations that provide high-level services such as shared cataloging or interlibrary loan; these services usually are based on a computer network of some sort, but the justification for a library network is the service it provides, not the communication facility itself.[2]

A network may be thought of as either a formal or an informal linkage of discrete library units and other information-dispensing agencies for the purpose of exchanging or transferring recorded information. Exchanging and transferring is emphasized, implying two-way communication and some sort of switching mechanism.[3]

Networks may be used for various cooperative ventures—cataloging and processing, reference services, collection development, resource sharing, and others. The ILL function is dependent on efficient methods of transmission of requests and document delivery. Whenever a group of libraries can agree on a formal procedure of transmission and delivery, improvement in service is almost always reached. Ron Miller stated that, at the very least, a self-respecting network should have plans for computerization even though it can call itself a network if a delivery system or regional ILL arrangement has been agreed upon.[4]

The network concept includes the development of cooperative systems of libraries on geographical, subject, or other lines, each with some kind of center that not only coordinates the internal activities of the system but also serves as the system's outlet to, and inlet from, the centers of other systems. The concept is also hierarchical in that the centers of smaller systems are channels to centers of larger networks at state, national, and even international levels.[5]

# Needs and Development

One of the most common types of traditional networks is the ILL network in which groups of libraries agree to provide lending privileges to each other; this agreement often contains a mechanism to identify holdings to facilitate lending and borrowing.

The concept of networking is intertwined with the history of interlibrary loan. Early sponsors of interlibrary loan described it without calling it by name. Networking began to develop on a national scale with the activities of the LC. The communication mechanism, or location tool, was born in 1901 when the LC began producing and distributing catalog cards. Resource sharing exploded when the LC again led the way by designing and then receiving national and international acceptance of the MARC format. It began distributing these data in 1969.

Other factors accelerated the trend toward networks. The quantity of materials being published is only one of them. In the past, libraries served their patrons from their own collections as much as possible, using interlibrary loan as a supplement. Decreasing purchasing power and increasing service to patrons have caused libraries to view a collection as being not only materials owned by an individual library but materials owned by other libraries as well.

Before 1970, the two primary ways of transmitting information were the postal service and teletypewriters. At the same time, the bibliographic tools used in ILL work were the NUC or regional or local catalogs.

## Communication by Teletype

In 1927, the Free Library of Philadelphia used a teletypewriter as part of a closed circuit to communicate information from the loan desk in the main reading room to and from the stacks. In the 1940s, Michigan librarians connected two different city libraries with a teletypewriter.[6]

The result of a fire in the Michigan State Library was the installation of a teletype circuit tying together the resources of most of the major libraries in Michigan. Each of the libraries paid the charges for its own requests. The teletype was used for other purposes as well, but its ability to improve library cooperation and speed interlibrary loans so inspired librarians that they encouraged others to install teletype machines. It was reported in 1968 that a "hot line" teletype system, coupled with a speedy delivery system, was being used by Western Michigan University libraries to get interlibrary loans to their extension students.[7]

The system used in the state of Louisiana, the Louisiana Rapid Communications System, combined the features of the TWX and the Wide Area Telecommunications Service (WATS) in a manner providing each library in the state with almost instantaneous communication with any other library in Louisiana, using the state library as a relay station. Even with such rapid communication available, however, Kleiner reported that the system was slow to catch on. Some libraries lost their machines because they used them so seldom that the cost per transaction was prohibitive. Many continued to place requests via mail, although a TWX or WATS number was available to them.[8]

The Texas State Library Communication Network began in 1968. Administration of the network was the responsibility of the state library. It and major resource center libraries were compensated by LSCA (Library Services and Construction Act) funds. When an area library could not fill requests from its community libraries, these and its own requests were referred to its major resource center library. If that library was unable to comply, the requests were referred to the Texas State Library. If it did not own the material, it sent the request to the other major resource center libraries or (for scholarly materials) to the University of Texas at Austin.

In every stage of a transaction there was both downward and upward activity—downward when a borrowing library's request could be filled and upward to a library with greater resources if a request could not be filled. As a request progressed upward, resources became greater and the possibility of its being filled increased. The community, area, and major resource libraries communicated by telephone; the major resource center libraries and the Texas State Library communicated by teletype.[9]

The Iowa Library Information Teletype Exchange (I-LITE), begun in 1969, noted that a filled request might cost as much as $5.21. The greatest problem was the length of time required for the requests to make a complete circuit and for unfilled requests to be returned to originating libraries.[10]

Upon the advice of its consultant, the Montana State Library replaced its TWX equipment with microprocessor-based equipment in order to save money and speed up ILL transactions. The software package selected to format, edit, and transmit ILL requests was MicroCourier, developed by MicroCom.

MicroCourier allows the operator to prepare and edit interlibrary loan requests during working hours and send them automatically during evening hours, when telephone rates are lower. The microcomputer also acts like a computer terminal to send messages to libraries that subscribe to the Ontyme II electronic mail (E-mail) service and to interact with other host computers like Montana University system computers.

The microcomputer systems were installed in 1981 at the Montana State Library and at the headquarters buildings of six public libraries. Batches of requests are sent in round-robin fashion. As many requests as possible are filled in-state before being sent to out-of-state libraries. By the time a request reaches the last stop, it will have been checked against the holdings of four public libraries, two university libraries, and the state library. The state library checks the remaining requests against the Western Library Network (WLN) database.

The microcomputer has also simplified use of the Ontyme II E-mail service. Messages are prepared off-line and stored on diskettes. On a given day, several ILL request files, each for a different library, are created and sent. Incoming and outgoing messages are also stored on diskette. A detailed transaction log became a necessary part of the interlibrary loan E-mail procedure.

It was found that the microcomputers functioned with more ease and speed than did the TWX machines, even though there were drawbacks with the software, which is basically a business application package. Telecommunication costs were considerably less for microcomputers than for TWX—about $.20 per request for microcomputer-to-microcomputer transmission compared to over $1.25 per request for TWX machine operation. The editing features of the microcomputers saved time, and the working environment improved. Microcomputers are also capable of being used for a variety of other library programs.[11]

## Communication by Telefacsimile

Librarians began experimenting with telefacsimile, or fax, in the 1960s, using it mainly to send interlibrary loan requests and brief journal articles. The early machines required up to six minutes to transmit one page of text. The equipment was expensive and unreliable, produced low-quality copies, and was not serviced by its manufacturers. It also did not always reduce the time involved in document delivery. Most of the networks that used fax only for communicating the actual loan requests replaced the systems with TWX or telephone.

In 1978 TALINET (Telefax Library Information Network) was designed to assess the use of fax in document delivery to remote communities in Colorado, Kansas, Montana, Wyoming, and South Dakota. The study concluded that the technology was suitable, but the cost was still too high in light of the limited demand for that kind of service.

In 1981, when high-speed digital fax machines were becoming available, another study concluded that fax was still not very successful due to expense, staff time, and the need to improve the technology. Since the mid-1980s, however, interest has increased and a variety of studies and projects conducted in the Denver Public Library, Texas A&M University's College of Medicine, the Western Council of State Libraries, New York and Columbia universities, Texas College of Osteopathic Medicine, the National Library of Canada, and the College of Physicians of Philadelphia indicate librarian and user satisfaction.[12]

Pennsylvania libraries installed fax equipment to speed document delivery. Requests may still be placed through bibliographic utilities. Protocols and guidelines were drawn up to supplement procedures outlined in ILL codes. The ALA form is used for requests sent by fax rather than through bibliographic utilities. Subject requests are sent only to those libraries with whom a prior agreement has been made.[13]

Many other libraries are presently using fax to speed document delivery. Guidelines vary, but the basic procedure is about the same. Some libraries send materials by fax only on a rush basis.

So extensive is the fax network that publications have been written on the applications of fax in libraries, comparisons of E-mail and fax, telecommunication costs, ILL guidelines, and directories of fax numbers. Two such publications exist in Ohio, *The Authoritative Guide on the Use of Telefacsimile in Libraries* and *Telefacsimile Directory of Ohio Libraries*. Directories of fax numbers are available for the Rocky Mountain area (*Action for Libraries*), for the New England area (*Directory of FAX Numbers in New England Libraries*), and, indeed, for the entire North American area (*Directory of Telefacsimile Sites in North American Libraries*).[14]

## Communication by Computer

The by-product of on-line shared cataloging was the ability to verify and transmit interlibrary loans on-line. Automated ILL systems exist in every major bibliographic utility.

The successful on-line network requires a significant level of financial and organizational commitment from participants; it is based upon agreement within the group of participants that specific tasks should be performed and specific guidelines adhered to; and it provides an immediate facility for access, through computer and communications technologies, to databases that may stem from both the public and private sectors of the information community. Because involvement entails a sizable financial commitment, representing both direct and indirect costs, libraries that are network participants must actively use the network's services in order to derive benefits commensurate with their levels of expenditure.[15]

In the United States, the 1960s was a period of affluence compared to the leaner years of the 1970s, when funds to start new projects or to expand those already begun were limited. During the 1970s, there were fewer systems for automating the operations of a single institution. Efforts were concentrated on building systems to use a single computer-based file to serve the processing and public-service needs of many institutions.[16]

Since the advent of the automated library network in the 1970s, it is no longer easy to distinguish between the traditional network and the computerized network. The traditional network has changed to meet modern needs. Werking concluded that the introduction of on-line library automation into liberal arts college libraries lagged behind the same phenomenon in the ARL libraries, but automation caught on rapidly with this group during the 1980s.[17]

There are very few libraries in the United States now that do not belong to some sort of network, either formal or informal. Public library systems represent a particular type of cooperation. Within a given geographic region, public libraries may join together to establish and maintain a union catalog in order to provide information for patrons using a library in another part of the geographic region. This type of agreement is often accompanied by a delivery mechanism.

Special libraries also group together in order to cooperate. Throughout the country are found groups of medical libraries, law libraries, research libraries, public documents libraries—all attempting to share materials, to solve common problems, or to set standards affecting their special group.[18]

Many libraries belong to more than one network, taking advantage of the various services of each. Libraries may belong to a local network and a state network; they may also belong to a regional or national network.

Union catalogs, made available through networks, have made possible the "extended library." Individuals or libraries can use on-line terminals to identify a book, its location, and, in some cases, its availability.

The cost of an interlibrary loan, including the cost of telecommunication, is usually less than the cost of the material being borrowed. Computer equipment costs have either decreased or remained stable; staff and materials costs have risen. Networks flourished during the 1960s when the federal government began providing large sums of money to libraries, especially through the LSCA. During the 1970s, funding decreased, however, causing even closer cooperation. Improvements in telecommunications technology also spurred the growth of networks.[19]

A special conference held in Virginia in 1970 on interlibrary communications and information networks recommended that a new National Commission on Libraries and Information Science be made a focal point for devising a national network of libraries and information centers.[20] An important foundation for the effective sharing of information resources nationwide was established with the development of procedures and protocols for sharing authority records among the bibliographic utilities. These procedures and protocols will facilitate the uniform use of names and subject headings throughout the library community, not merely within individual collections.[21] Libraries require networking links for two different aspects of their operation: They need links with other libraries and with bibliographic utilities to support their traditional processes, and they need links with the academic community to carry out their primary mission of providing students and scholars with access to information. Until now, most libraries have concentrated on the former because patrons usually would come to a library to use its services. Independent networks were needed because the emerging general-purpose computing reached only a small number of academic institutions. Bibliographic utilities developed independent, dedicated networks to support access for libraries to their centralized services.[22]

## Organization and Finance

If we limit the consideration of networks to only those organizations using telecommunication devices, the formation and establishment of library networks has been prompted by four federal laws: 1) Library Services and Construction Act, Title III; 2) Higher Education Act, Title II; 3) State Technical Services Act; and 4) Medical Library Assistance Act. Each of these laws may be called enabling legislation because funds are provided to develop networks to achieve some specific purpose outlined by the law. By accepting federal funds, the state agencies give precedence to federal laws over state laws. State rulings are adjusted to allow for the implementation of the federal law. Each state usually prepares a state plan, which must be reviewed and approved by the federal agency administering the program. Existing networks are quasi-official organizations with questionable legal identity and with powers resulting from a long series of contracts generally following this pattern and subject to legal interpretation of the following: 1) enabling federal law, 2) U.S. Bureau of Budget rules, 3) guidelines to the federal law, 4) state agency rules and the grant agreement between the federal and state agency, 5) state plans for that particular law, 6) the qualifying host institution's contract with the state agency (or federal agency), 7) the host institution regulations, and 8) the agreement between the network administrator and the host institution.

Duggan reviewed membership agreements or state contracts being used by 17 networks operating in one state. She found that no two networks had a similar instrument and that the lack of standardization was obvious even within the boundaries of one state. To avoid legal questions concerning sales tax for photocopy charges or other fees, liability for incomplete services to network users, and other matters, some networks call their contracts membership agreements. Formal written agreements of some type are considered essential in operating a successful network. Appendix B contains various types of written network agreements.

Legal questions may arise concerning who owns the databank used in a network, or from the procurement of an information bank by a network from a commercial agency, or even concerning a federal information bank. New academic institutions seeking accreditation by network access to collections can also present legal problems. Perhaps the most complex legal problems arise with network interfacing where incompatibility of operational policies, fee structures, users' access, funding base, and so forth become evident.[23]

Any formula for network support requires consideration of cost elements, and these are embedded in the structural and operational decisions of network construction. The questions of what kind of network, the projected stages of development, and who pays for what must be answered before a viable formula can be advanced; otherwise, we would be prescribing a fiscal remedy without benefit of diagnosis. Communication costs must be specified in terms of equipment, routing, channels, volumes, and outlets.[24] S. Gilbert Prentiss, in describing the New York State Inter-Library Loan Network (NYSILL), suggested that a one-to-one charge from lender to borrower might be a simpler, less costly method of handling interlibrary loans than network membership fees or the passing of federal monies to the state agencies.[25]

Some loss of autonomy seems to be necessary if useful cooperation is to occur. The very fact that member libraries divert local funds to the consortium or the network means that some local leverage is sacrificed—fewer books can be purchased, a new staff member cannot be hired, a new machine cannot be purchased or rented.[26]

## Types of Networks

Edward Walters has identified five forms of library networks: 1) the unit-cost networks, or bibliographic utilities—such as the Online Computer Library Center (OCLC) or the Research Libraries Information Network (RLIN)—with the size and revenue sources to raise capital for development; 2) the multistate regional auxiliary enterprise networks, such as AMIGOS (meaning friends) or the Southeastern Library Network (SOLINET), with their low capital investment and fee-based assessment and a more limited ability to amass capital; 3) the authority-sanctioned networks, such as ILLINET and FEDLINK (Federal Library Network), established by governments that have jurisdiction and draw on their authority to coerce the acceptance of standards and capital for new projects; 4) the discipline and type-of-library networks that are created for the purpose of sustaining either a discipline (law, medicine, or agriculture) or an institutional form (university or corporation); and 5) local consortia or proximity networks that are founded and sustained because geographical proximity makes library cooperation more timely and often more effective. These latter vary greatly in the kinds of organizations they include and in size, governance, and programs.[27] A consortium is defined as a group formed through contractual arrangements. In 1934 a study of interinstitutional agreements indicated there were 113 such agreements.[28]

Most consortia are established for special purposes. Members are allowed to resign when the group's purposes are no longer relevant. Most consortia ask for membership fees from the participating institutions, yet they are generally supported by federal money or a foundation grant. A distinct benefit of a consortium is the modest cost of participation for a much greater extension of resources and services.[29]

Each of the five types of library networks is part of a national library "network picture" that is interlocking in its services. One cannot talk about a type of network without defining its relationship to the others.[30] The five types of networks, as defined earlier, are discussed in more detail throughout this chapter.

## Bibliographic Utilities

During the late 1960s and early 1970s several cooperative organizations were founded to support, through computer systems, shared cataloging, retrospective conversion of catalog records to machine-readable form, and interlibrary lending. Initially, they were based on batch-processing systems, but on-line services soon followed.

Four major bibliographic utilities serve North American libraries. They are known by the acronyms OCLC, RLIN, UTLAS, and WLN. Each has its own characteristics and special mission. For example, OCLC grew from a consortium (Ohio College Library Center) to support shared cataloging for libraries in Ohio into a worldwide organization with thousands of member libraries (Online Computer Library Center). UTLAS (University of Toronto Library Automation Center) began as a project to develop a union catalog for five new universities in Ontario, Canada. It evolved into a mission to support the Canadian library community in general, but it expanded to serve libraries in the United States and other countries. In 1985 it was sold to the International Thomson Organization and became a for-profit corporation. WLN began as the Washington Library Network and later became the Western Library Network. It is still a regional organization and provides a more limited range of services and products than does OCLC or UTLAS.[31]

The libraries of the 1970s used the three large bibliographic utilities—WLN, OCLC, and RLIN. Though some were using COM, the local library catalog was primarily still a card catalog, with the cards being supplied by the utilities. The basic service of all three utilities was providing LC and member records for use in cataloging and to which holdings could be attached.

### Online Computer Library Center (OCLC)

The largest and most famous bibliographic utility was established in 1967 as the Ohio College Library Center to serve as a computerized regional processing center for libraries in Ohio. The goals of OCLC were 1) to support the member institutions by suppling information to them when and where they needed it, making it possible for them to cooperate in the educational and research activities of their individual users; and 2) to make the resources of all member libraries available to the faculty and students at each institution by means of an on-line union catalog.[32] An off-line card production system was begun in 1970, followed by an on-line system for shared cataloging in 1971. The database consisted of Library of Congress MARC records plus original cataloging contributed by participating libraries.

In 1973 OCLC offered membership to libraries outside Ohio, and the name was changed twice to reflect a larger outreach. During the 1980s OCLC began serving libraries in England and Japan.

Libraries with not enough activity to justify special workstations, leased telephone lines, and high-speed modems can use video-display terminals or microcomputers to access OCLC through the regular telephone network and through a telecommunications gateway.

OCLC's Union List Component supports the efforts of groups creating and maintaining national, state, and regional union lists of serials. Interlibrary loan participants can display these holdings through OCLC's interlibrary loan subsystem.

The interlibrary loan subsystem enhances communication. The electronic mailing of requests reduces turnaround time, and requests are sent to libraries known to hold the requested items. Studies have shown that the subsystem processes loan requests faster than TWX, the U.S. Postal Service, or package-delivery services.

Interlibrary loan requests are verified in the on-line union catalog, eliminating the need to search multiple sources to identify an item and find out who holds it and whether it can be borrowed. Bibliographic information from the on-line union catalog, as well as borrower and lender constant data, transfer automatically to an on-line ILL record, virtually eliminating the need for typing.

Up to five potential lenders per request may be chosen, with the system forwarding the request to each potential lender, in turn, until it is filled. The status of the request can be checked at any time in the subsystem's electronic message file, which contains notices of new requests, recall and renewal notices, and other pertinent information. The system automatically notifies borrowers and lenders when items are overdue or lost. Policies and procedures for libraries and document suppliers can be obtained on-line in the name-address directory.

OCLC offers lending credit for each item loaned through the OCLC interlibrary loan subsystem. The credit is recorded when the status of the record is changed to "shipped". Borrower and lender statistical reports can be ordered to keep up with ILL activity.

The Micro Enhancer software package helps save staff and terminal time by performing routine ILL record-keeping functions such as printing and batch updating ILL records. The Micro Enhancer software can be set to automatically dial up and log on to the OCLC on-line system, update ILL records entered off-line, and download and print ILL records. The updating functions that can be performed are shipping, receiving, returning, completing, canceling, recalling, and saying yes or no to "Pending," "Retry/Pend," and "Cond/Pend" requests, among other things.

The system is somewhat more cumbersome for the lender than for the borrower. The lender must enter a status response, return address, and shipping date in order not to lose a transaction from the file.[33] With the addition of its EPIC on-line service, OCLC greatly expanded the search and retrieval capabilities of the OCLC database. Searching the OCLC database on EPIC provides subject access to the full database for the first time, in addition to allowing retrieval by many more access points.[34] A growing number of document suppliers like the LC, National Agricultural Library, British Library Document Supply Centre (BLDSC), and University Microfilms International are part of the OCLC's ILL network.

In August 1991, OCLC was 20 years old. Its database contained at that time information on 24 million pieces of library materials held by 4,600 member libraries. More than 13,000 libraries in 41 countries use OCLC for cataloging, interlibrary loans, and reference. A new on-line computer system has been installed in anticipation of future needs.[35]

### Research Libraries Information Network (RLIN)

The Research Libraries Group (RLG) was formed in 1974 to meet the needs of research libraries. In 1988 its membership consisted of 36 major U.S. universities and research institutions, each with a seat on the board of governors. After concluding that they needed to share a computer-based bibliographic processing system, RLG acquired BALLOTS (Bibliographic Automation of Large Library Operations Using a Time-Sharing System), the library automation system developed in the late 1960s and early 1970s for the Stanford University libraries. BALLOTS was replaced in 1982 by a large application program known as the Integrated Technical Processing System (ITPS).

RLG operates an international computer network and a large mainframe computer system to provide the infrastructure for the RLIN. RLIN services, which include acquisitions, cataloging, and interlibrary loan, are provided by RLG members to institutions worldwide through the Cooperative Library Authority for Systems and Services (CLASS), based in San Jose, California.[36]

Users can create and send loan requests through RLIN. Bibliographic information can be copied from an existing record to expedite the creation of requests. Borrowers can be notified that a request is being filled. Unfilled requests can be forwarded to another library. Users may check status of requests, renew, recall, send overdue notices, and collect statistics.[37]

In addition to the RLG member library holdings, records are loaded into the database from the LC, CONSER (the CONversion of SERials project), the National Library of Medicine, the Government Printing Office, and the British Library. Special databases in this network are the On-Line Avery Index to Architectural Periodicals, the Sales Catalog Index Project Input On-Line (SCIPIO), the Eighteenth Century Short Title Catalogue (ESTC), and the RLG Conspectus On-Line.

The On-Line Avery Index to Architectural Periodicals is produced and maintained by Columbia University. It indexes articles published since 1979 in over 1,000 journals in the fields of architecture, architectural design, history and practice of architecture, landscape architecture, city planning, historic preservation, and interior design and decoration. SCIPIO is a listing of art-sales catalogs. The database is maintained by the Art Institute of Chicago, the Cleveland Museum of Art, the Metropolitan Museum of Art, the Getty Center for the History of Art and the Humanities, the National Gallery of Art, the Clark Art Institute, the Nelson-Atkins Museum of Art, and the University of California at Santa Barbara. These catalogs are used to trace art sales, to establish collecting patterns, and to analyze the art market.

The ESTC database contains bibliographic records for eighteenth-century publications from Great Britain and its colonies, as well as for English-language materials printed anywhere in the world during the same period. The British Library created the initial database, and the North American Center for ESTC, which is located at the University of California in Riverside, is adding North American holdings information as well as creating new bibliographic records for British imprints held by North American libraries. The American Antiquarian Society is also compiling American imprints in the North American Imprints Project.

The RLG Conspectus On-Line is used to analyze RLG collections. Although it is primarily for collection-development librarians, it can also be useful in locating materials because it identifies libraries with strong collections in many fields.[38]

### Western Library Network (WLN)

The Western Library Network is the youngest and smallest of the on-line networks and began as the Washington Library Network. Several years of study preceded its development. It was established by state legislation in 1976 and began operations the following year. It was designed to serve the libraries of the state of Washington. Each library within the cooperative has the right to be represented in the development of goals, objectives, and day-to-day regulations and rules of the organization. Like OCLC and UTLAS, the WLN uses computer systems to support shared cataloging, retrospective conversion of catalog records to machine-readable form, and interlibrary lending. It is essentially a multitype library venture on a statewide basis that includes computer services, telecommunications services, interlibrary services, and reference and referral services.

WLN is subject to more governmental regulations than the other systems, because its headquarters is the Washington State Library. Its database is also smaller than those of the other systems. As a system, however, its quality is considered very high. The WLN software has been purchased by the University of Illinois at Urbana-Champaign and SOLINET, among others.

In the mid-1970s WLN introduced its on-line cataloging system and expanded to include the University of Alaska. It was one of the original participants in 1980 in the Linked Systems Project (LSP), a computer-to-computer linkage for the exchange of library information, which was to be used to create a national bibliographic network. It is, however, no longer a participant.

WLN, like RLG, provides on-line computer processing services to its members from the central offices. Others contract for the supply of network resources to their member libraries. Compared to other networks, WLN pricing is high.

Laser Cat, a CD-ROM product, is a subsystem of the Western Library Network's database containing location and call number information. It is used to locate holdings information to facilitate regional resource sharing.[39]

### University of Toronto Library Automation System (UTLAS)

UTLAS uses computer systems to support shared cataloging, retrospective conversion of catalog records to machine-readable form, and interlibrary lending. In the beginning, batch-processing systems were used, but on-line services followed.

UTLAS began as a project to develop a union catalog for five new universities in Ontario, Canada, developed into the University of Toronto Library Automation System to support libraries in Canada, and then expanded to serve libraries in other parts of the world. In 1985 UTLAS was sold to the International Thomson Organization and became a for-profit corporation.

The University of Toronto updated its microform catalog by use of the UTLAS system. The university began converting its catalog records to machine-readable form in 1959. Shortly thereafter efforts to form consortia among Ontario libraries were initiated. UTLAS network organization efforts paralleled system development efforts. It is now used in hundreds of libraries across Canada. By the mid-1970s UTLAS had a large on-line technical processing support system in operation. In 1980 Rochester Institute of Technology became the first library in the United States to use UTLAS.

Each user of UTLAS owns its own database and may decide whether to charge other libraries a royalty for using its records. Annual costs are, therefore, unpredictable, and the costs of specific products and services are unstable.

The major database resources are available through UTLAS—MARC, CAN-MARC, BNB (British National Bibliography) and others. From the on-line database other resources, including microform and book catalogs, are made available. The now-commercial UTLAS has a copyright on its database but makes it available to nonmember institutions.[40]

## Regional Networks

Regional networks arose from library consortia, taking advantage of available technology and technical expertise. The regional networks made major contributions by developing approaches to the organization, governance, and financing of decentralized cooperative efforts.

Regional or multistate networks are usually privately funded by their own members. The political constraints and geographical boundaries of a statewide network do not apply. Examples of such networks are AMIGOS, which serves the Southwest; CAPCON (Capitol Consortium), which serves libraries in the Washington, D.C. area; NELINET (New England Library Information Network); OHIONET; PALINET (Pennsylvania Area Library Network), which serves libraries in Pennsylvania, Delaware, Maryland, and New Jersey; SOLINET; and others. Federal libraries scattered all over the country have their own network called FEDLINK.

These brokers serve as liaisons between member libraries and OCLC, contracting for OCLC services on a time-sharing basis. They assist with OCLC installation, provide operators' manuals and newsletters, conduct training sessions, and collect fees for OCLC usage. Regional networks add a surcharge to OCLC rates. Following is a closer look at several regional networks.

### Midwest Region Library Network (MIDLNET)

The Midwest Region Library Network (MIDLNET) was established to solve the resource-sharing problems of four net lenders—the University of Illinois at Urbana, the Illinois State Library, the Minnesota Interlibrary Telecommunications Exchange (MINITEX), and the Wisconsin Interlibrary Loan Service (WILS). The libraries placing requests through MIDLNET experience the advantages of comprehensiveness, speed, and reliability not available to institutions borrowing and lending independently.[41]

### Pennsylvania Area Library Network (PALINET)

PALINET, with offices in Philadelphia, is an outgrowth of the Union Library Catalogue of Pennsylvania. The catalog was microfilmed and sold to major libraries in the area when the OCLC database was made available. Many of the member libraries began using the OCLC database. PALINET provides the usual network services—training, documentation, consultation, and general support services.

PALINET is not the perfect answer to interlibrary loan, however. The associate director of the network, Dorothy Russell, indicated in early 1982 that there were five major factors working against perfect interlibrary loan in the PALINET region: 1) not all libraries belong to the same bibliographic network—most belong to OCLC, but some belong to RLIN; 2) not all libraries choose the same form of transmission for ILL requests (OCLC, TWX, mail, or telephone); 3) the multistate and multiinterest nature of the network means that interlibrary loan is not as controllable and definable as it is in some single-state networks. Interlibrary loan codes abound; 4) PALINET lacks a comprehensive and unified delivery service; and 5) funding problems.

The good news is, according to Russell, that members are integrating OCLC with TWX, mail, and other systems, and the OCLC network is expanding and participating in exchange agreements. An alternate method of document delivery, the Interlibrary Delivery Service (IDS), has been developed through LSCA funds and membership fees. Overnight delivery is provided through Purolator.[42]

## Multitype Area Networks

*Networking* and *multitype library cooperation* are not synonymous terms. Multitype library *cooperation* is defined as the cooperation of two or more legal library entities in sharing resources, personnel, facilities, and/or programs with a library or libraries of other types and having different legal bases. A multitype library network is a cooperative structure that crosses jurisdictional, and often political, boundaries to join several types of libraries (academic, school, special, and public) in a common enterprise. The multitype library *network* is usually an interface between two more or less highly articulated single-type library cooperatives. In many areas of the country, the definitions of these two multitype functions are not so precise and blend into one.[43]

Publicly funded networks, usually statewide, are often supported with LSCA funds through a state library agency. Some doubt is expressed that these diverse institutions can really share services. There was also concern that enabling legislation and tax support, or hard money, is not as easily obtained as the soft start-up money received from the federal government through LSCA. The statewide networks, such as the Indiana Cooperative Library Services Authority (InCOLSA), MINITEX, and ILLINET, are multitype.

Often school libraries are not included in networks because it is assumed they have little to contribute but will be frequent borrowers. A survey conducted by Betty Turock in New York State looked at the Rochester Area Resource Exchange (RARE), a multitype network including public, academic, special, and school libraries.

The study showed that the involvement of 243 schools increased ILL requests by only 3.6 percent in 1981 and 3.7 percent in 1982. It confirmed the belief that different types of libraries satisfy requests among themselves rather than going to other types of libraries.

The addition of the schools, however, did bring 116 unique periodical titles into the network's resources. None of the titles in this particular study attracted requests, so they were only a *potential* resource that did not change supply.[44]

The effects of LSCA funding on the development of multitype cooperatives are far-reaching. LSCA requires that funds be administered through state agencies and that these agencies produce long-range plans, coordinating agency programs with library programs in colleges and schools and other public and private institutions offering library services.

A statewide network can be a single-function (for example, interlibrary loan) or a multifunction network. Many types of governance structures are possible. Many complex legal, technical, and philosophical issues are involved.

In contrast to the informal union list type of cooperative, multitype library networks that provide ILL service are usually formal in structure. They have a paid staff, continuous funding by state and federal appropriations, and perhaps membership fees, and they usually compensate resource libraries. There are many examples of such statewide, single-function, multitype library cooperatives. Among them are NYSILL; ILLINET; TIE (the Texas Information Exchange); and FLIN (Florida Library Information Network).

During the 1970s the previously slow growth of multitype library networks accelerated dramatically. By 1984, the fifth edition of *The Report on Library Cooperation* indicated an increase of 184 percent over the figures reported in the first edition of the report published eight years earlier.[45] Turock reported in 1986 that multitype networks were the fastest growing type of cooperative in the United States.[46]

Several studies have concentrated on multitype networks within a state or region.[47, 48, 49] Van House pointed out that school and special libraries have different priorities than do public and academic libraries and that they are more constrained by their parent organizations.[50] Libraries involve themselves in multitype networks to reach their own objectives, even though they differ widely in political sophistication and financial backing. It is necessary to know the environment in which each type of library operates and what its objectives are to know what the advantages of participating in a multitype might be. Libraries entering networks should be analyzed to determine their constraints, their support systems, their social and economic backgrounds, their services, their expertise, their resources, and their expectations. Such preparation will assist multitype originators in creating networks responsive to situational needs instead of creating networks defined by what convention says they should be.[51]

There appear to be three primary approaches to network building. One approach has the primary focus of activity at the state library agency, another has the activity focus at academic libraries, and the last uses a nonprofit corporation with a relationship to the state library. Concerning state networks, there are questions that arise regarding enabling legislation, relationships among libraries of various types and sizes, funding, organization and administration, and relationships with vendors. To be more specific, one of the first questions that must be answered is whether the state library will play a major role. These agency heads are often public library oriented, and they may even be politically motivated. Political problems, including funding and governance, are more difficult to overcome than are technical problems.

States having regional, multitype library systems may be more likely to develop statewide networks because the fear of losing control has already been addressed. The all-important question then becomes, "Will state governments assume the responsibility for funding statewide library networks?" LSCA funds are also obtained through grant proposals written by the state library.

What happens if large libraries do or do not participate in state networks? Some have not, thinking they would become net lenders, increasing their work load disproportionally. Those who did join were often pleasantly surprised to learn that the pooled resources of the smaller libraries met the needs, for the most part, of the patrons of the smaller libraries, and they were not called upon as often as they had anticipated. They also reaped some benefits of being able to borrow from smaller, specialized libraries. There is some indication, however, that all librarians involved have not acquired the spirit of the true multitype network.

Major Owens was right when he predicted in an article in the *Library Journal* in 1976 that local and city powers would diminish and state powers would increase. He further predicted the importance of multitype networks, expressing a need for a state agency to act as coordinator.[52] This approach to state-based networking has been adopted by many states. Leadership in automation and networking has been provided by Illinois, New York, California, Colorado, and Indiana. Much of the activity in those states has been reported in the professional literature. State-based networking in 10 other states (North Carolina, South Carolina, Alabama, Virginia, Florida, New Jersey, Connecticut, Kentucky, New Hampshire, and Michigan) was described in 1987 by Ruth Katz.[53] Further developments in some of these states also appear in the professional literature. Highlights of some of the statewide networks appear as follows.

### New York State Interlibrary Loan Network (NYSILL)

NYSILL, begun in 1967, assigns to the state library the responsibility for switching and screening messages. Public library systems and other consortia (SUNY biomedical network, FAUL, [Five Associated University Libraries], METRO, and others), as well as academic libraries, were expected to fill as many requests within their own jurisdictions as possible. Participation grants were provided to referral libraries, as well as reimbursement of costs for each transaction to subject resource libraries. School libraries were not included because age limit was restricted to 18. Other libraries were arranged in hierarchical tiers. Each referral library had a TWX installed to speed communications.

Several revisions to the system were made, including allowing large academic institutions to borrow from one another without going through NYSILL, thus speeding up service. Copies of the requests had to be sent to the state library to ensure reimbursement. The system was at first, however, time-consuming and costly, with only 55 percent of requests being filled. Average cost per request filled was $15.80.

Further refinement of the system resulted in improvement in the four factors by which system performance may be measured—volume, filling rates, elapsed time, and decrease in costs. Local delivery systems (UPS) and first class mail for photocopies improved delivery.[54]

Nelson Associates conducted a survey of borrowing among the multitype libraries in the state in order to assess NYSILL's contributions to overall interlibrary loan in the state. Forty-four separate findings were reported in this very detailed study. Of the 16 recommendations, the first was that NYSILL should be funded as an ongoing system, not as an experimental program. Other recommendations were that more administrative and planning help should be obtained from the state library, the teletype format should be revised, interfacing with other systems in the state should be studied, automation of recordkeeping should be implemented, and an analysis should be made of requests not filled. The final recommendation advised the state library to delay plans for a proposed delivery system until the volume of interlibrary loans increased.[55]

### Illinois Library and Information Network (ILLINET)

ILLINET, which began operations in 1967, is an intertype network established under the Illinois Library Systems Act of 1965. It was set up as a network of public library systems administered by the state library with backup interlibrary loan and reference services provided by four libraries serving as research and reference centers—the Chicago Public Library, the Illinois State Library, the University of Illinois at Urbana, and Southern Illinois University at Carbondale.

The network was evaluated in 1974 to identify problems, to make recommendations for solutions to the problems, and to develop a model for continuous evaluation of the network. Information was sought about the requesters as well as about the handling of the requests. Member libraries were stratified by type, and a random sample was drawn from each type.

Over two-thirds of all requests during February 1975 were for adults. Almost twenty-five percent were for college students; 8 percent were for high school students; and 2 percent were for elementary school students. Eighty-four percent of the requests analyzed were for authors and titles. Eleven percent were information requests, most of them going to system-headquarters libraries.

Requests were further analyzed by type and subject, by type of library submitting requests, and by other criteria. One of the findings was that almost two-thirds of the public library serial requests were for items published in the previous five years. Half of the public library monograph requests were for books published in the previous five years.[56]

## Florida Library Information Network (FLIN)

Florida has a statewide network with the Bureau of Interlibrary Cooperation established at the Florida State Library and a network advisory committee to coordinate activities. Clusters of libraries also work together within the state to form consortia. One example is the Southeast Florida Library Information Network (SEFLIN). It includes populous Broward County and nearby areas and provides document delivery services.

Ninety-four FLIN libraries provide free exchange of materials among many of the most significant libraries in the state. The network includes multitype libraries—the state library, public libraries, academic libraries, special libraries, and the School Board of Pinellas County Library.

FLIN public on-line libraries use protocol tiers to prevent any library from becoming overburdened and to distribute the work load equitably. Local reciprocal and other agreements for resource sharing take precedence over FLIN protocols. For example, members of SEFLIN will exhaust its resources before going to FLIN and following FLIN protocols. These local agreements make up the first protocol tier. The State Library of Florida is the second tier; the third tier is composed of regional resource centers (large public libraries); the fourth tier is composed of public library systems and school libraries; the fifth tier is composed of non-ARL academic libraries; the sixth tier is composed of ARL libraries; and the last tier is special libraries.

A different set of tiers is used for academic libraries, with the second and third tiers being composed of those libraries, and the state library being moved to the fourth tier. There is also some shifting in the other tiers. Similarly, the community college libraries, the private academic libraries, and the special libraries have their own set of rearranged protocols, allowing types of libraries to borrow from each other as much as possible.

During the July 1991 to June 1992 time period, 190,008 items were supplied through FLIN for requests submitted through OCLC, U.S. mail, and courier. This figure represents an increase of 20,078 items (12 percent) over the number of items supplied from July 1990 to June 1991. Improved networking and regional library consortia are two reasons resource sharing figures continue to rise in Florida.

Books were 67.9 percent of the items supplied, and 32.1 percent were photocopies. The State Library of Florida supplied 19.1 percent of the total. It not only supplies material from its own collection but also refers requests for FLIN libraries that are not on-line to OCLC. Other items were supplied by multitype libraries as follows: 1) regional resource center libraries, 20.4 percent; 2) Florida State University (working under a grant with the state library), 9.6 percent; 3) other state university system libraries, 24.8 percent; 4) private academic libraries, 11.7 percent; 5) public libraries, 7.3 percent; 6) community college libraries, 3.9 percent; and 7) special libraries, 2.5 percent. A new group called Selective User Libraries supplied 0.8 percent.[57]

## Other State Networks

Automation has precipitated large-scale development of statewide networks, many of them evolving from a TWX or other system. Some states have found automation provided through bibliographic utilities too expensive and thus have worked to develop an individualized system. In Connecticut the five largest public libraries were, in the beginning of the state network, on a teleprinter circuit joined to the state library. The network was reinforced by United Parcel delivery, in addition to mail service. Like many other statewide networks during the 1960s, the state library also maintained a TWX system to exchange bibliographic information. At first it exchanged with Rhode Island. The TWX exchange was further expanded by the state universities of New England through NELINET.[58]

The KIC (Kansas Information Circuit) Interlibrary Loan Network, has proved to be a low-cost alternative to OCLC's interlibrary loan subsystem, and by maintaining most of OCLC's features, it has become the preferred transmission method for in-state requests by even those libraries with OCLC capability. For those libraries in Kansas that exclusively used ALA forms or the old Texas Instruments network, KIC has been hailed as the most significant resource-sharing advance since the COM union catalog was introduced in 1977. It did not come easy, however. The amount of effort required to bring each library on-line and to maintain the network was horrendous, according to the system administrator.[59]

Massachusetts' first formal statewide automation plan was approved by the board of library commissioners in 1983. Fifteen million dollars in state and federal funds were allocated to automated resource sharing in Massachusetts. Funding was used for system planning, for central site hardware and software for 12 circulation and ILL systems, for telecommunications plans and equipment, for expansion of dial-up access micros, and for union lists of serials.

Within two years, it became apparent that a new planning and policy document was needed. A network advisory committee, through a series of town meeting forums in which members of the library community were asked for input, completed a new document in 1987. The development and implementation of 12 automated resource-sharing cooperatives changed the primary focus of statewide planning from basic development to coordination and enhancement of automated services.[60]

## Five Associated University Libraries (FAUL)

FAUL is an example of a network that was not really a network in its own right, so it did not survive. It was a consortium dependent on NYSILL, national ILL codes, TWX, telephone, United Parcel Service (UPS), the U.S. Post Office, and the like.

FAUL adopted its constitution in 1967. It was composed of the libraries of the five largest universities in upstate New York: SUNY-Binghamton, SUNY-Buffalo, Cornell, Syracuse, and the University of Rochester. Some of the universities already had centers, but they were not involved in networks.

There were four primary reasons for the formation of the consortium: 1) the rapid growth of SUNY and the New York State Library; 2) the bandwagon growth of library consortia; 3) the promise of federal and private funding of library consortia; and 4) a belief by the chief librarians that the problems of academic research libraries are unique insofar as libraries go but are fairly similar among themselves. Shared resources was only one of the services expected to be derived from this cooperative arrangement.

Financial support was provided by member libraries. Their dues ($13,000 in 1970) provided central office staff salaries, travel, equipment, space rental, consultants, and small research and development projects. FAUL was ineligible for New York State funds, because it was not incorporated.

The chief librarian and the academic vice president (ex officio) from each member institution formed the board of directors. The board hired employees, acquired property, and made contracts.[61]

## Single-Type Networks

Many networks began as single-type networks designed to foster cooperation and communication among libraries serving the same general purpose. Public libraries within a state or region, because they are funded with public money and because they serve the same type of clientele, have cooperated for a long period of time.

Groups of research libraries have also created single-type networks. Research libraries, like public libraries, have common goals with a very specific group of borrowers to serve. Two examples of this type of network are the Association of Research Libraries (ARL) and the Center for Research Libraries (CRL).

Single-type networks predominated until expensive computer systems began to be used. OCLC, especially, caused single-type networks to gradually become multitype.[62]

The National Library of Medicine coordinates a national biomedical library network called DOCLINE, which provides document delivery and supports an automated document routing and referral system. DOCLINE, which was implemented in 1985, is similar in operation to the OCLC ILL subsystem. Users may create and receive requests, monitor request status, update requests, receive messages, and receive statistical reports.

The DOCLINE database was created in 1974 and used for a prototype referral system with the British Library Lending Division. Following that, additional databases were added, gradually leading up to the development of an automated document request routing system.

Before DOCLINE was implemented the Regional Medical Library Network handled millions of requests in the traditional way. By building on an already existing network, DOCLINE developers could concentrate on technical problems and avoid many of the organizational and policy issues associated with network development.[63]

## Local Area Networks

In the 1980s the microcomputer became widely available, and the librarian's dream of having an integrated on-line system began to seem possible, even for smaller libraries. The problem with creating local on-line systems is that we are still tied to the bibliographic utilities. Martin believes that we must measure the level at which we can afford to be "good citizens," contributing standard data to a nationwide database.[64]

The idea for local cooperation among health sciences libraries in St. Louis originated from the databases and technology that had existed in the area since 1962—the Washington University PHILSOM system (Periodical Holdings in Libraries of Schools of Medicine)—which included the machine-readable holdings records of most St. Louis health-related libraries. The network was provided by OCTANET, a regional ILL system developed by Washington University and administered by the Midcontinental Regional Medical Library Program.

OCTANET was the prototype for DOCLINE, the National Library of Medicine's ILL system. When DOCLINE became available in 1987, OCTANET was discontinued. Holdings of the smaller health sciences libraries in the region were not yet in DOCLINE, however, and the St. Louis medical librarians consortium was reluctant to give up electronic access to local collections.

Washington University responded positively to their requests for a local network, on several conditions. The consortium would have to guarantee financial support, and the system would have to pay for itself. It would also operate on a trial basis, during which time members would determine if a local system, in addition to DOCLINE, was needed.

The consortium agreed and PHILNET began operating with 28 institutional members. Hospital libraries found that local sources filled most of the requests. Local control also allowed flexibility and responsiveness to user needs.

In the beginning, PHILNET's primary purpose was shared document delivery. Its success encouraged network members to expand its capabilities beyond interlibrary loan. By 1983, Washington University's Bibliographic Access and Control System (BACS) was available to offices, laboratories, and other remote locations through a hard-wire network and dial-in access. Through the BACS consortium, serials control, cataloging, on-line public access catalog, circulation, management reports, E-mail, and access to bibliographic databases are now available in addition to automated interlibrary loan. BACS and PHILNET demonstrated that by using technology and databases already in place, local libraries can benefit by working together within large networks.[65]

Since the early 1980s, librarians have shifted from total cooperation to strong support of local systems. There are several reasons for this: 1) microcomputers make it possible for libraries to accomplish locally what once could be achieved only by cooperating with others; 2) librarians have discovered that the autonomy of a local system is often preferable to the requirement of operating in a specified manner according to network procedures; and 3) the private sector has discovered the library market to be profitable and is offering services that may compete with network services. All of this does not mean that the bibliographic utilities will no longer be needed, but rather that they will need to continue.[66]

What used to be done on a TWX machine can be done using a microcomputer. Interlibrary loan networking went from the TWX machine to participation in bibliographic utilities using mainframe databases. Now the whole thing is being localized using microcomputers and communications networks. LANS (local area networks) are being used to connect personal computers. The network is restricted to an area the size of an office or campus. The networks are an attempt to provide resource-sharing capabilities to the end user who has access to a personal computer.[67] Individual patrons may access the library catalog from their home terminals. It requires the addition of modems and ports to the computers and the appropriate software.

Brigham Young University's Law School and Law Library has gained national recognition for its own local, integrated computing facilities, which are linked to other campus facilities to form a local area network. The University of Delaware has expanded its computerized library system to offer statewide toll-free access to the on-line system on the Newark campus. Individuals throughout the state can now dial from home computers to search through the system's bibliographic records. A particular item can be requested at no charge through regular ILL procedures at a local public library.[68]

Interlibrary loan has been speeded up by widespread participation in bibliographic utilities available through remote mainframe databases. The whole system can be localized using microcomputers and communications networks. Interfaces can save personnel time by transferring and reformatting MARC records from a bibliographic utility into a local database. Accuracy can be increased by eliminating rekeying, and records can be made available instantly.[69]

Interfaces used with the NOTIS (Northwestern University) software allow users in several statewide systems to access public catalogs of large university libraries in their state. Users in Indiana public, school, and special libraries access the catalogs of eight Indiana research libraries using SULAN/LINKWAY, a point-and-click user interface to the NOTIS on-line catalog. SULAN is an acronym for the State University Library Automation Network, and LINKWAY is an IBM hypermedia software product. SULAN/LINKWAY intercepts NOTIS screens, processes them, and redisplays them using color graphics. The increased visibility of research library collections increases the demand for the items in those collections. SULAN/LINKWAY will also form the platform for many new services such as expert systems and links to other types of data.[70]

Microcomputers have led to more widespread cooperation in foreign libraries, as well. Italian libraries, for example, had very little cooperation because of a lack of funding. In 1985 two public libraries near Florence automated their services using microcomputers. Data are exchanged using floppy disks, thereby creating a Floppy Disk Local Area Network, or FLAN. The software program TINlib, which is based on the database TINman, was translated and adapted to the needs of Italian libraries.

Each library runs the same copy of the program on two separate databases— its own catalog and the collective catalog. Periodically each library transfers data relative to the latest acquisitions onto a floppy disk and sends it to the project coordinating office. The data are loaded into the union catalog from the disk using TINlib's import procedure. Thus gradually the participating libraries' union catalog is being constructed.

Every month the union catalog data contained on a tape cassette are sent to the libraries where, using a tape streamer, operators load it in a few minutes into the second database present in TINlib. As the collective catalog is updated only by the coordinating office, each copy sent to the libraries completely supersedes the previous one. This catalog is consulted in the same way as is the library's own local catalog.

Searching is done through an on-line public access catalog (OPAC), which allows Boolean searching, as well as searching by author, title, subject, DDC, ISBN/ISSN, keyword, and serials. Materials are bar coded and, as this procedure is integrated with the search module, one can see from the catalog whether the material is available.[71]

## A National Network

In the mid-1970s, most people saw the need for a national network with the major players consisting of large research libraries such as the LC, bibliographic centers such as WLN and OCLC, the regional networks such as SOLINET and NELINET, and private-sector suppliers of library services.[72] Gordon Williams, director of the CRL in Chicago, believed that a single dedicated ILL center, providing fast access to all libraries and providing access as a right rather than as a privilege, would greatly improve ILL access. It is not certain, he said, whether one or more centers are needed or where they should be located. He suggested that until more information was made available, it would be best for the United States to copy the British Library Lending Division model, even though our greater population and greater landmass might present some problems.[73]

After a thorough study of interlibrary loan problems in all types of libraries, Rolland Stevens concluded that a periodicals lending center along the lines of the British Library Lending Division (Boston Spa) is not the total solution to our lending problems. The differences in geography and library resources between the United States and Great Britain argue against the success and the need for such a center in this country. Our money and efforts, according to Stevens, would be better spent on improving bibliographic and local information and on building a hierarchical lending system based on present library resources.[74]

To build a national network it will be necessary to standardize the policies and procedures, including prices, of libraries involved in that network. Despite the interlibrary loan code, there are almost as many policies and prices as there are libraries. It will be impossible to ask the government to subsidize a network with all sorts of variant rules.

John Berry made an interesting point when he said that it is difficult to refute the argument that the first priority of academic research libraries is to serve their own members, yet according to a survey of 10 Ivy League RLG libraries, few, if any, exist without direct aid from government in one form or another. Not one of them pays local, state, or federal taxes. Gifts of money and materials are tax deductible. Lower postal rates and copyright protection are also provided to libraries through the government.[75]

Fourteen libraries across the United States participated in a pilot project to test the feasibility of making the LC database available on-line. Sandra McAninch and others reported on Kentucky's experience participating in the project. They also made recommendations for improvement. The system should be less expensive and more user friendly.

The LC database, called LOCIS (Library of Congress Information System) is subdivided into two segments called SCORPIO (Subject-Content-Oriented Retriever for Processing Information Online) and MUMS (Multiple Use MARC System). SCORPIO contains books, citations for selected periodical articles and U.S. government publications since 1976, federal legislation since 1973, copyright registrations since 1978, and referral information on organizations. MUMS contains 1) books cataloged, books being cataloged, books on order, and some books located in other libraries; 2) serials cataloged and owned by LC or selected other research libraries; 3) maps cataloged and owned by the LC and some cataloged by other libraries; 4) recorded sound materials and music scores; 5) visual materials; 6) files with records for several types of items, such as manuscripts, NUC holdings, in-process material at the LC; and 7) records with authorized name and subject headings, and cross-references, used for LC cataloging.

LOCIS was called a powerful cataloging tool, and the authors indicated that they had been able to provide public services that were unavailable before having access to LOCIS. The ILL unit at the University of Kentucky used SCORPIO and MUMS for title verification and for electronic transmission of requests. Users in the unit concluded that for libraries not already using an electronic method of transmission such as OCLC or RLIN for obtaining materials, the LC on-line system of transmission (FETCH) would be worthwhile in expediting ILL requests. Their experience suggested that for a large research library, processing ILL requests via a bibliographic utility—OCLC or RLIN—seems to be the best solution.[76]

If the United States had started with a centralized national system, it can be assumed that we would certainly have a national library today. Instead of pursuing a physical national structure, the united States is now expanding efforts to link systems, as with the LSP, or to provide technological gateways from one system to another.

In reviewing 20 years of national library network development in 1985, Barbara Markuson noted, "The reality is that our tremendous system of nationwide access to library holdings would stop dead in its tracks without constant local commitment and financial support."[77] Because the libraries that participated in large-scale cooperative or automation efforts were large institutions geographically dispersed across the country, a national network seemed the most likely way to interconnect them. As the number of libraries involved in automation increased, small and decentralized clusters of libraries were needed. Regional service units were soon developed to meet the need.

Continued growth in library automation fueled by the availability of micro- and mini-computer-based turnkey systems and by the large number of bibliographic records and holdings data in standard formats has brought the current interest in further decentralization from national networks—or centralization at the state level.[78]

# Linking Networks

Although the LC would seem to be the appropriate source for a nation-wide network, as has been suggested many times, its primary influence has been with the development of the MARC record and the activity of the Network Advisory Committee (NAC). In 1976 the LC set up a special office to investigate how it could facilitate networking and perhaps derive benefits for itself. This office organized the NAC as a major planning tool. The LC Network Development Office, the NAC, and the NAC-sponsored Network Technical Architecture Group focused on two networking components that set the stage for the Linked Systems Project. The Network Advisory Group was formed from representatives of several ongoing systems to help the LC in coordination of the components of this evolving national system. The group, which met for the first time in February 1977, consisted of representatives from the ALA, AMIGOS, the ARL, BALLOTS, the Bibliographic Center for Research, the California Library Authority for Systems and Services, the Council for Computerized Library Networks, the Council on Library Resources, the Federal Library Committee, the LC; MIDLNET, NCLIS, National Library of Medicine, NELINET, OCLC, RLG, the Southeastern Library Network, the University of Chicago, WLN, and the Western Interstate Library Coordinating Organization.[79]

The primary focus of the group was to search for a way to enable cost-effective system-to-system communication that would facilitate sharing of the large resources of records building up at the three bibliographic utilities—WLN, OCLC, and RLIN. This could make the U.S. network configuration respond like a single system while retaining the advantages of a distributed (three-site) system.

The second major focus was on sharing authority records. Studies in these two areas of emphasis were carried out. An ad hoc computer-to-computer link was set up between the LC and the RLG computer system. Protocol specification work for linking computers was supported by NCLIS, and a program for sharing authority records was organized by the LC.

When libraries began to put their records into the bibliographic utilities, the situation began to change. This was largely because the utilities are basically competing organizations.

There are three major areas where standardization is needed as libraries move into the linked OPAC environment: data, communications, and user interface. Care needs to be taken to ensure that standards are specified in all system procurements.[80]

Much planning, experimenting, coordinating, learning, and implementing has gone into the LSP. In the early years, standards were not ready, but they were starting to appear when implementation began.[81] The first part of a fully linked system was operating in early 1985.[82]

## Choosing and Planning Networks

For a library just beginning to investigate the possibilities of networking, choices are available among systems with a long survival record. Because the networks are changing constantly, however, a library should not make a decision on a network by copying another library's decision unless it was a very recent one and the libraries are very similar in nature.

As more libraries are becoming involved in networks, network systems and organizations are viewed as vendors vying for the library's business rather than as partners. Librarians, therefore, are joining networks by signing contracts for specific services. If another vendor should offer better services at less cost, the library may change networks or vendors.

A combination of start-up expenses, fixed ongoing costs incurred regardless of a library's volume of cataloging activity, and variable costs that depend on the amount and nature of services used are incurred by libraries using bibliographic utilities. In the case of OCLC, for example, required start-up expenditures include those for workstations and their installation, site preparation, establishing the library's catalog card profile, and staff training. Examples of fixed ongoing costs include the cost of leased telephone lines, ongoing training, printed operators' manuals and other documentation, and network membership fees if the subscriber joins OCLC through a regional network.[83] A telecommunication system normally can be analyzed in terms of the costs and performance of three major hardware components: 1) user terminals, 2) communication lines, and 3) the central computer and data storage system. In addition, a substantial cost in most systems is associated with the software that enables the user to operate the system simply and efficiently. Maintenance and operating costs either can be associated with each of these subsystems or lumped as a single separate item.[84]

OCLC and RLG/RLIN are both on-line cataloging systems, yet they reflect tremendously on networking and interinstitutional cooperation. OCLC has not restricted itself to any one type of library. RLG focuses only on research library interests. OCLC's mission is directly linked to its database and its auxiliary systems such as interlibrary loan and acquisitions. For RLG, the RLIN database is only one of several tools developed to support programs for cooperation, preservation, and collection development. Comparison of the two systems is necessary, however, for library planning and decision-making because they do perform similar functions.

OCLC has a larger database, a broader financial base, and a more sophisticated ILL subsystem and regional structure. Twenty regional networks offer OCLC services. Until recently, one of the chief disadvantages of OCLC was its limited search capabilities. It has also been criticized for its

inability to perform as a local on-line catalog and its lack of interest in cooperation among the networks.

Its powerful searching capability, higher quality of records, and ability
to serve as a local on-line catalog are the features that have caused RLIN to
be praised as the system of the future, even though OCLC has the advantage
presently. RLIN is disadvantaged by a smaller database, slower growth, and
a more expensive system. It has promoted network cooperation and unrestricted
access to its database.[85]

It was announced on July 10, 1991, in the *Chronicle of Higher Education*
that the RLG rejected a proposal to connect its national electronic network
with that of the OCLC. The connection would have cut costs and reduced
duplication of library materials. Under the proposal, members of both organizations would have had access to the computer databases of the other while
continuing to maintain their own networks. Although admitting that the link
is a vision long held by the library community, RLG president James
Michalko said that his consortium objected to the basic features of the link
as proposed, its administration, and the timetable for establishing it. OCLC
would not commit to link the networks before 1994, but RLG wanted the
connection established sooner. Representatives of both groups held out the
possibility that they may yet reach an agreement.[86]

To help librarians in choosing a network, Rouse and Rouse prepared an
analysis aimed at providing a methodology for answering questions of
performance and cost. Using ILLINET as an example, the consultants presented
a procedure for quantitative assessment of the impact of computer technologies
and their various combinations on ILL activities.[87]

It is quite another matter to begin a new network. The first stage of network
implementation is planning. When agreement is reached on goals, network
planners must win support for their program from librarians, trustees, education officials, members of the state executive department, and the state legislature. It must be decided whether to select the legislation rather than the
appropriation route to achieve network funding goals. The legislation route will
be preferred for continuity of state funding through a legislated formula. The
appropriation route may ensure an earlier start of the network.

If the legislation route is selected, planners must be as precise as possible
in drafting the bill, including such information as the purpose of the program,
its administration at the state level, the types of network organizations
eligible for state aid, the standards for eligibility of networks, and state-aid
formula factors. Of key importance to state officials will be the maximum
state cost of the formula and the appropriation level for the first year of
operation. The network legislative bill must then be explained to and understood by those in state government who make the decisions on all "money
bills." The bill must be approved by the legislature and the governor.

The appropriation route is easier. It may be a small part of a much larger
agency budget. In many instances, only the approval of the state budget
agency is needed. If the appropriation is incorporated in the governor's
budget, the prospects for approval by the legislature are greater than if the
appropriation is sought in special library network legislation.[88]

# Notes

[1] R. C. Swank, *Interlibrary Cooperation Under Title III of the Library Services and Construction Act* (Sacramento: California State Library, 1967), 1.

[2] Ibid.

[3] Brigitte L. Kenny, "Network Services for Interlibrary Loan," in *Proceedings of the Conference on Interlibrary Communications and Information Networks*, ed. Joseph Becker (Chicago: ALA, 1971), 121.

[4] Ron Miller, "Network Organization—A Case Study of the Five Associated University Libraries (FAUL)," in *Proceedings of the Conference on Interlibrary Communications and Information Networks*, ed. Joseph Becker (Chicago: ALA, 1971), 266.

[5] Swank, *Interlibrary Cooperation*, 1.

[6] "Detroit Urges Use of Teletypewriters," *Library Journal* 52 (August 1951):1190.

[7] "Western Michigan TWX Serves Extension Students," *Library Journal* 93 (November 15, 1968):4234.

[8] Jane P. Kleiner, "The Louisiana Rapid Communication Network: A System for Improved Interlibrary Loan Service," *LLA Bulletin* 33 (1971):103-8.

[9] Ronald V. Norman, "The Texas State Library Communication Network Today," *Texas Libraries* 33 (1971):42-46.

[10] R. M. Stump, "The Iowa Library Information Teletype Exchange (I-LITE)," *Iowa Library Quarterly* 21 (October 1970):142-45.

[11] Beth Givens, "Montana's Use of Microcomputers for Interlibrary Loan Communications," *Information Technology and Libraries* 1 (September 1982):260-64.

[12] Richard W. Boss and Hal Espo, "The Use of Telefacsimile in Libraries," *Library Hi Tech* 5 (Spring 1987):33-38.

[13] M. P. Wilson, "How to Set Up a Telefacsimile Network—The Pennsylvania Libraries' Experience," *Online* 12 (May 1988):20.

[14] "Library to Library," *Wilson Library Bulletin* 64 (October 1989):91.

[15] Susan K. Martin, *Library Networks, 1981-82* (White Plains, N.Y.: Knowledge Industry, 1981), 2.

[16] Henrietta D. Avram, "U.S. Library of Congress Networking Activities," *UNESCO Bulletin for Libraries* 32 (March-April 1978):71-80.

[17] Richard Hume Werking, "Automation in College Libraries," *College and Research Libraries* 52 (March 1991):117-23.

[18] Martin, *Library Networks, 1981-82*, 91.

[19] Ibid., 2-7.

[20] Joseph Becker, ed., *Proceedings of the Conference on Interlibrary Communications and Information Networks* (Chicago: ALA,1971), 4.

[21]Caroline Arms, ed., *Campus Strategies for Libraries and Electronic Information* (Bedford, Mass.: Digital Press, 1990), 30.

[22]Ibid.

[23]Maryann Duggan, "Legal and Contractual Aspects of Interlibrary and Information Service Operations," in *Proceedings of the Conference on Interlibrary Communications and Information Networks*, ed. Joseph Becker (Chicago: ALA, 1971), 222.

[24]J. W. Emling, J. R. Harris, and H. J. McMains, "Library Communications," in *Libraries and Automation, Proceedings*, ed. Barbara Evans Markuson (Washington D.C.: United States Government Printing Office, 1964):203-19.

[25]S. Gilbert Prentiss, "The Evolution of the Library System (New York)," *Library Quarterly* 39 (January 1969):85.

[26]Miller, "Network Organization," 266.

[27]Edward M. Walters, "The Issues and Needs of a Local Library Consortium," *Journal of Library Administration* 8 (Fall-Winter 1987):15-24.

[28]Daniel Sanford, Jr., *Inter-Institutional Agreements in Higher Education: An Analysis of the Documents Relating to Inter-Institutional Agreements with Special Reference to Coordination* (New York: Columbia University Teachers College, 1934), 112.

[29]David C. Weber and Frederick C. Lynden, "Survey of Interlibrary Cooperation," in *Proceedings of the Conference on Interlibrary Communications and Information Networks*, ed. Joseph Becker (Chicago: ALA, 1971), 78.

[30]Walters, "Issues and Needs," 15-24.

[31]Arms, ed., *Campus Strategies*, 17.

[32]Frederick G. Kilgour, "Objectives and Activities of the Ohio College Library Center," in *Indiana Seminar on Information Networks*, eds. Donald P. Hammer and Gary C. Lelvis (West Lafayette, Ind.: Purdue University Libraries, 1972), 34.

[33]Danuta A. Nitecki, "Online Interlibrary Services: An Informal Comparison of Five Systems," *RQ* 21 (Fall 1981):7-14.

[34]Laurie Whitcomb, "OCLC's Epic System Offers a New Way to Search the OCLC Database," *Online* 14 (January 1990):45-50.

[35]"Online," *Chronicle of Higher Education* 38 (September 4, 1991):A26.

[36]David Richards, "The Research Libraries Group," in *Campus Strategies for Libraries and Electronic Information*, ed. Caroline Arms (Bedford, Mass.: Digital Press, 1990), 61.

[37]Ibid., 68.

[38]Ibid., 64-66.

[39]Nancy L. Eaton, Linda Brew MacDonald, and Mara R. Saule, *CD-ROM and Other Optical Information Systems: Implementation Issues for Libraries* (Phoenix, Ariz.: Oryx Press, 1989), 116.

[40]Martin, *Library Networks, 1981-82*, 40-42.

[41]"MIDLNET Goes Interstate with ILL Program," *Library Journal* 106 (December 1981):2274.

[42]Dorothy W. Russell, "Interlibrary Loan in a Network Environment: The Good and the Bad News," *Special Libraries* 73 (January 1982):21-26.

[43]Roderick G. Swartz, "The Multitype Library Cooperative Response to User Needs," in *Multitype Library Cooperation*, eds. Beth A. Hamilton and William B. Ernst, Jr. (New York: Bowker, 1977), 12.

[44]Betty J. Turock, "Performance Factors in Multitype Library Networking," *Resource Sharing and Information Networks* 3(1) (1985-1986):15-38.

[45]N. Wareham, *The Report on Library Cooperation, 1984*, 5th ed. (Chicago: ALA, 1984), v.

[46]Betty J. Turock, "Organization Factors in Multitype Library Networking: A National Test of the Model," *Library and Information Science Research* 8 (1986):117-54.

[47]B. Imroth, "The Role of the School Library Media Program in a Multitype Library Network," (Unpublished dissertation, University of Pittsburgh, 1980).

[48]W. Rouse and S. Rouse, *Management of Library Networks: Policy Analysis, Implementation and Control* (New York: Wiley, 1980).

[49]N. Van House, *California Libraries and Networking: Report of a Survey* (Belmont, Calif.: Peninsula Library System, 1985).

[50]Ibid.

[51]Turock, "Performance Factors," 143.

[52]Major R. Owens, "The State Government and Libraries," *Library Journal* 101 (January 1, 1976):22.

[53]Ruth M. Katz, "Trends in the Development of State Networks," in *Advances in Library Automation and Networking; A Research Annual*, ed. Joe A. Hewitt (Greenwich, Conn.: JAI Press, 1987), 169-88.

[54]Kenny, "Network Services for Interlibrary Loan," 125.

[55]"Summary of Nelson Associates' Second Study of the NYSILL Network," *Bookmark* 28 (May 1969):239-47.

[56]Herbert Goldhor, "An Evaluation of the Illinois Interlibrary Loan Network (ILLINET)," *Illinois Libraries* 61 (1979):13-18, 58.

[57]*Florida Library Information Network Statistical Report for July, 1991-June, 1992* (Tallahassee: Florida Department of State, Division of Library and Information Services, 1992), 1-5.

[58]Wyman W. Parker, "The Network Concept: CONVAL," *Connecticut Libraries* 12 (1970):11-12.

[59]Bruce Flanders, "Interlibrary Loan in Kansas: A Low Cost Alternative to OCLC," *Wilson Library Bulletin* 61 (March 1987):31-34.

[60]"Sidebar: Revision of the Massachusetts Automated Resource Sharing Plan," *Library Hi Tech* 6 (1988):35-36.

[61]Miller, "Network Organization," 266-68.

[62]Susan K. Martin, *Library Networks, 1986-87; Libraries in Partnership* (White Plains, N.Y.: Knowledge Industry, 1986), 4.

[63]Gale A. Dutcher, "DOCLINE: A National Automated Interlibrary Loan Request Routing and Referral System," *Information Technology and Libraries* 8 (December 1989):359-70.

[64]Susan K. Martin, "Technology and Cooperation: The Behaviors of Networking," *Library Journal* 112 (1987):42-44.

[65]Candace W. Thayer and Kathryn P. Ray. "A Local Network for Sharing Resources and Technical Support: BACS/PHILNET," *Bulletin of the Medical Library Association* 76 (October 1988):343-45.

[66]Susan K. Martin, "Library Networks: Trends and Issues," *Journal of Library Administration* 8(2) (Summer 1987):16.

[67]W. Scott Currie, *LANs Explained; A Guide to Local Area Networks* (New York: Halsted Press, 1988), 15-17.

[68]"DELCAT Goes Statewide," *Wilson Library Bulletin* 63 (April 1989):10.

[69]David C. Genaway, "Microcomputers as Interfaces to Bibliographic Utilities (OCLC, RLIN, etc.)," *Online* (May 1983):21-27.

[70]Julie Bobay, et al., "Library Services for Remote Users with Linkway," *Reference Services Review* 18 (1990):53-57.

[71]Susanna Giaccai, "FLAN: Virtual Inter-linking Using Floppy Disks as a Local Area Network," *Electronic Library* 7 (June 1989):160-62.

[72]Katz, "Trends in the Development of State Networks," 170.

[73]Gordon Williams, "Interlibrary Loan Service in the United States," in *Essays on Information and Libraries,* ed. Keith Barr and Maurice Line (Hamden, Conn.: Linnet Books, 1975), 204-5.

[74]Rolland Stevens, "Other Answers to ILL Problems," *American Libraries* 10 (November 1979):582.

[75]John Berry, "Interlibrary Loan and the Network," *Library Journal* 103 (April 15, 1978):795.

[76]Sandra McAninch, et al., "Online to the Nation's Library: Kentucky's Experience with the Library of Congress Information System," *Online* 14 (November 1990):70-74.

[77]Barbara E. Markuson, "Issues in National Library Network Development: An Overview," in *Key Issues in the Networking Field Today, Proceedings of the Library of Congress Network Advisory Committee Meeting, May 6-8, 1985* Network Planning Paper no. 12 (Washington, D.C.: Library of Congress, 1985), 9-32.

[78]Katz, "Trends in the Development of State Networks," 170.

[79]Avram, "Networking Activities," 71-77.

[80]Sally H. McCallum, "Standards and Linked Online Information Systems," *LRTS* 34(3) (July 1990):360-66.

[81] Avram, "Networking Activities," 71-77.

[82] Martin, *Library Networks, 1981-82*, 29.

[83] William Saffady, *Introduction to Automation for Librarians*, 2d ed. (Chicago and London: ALA, 1989), 233.

[84] Duggan, "Legal and Contractual Aspects," 222.

[85] Jean Slemmons Stratford, "OCLC and RLIN: The Comparisons Studied," *College and Research Libraries* 45 (March 1984):123-27.

[86] "Computer Notes," *Chronicle of Higher Education* 37 (July 10, 1991):A16.

[87] William B. Rouse and Sandra H. Rouse, "Assessing the Impact of Computer Technology on the Performance of Interlibrary Loan Networks," *Journal of the American Society for Information Science* 28 (March 1977):79-88.

[88] Harold S. Hacker, "Implementing Network Plans in New York State: Jurisdictional Considerations in the Design of Library Networks," in *Proceedings of the Conference on Interlibrary Communications and Information Networks*, ed. Joseph Becker (Chicago: ALA, 1971), 228.

# chapter 4

# Copyright

Much has been written about the new copyright law and its impact on libraries. Books, chapters in books, and journal literature in the library field abound. The entire fall 1983 issue of *Library Trends* was devoted to copyright. Articles on public lending rights appeared in the spring 1981 issue of *Library Trends*.

Each of the major library associations has a copyright committee, and much of the literature has either been published or gathered together by these and professional education associations. The ALA produced the special *Librarian's American Library Association Copyright Kit*. The ARL sponsored at least two copyright kits—*Copyright Policies in ARL Libraries, Special Kit 102*, and *University Copyright Policies in ARL Libraries, Special Kit 138*. The Special Libraries Association (SLA) published *Library Photocopying and the U.S. Copyright Law of 1976*. The ALA also published *Comments of the American Library Association on the Report of the Register of Copyrights to Congress: Library Reproduction of Copyright Works; Libraries and Copyright: A Summary of the Arguments for Library Photocopying* and, in conjunction with the National Education Association and the National Council of Teachers of English, *New Copyright Law: Questions Teachers and Librarians Ask*, among others.

Books have also been written by individual authors on how the law affects libraries. Jerome Miller has been quite prolific in his writings on the subject. His *Applying the New Copyright Law: A Guide for Educators and Librarians*, published by the ALA, digests the legal jargon of the copyright law into academic language and application. Other writers have done the same. During this time frame, Henry Tseng wrote *New Copyright USA: A Guide for Teachers and Librarians*. More recent books on the subject are Heller and Wiant's *Copyright Handbook* and *Copyright Primer for Librarians and Educators* by Mary Hutchings Reed, legal counsel for the ALA.

One of the reasons interlibrary loan is on the rise is that prices of printed books and journals are increasing more rapidly than inflation rates. A study conducted at Louisiana State University of three major international scientific publishers revealed that prices doubled in about 6 years and journal contents doubled in about 12 years.[1]

It is also likely that much of what is photocopied and shared by libraries can no longer be purchased because increasing numbers of publications are produced in short runs. Librarians must always be mindful, however, of the legalities of copyright.

The system of copyright creates legal rights similar to property rights. Intellectual property, however, lacks the tangible qualities of real property, and an author owns only those portions of a work that are completely original. Applying this law can be very difficult, so we must rely as much as possible on works in the public domain—works published before the copyright law was enacted, works with an expired copyright, works that were never copyrighted because they were written by foreign nationals, or works that for some other reason fell through the cracks.

Two fundamental beliefs of the framers of the constitution are embodied in the copyright clause: society is benefited by the production and dissemination of creative works, and in order to guarantee the greatest production and disclosure of such works, creators should be provided with economic incentives through copyright. The common-law doctrine of fair use is the tool used by the courts to restrict copyright owners' rights where societal interest in dissemination outweighs the interest in the creator's incentives.[2]

Courts have traditionally viewed copyright as an instrument for encouraging creative activity. By giving authors the ability to prevent others from reproducing, distributing, performing, displaying, or basing new works on original material, copyright creates a property right that authors may exploit commercially. The possibility of realizing such financial gains gives authors incentives to create new works from which the public may benefit. Copyright law limits the duration of an author's copyright and allows a significant degree of borrowing from every work even during the life of the copyright. This basic structure often leads courts to determine the extent of an author's rights under copyright law by engaging in an intuitive cost-benefit analysis. To avoid interference with the creative process, three doctrines were written into the copyright law—the rule that copyright does not protect ideas but only the expression of them, the rule that *facts* are not protected, and the Fair Use Doctrine, which allows a single research copy to be made.

The stated intent of the 1909 Copyright Act was to promote the progress of science and the useful arts. Copyright law, for authored works, seeks to identify intellectual property as "works fixed in a medium of expression" such as writing, music, and art. The law was meant to protect the expression of an idea while encouraging dissemination of the idea. The law gives—for 50 years or more—the right to produce, reproduce, distribute, perform, or display. Authors often sign these rights over to the publisher.[3]

## Historical Background of Copyright

A U.S. copyright law is based somewhat on laws that precede it. Copyright originated in Italy in the early Renaissance when the city-states granted exclusive rights to authors, inventors, and merchants. The first known copyright for a specific title was received by Marc Antonio Safellico in 1486 for *Decades rerum Venetarum*, and the practice soon spread to other parts of Europe. The printers, not the authors, owned the copyright. Publishers paid for the right to publish. The state, therefore, received revenue from and exercised censorship over the printing of books.[4]

An early form of copyright protection was present for German-speaking natives. Over 350 "authors privileges," or copyrights, were granted by the Holy Roman emperors. In Great Britain when the Stationers' Company charter, which had been renewed a number of times, expired in 1695, printers appealed for a continuation of the system. Finally, in 1710, the Statute of Queen Anne, which revised the British system of copyright and formed the basis of modern copyright, was passed. The statute was brought about to reconcile Scotland and England in their commercial ventures, not by English publishers concerned about legal copyright protection.[5]

The author of a work was granted protection for 28 years by the Statute of Anne. Most of Europe wanted broader protection for the author. At the Berne Convention for the Protection of Literary and Artistic Works (1886), it was established that copyright should benefit the author primarily. Protection should be broad and for as long as possible. In 1952 the Universal Copyright Convention gave only enough protection to the author to encourage creative writing.[6]

The Massachusetts Bay Colony had passed two laws predating the Statute of Anne, but they did not meet all of the tests for a true copyright law. The Statute of Anne was used in the English colonies, but the American Revolution terminated British copyright law. Following the war, American states began passing copyright laws, all somewhat different but based on each other's laws, as well as the British law.

The problem of enforcing so many laws was solved when copyright responsibility was given to the federal government. The first U.S. copyright law, passed during the second session of Congress in 1790, was based on the state laws and the Statute of Anne.

## U.S. Copyright

In 1790 Congress enacted the first federal copyright statute following England's Statute of Anne guidelines. The copyright laws are covered in 17 U.S. codes, sections 101 and following.

Section 104 protects unpublished works and continues the protection upon publication if 1) at that time the author is a national or resident of a foreign nation that is a party to a copyright treaty to which the United States is also party, or the person is stateless; 2) the work is first published in the United States or in a foreign nation that is a party to the Universal Copyright Convention; or 3) the work is published by the United Nations or its agencies, or by the Organization of American States; or 4) the work comes within the scope of a presidential proclamation. Under section 108, it is not an infringement of a copyright for libraries:

1. to reproduce no more than one copy, or to distribute such copy, if

   a. the distribution is made without profit,

   b. the copy is included in collections of the library open to the public, and

   c. the reproduction includes a notice of copyright; and

2. to make copies for replacements and security, for preservation of material, or for interlibrary loans. Also, certain performances for teaching or for religious ceremonies are exempt under section 110.[7]

The law has undergone four revisions—in 1831, 1870, 1909, and 1976—and has been amended many times. Changes were made in lengths of copyright, the housing of depository copies, and the types of works copyrighted. With the second complete revision of the law, passed in 1870, the entire copyright function was given to the LC, where it still remains. Depository collections housed in the Department of the Interior and the Smithsonian Institution were transferred to the LC.

The 1891 amendment was the so-called International Copyright Act. It became the legal basis for participation in copyright with other countries. A voluntary and nonbinding agreement called the Gentlemen's Agreement was developed in either 1935[8] or 1937[9] by the Joint Committee on Materials for Research of the American Council of Learned Societies, the Social Science Research Council, and the Association of Book Publishers. Introduction of fast, simple, and inexpensive copying machines in the 1960s caused an explosion of copying that necessitated the revision of the copyright law. The issue of excessive photocopying was brought to the forefront when the publisher Williams and Wilkins sued the National Institutes of Health and the National Library of Medicine for copyright infringement through interlibrary loan.[10]

An amendment in 1954 allowed the United States to ratify the Universal Copyright Convention of 1952. At this time, the Copyright Office began studying a major revision of the 1909 copyright law. It was finally passed, after much debate and revision, in 1976, with most parts of the bill going into effect in 1978.

The Berne Convention was signed in 1886, but the United States could not participate because it denied copyright protection to foreigners. The U.S. requirements preventing adherence were notice and registration of copyright and domestic manufacture.

The convention is administered by the World Intellectual Property Organization (WIPO) and is the oldest and most important multilateral copyright treaty. The members pledge to maintain high levels of protection for the rights of authors in artistic and literary works. Works include books, motion pictures, music, video cassettes, and computer works.[11]

In 1988, the U.S. Congress passed the enabling legislation and the Senate ratified the Berne treaty, which became effective in 1989. International copyright protection, strengthened U.S. trade negotiations, and better protection of new technologies were among the reasons for making changes in the U.S. Copyright Statute, the chief reason being that the Berne treaty required removal of formalities for foreign works.

## Foreign Copyright

Other countries continue to review or develop their copyright laws, as we do in the United States. In the European Community, although copyright legislation had long been discussed, little happened until 1988, when a paper was issued that concentrated on such issues as databases, home taping, and computer programs.

New legislation became law in the United Kingdom in 1989, the first since 1956, which was poor to begin with and did not cover modern trends. Provision for "fair dealing" was defined in this law and was associated with any kind of research or private study. Fair dealing can be claimed only by individuals, not by libraries. Users may be supplied with only one copy and not more than one article from a periodical, but under the new law, they must sign a statement that they are not aware that anyone plans to request substantially the same material for substantially the same purpose.[12] If a researcher in a company, for example, asks for a journal article to be supplied through interlibrary loan, a second researcher would have to be refused. The second researcher would have to borrow the copy from the first researcher. Audiovisual materials may not be loaned without a fee. Archival copying is allowed. The moral rights provisions added to the 1988 U.K. Act—the right to be identified, the right to object to derogatory treatment of a work, and the right to privacy—do not increase protection for authors.[13]

Fair dealing was also introduced into a new copyright law passed in Spain in 1987. In Portugal, Denmark, and Italy there continues to be debate on copyright that leans in the direction of the author.

In South Korea a new copyright law came into effect in 1987. The only direct reference to interlibrary activity is that permission to copy for conservation extends to one library copying for another when the work is scarce, out-of-print, or otherwise not available for purchase. South Korea has now joined the Universal Copyright Convention. A treaty with the United States means that only American publications will be given retrospective protection for 10 years. This is seen by other countries as unfair.

Also in 1987, Malaysia passed a copyright act dealing with fair practice, as did Singapore. The Singapore law is more like the U.S. copyright law than it is like the Malaysian law, which prevents a library in a for-profit organization from fair practice. Singapore does not benefit from belonging to the Berne Convention, so foreign nationals must rely on regulations made under the Singapore Copyright Act for protection of their works unless first published in Singapore.

China is working slowly toward laws on fair dealing. Taiwan has a copyright law but does not belong to the copyright conventions, so protection of foreign nationals is negotiated by treaty.

Canada has worked for several years on the revision of copyright laws. In 1984, amendments were passed in Australia allowing libraries to copy for remote users with declarations from the users.

The Dominican Republic and Mauritius both introduced new legislation in 1986 allowing for "fair use." In the Dominican Republic, however, only public libraries may copy for interlibrary purposes. There is increasing pressure on those countries outside the framework of international copyright treaties to reform or introduce laws so that they can join.[14] Copyright laws of countries of the world were compared in an article by Sobel.[15] He also provided the framework for an international copyright system that would determine whether and to what extent a copyrighted work from one country would receive copyright protection in another.

# U.S. Copyright Law of 1976

After more than 20 years of debating the issue, Congress enacted, in 1976, the first revision of the Copyright Act since 1909. Problems created by new technologies, especially photocopying machines, provided impetus for the revision of the law. In 1974 Congress dealt with the problems by creating the National Commission on New Technological Uses of Copyrighted Works (CONTU). CONTU was established to help develop a national policy for both protecting the rights of copyright owners and ensuring public access to copyrighted works used in computer and machine duplication systems. The changes became effective in 1978.

Under the Copyright Law of 1976, rights fall into two groups—owners' and users'. Additional types of work were included, the duration of the copyright was extended to the life of the author plus 50 years, and the manufacturing clause of the earlier law was to be phased out. Insofar as the user is concerned, the law gave statutory force to what had been judicial interpretation of fair use. Special exceptions for photocopying were given to schools, libraries, and archives. The copyright office is required to conduct periodic studies of the law and to make recommendations for amendments to Congress.

Section 106 of the 1976 act gives the following rights to copyright holders: 1) to reproduce the work, 2) to prepare new versions, 3) to distribute copies, 4) to perform the work publicly, and 5) to display the work publicly.

Section 107, perhaps the most significant change in the law, indicates that fair use of a copyrighted work is not an infringement of the copyright. Section 108 allows libraries and archives to make single copies of copyrighted works for security or research purposes. Section 110 authorizes the performance of a work in face-to-face teaching situations in a nonprofit educational institution.[16]

## Ownership of Copyright by Publisher

Papers published in technical journals are most useful when copyrights are owned by the publisher. Under the new copyright law, copyrights must be transferred to the publisher. The publisher can ensure consistent reprint and republication policies, can enable legitimate copying that the new law would otherwise prohibit, and can collect and set copying fees when appropriate.[17]

Photocopying for interlibrary loan was the most controversial part of the law on library photocopying. Specific guidelines were developed by CONTU.

The five-year limitation set on photocopying from periodicals does not apply to books. Otherwise the guidelines are the same.

## Section 107

In section 107 of the Copyright Law of 1976, the Fair Use Doctrine is given statutory recognition for the first time.[18] Many legal scholars and copyright attorneys urged Congress not to legislate the question of fair use but to let the courts continue to handle it. Publishers, media producers, educators, and librarians, however, insisted on having the issue clarified by statute.

What constitutes fair use is spelled out in Section 107. Four factors or criteria are used to determine fair use of copyright-protected material. The four criteria can be explained in more detail by House Report no. 94-1476 and Senate Report no. 94-1733. All of the criteria must be considered in each application of fair use.[19] They are as follows:

1. The purpose and character of the use, including whether such use is of a commercial nature or is for nonprofit educational purposes;

2. The nature of the copyrighted work;

3. The amount and substantiality of the portion used in relation to the copyrighted work as a whole; and

4. The effect of the use upon the potential market for or value of the copyrighted work.[20]

## Section 108

Section 108 covers photocopying in libraries with collections accessible to the public. The section also includes copying for interlibrary loan and requires that copying be made without profit.[21]

Section 108 defines the conditions and limitations under which libraries may copy for their own use and for interlibrary loan. Nothing about it limits a library's right to fair use of copyrighted works. In fact, the new law reconfirms and extends librarians' rights to fair use. What it does prohibit is systematic copying, and even though it is possible that such copying could occur on a library copy machine, librarians are not held responsible. The literature shows that violation in this area has been by faculty and by photocopying stores.[22] Miller identifies, from the long and complicated section, 10 basic requirements of the law concerning library photocopying:

1. Photocopies are made and distributed without direct or indirect commercial advantage.

2. The collection is open to the public or open to researchers from outside the sponsoring firm or institution.

3. The reproduction includes a copyright notice.

4. Copying is limited to a single copy of an article from a periodical or to a small part of other works.

5. The copy remains the property of the patron for his or her private study or research.

6. The library displays a copyright notice at each self-service copying machine and at the place where orders are taken for copies.

7. A library cannot knowingly help a patron copy a large part of a work or make multiple copies of a part of a work by means of single or repeated copying.

8. A library may not enter into arrangements for the systematic duplication of single or multiple copies of a work.

9. The copyright law does not affect "contractual" obligations assumed at any time by the library or archives when it obtained a copy or phonorecord of a work in its collections.

10. With certain exceptions, a library may not reproduce or distribute copies of musical, pictorial, graphic, sculptural, or audiovisual work.[23]

Regardless of whether a particular use qualifies as fair under section 107, section 108 may still protect a library from an infringement claim.

The only individuals protected under section 108 are library employees; individuals who make use of the copying equipment located on the library's premises are not sheltered by section 108. Libraries are sheltered if reproduction equipment is unsupervised and if the equipment displays a copyright notice. Libraries and their employees are not shielded by section 108 from any liability incurred as a result of preparing derivative works from a copyrighted work.[24]

Libraries engaged in the reproduction and distribution of protected works must demonstrate the absence of any commercial advantage; libraries that are entirely private may not claim the benefits of section 108. Multiple requests for single copies of the same article (even if received on the same day) can be honored provided the requests are made by different patrons and appear to be unrelated.

Section 108(i) of the 1976 Copyright Statute calls for the Register of Copyrights to report to Congress every five years after 1978 on the effectiveness of the statutory balance as to "the rights of creators and the needs of users." Copyright owners, library users, and librarians are to be consulted.

## Relationship Between Section 107 and Section 108

Section 107 relates to fair use, which may be applied to everyone. Section 108 provides additional protection to certain libraries and archives and their employees. The fair use section applies to all rights covered by the 1976 Copyright Act, whereas the library exemption in section 108 is limited to reproduction and distribution.

Reproduction and distribution called unfair under section 107 may be satisfied by section 108. If, however, a library's use of a particular work falls outside the narrow categories of section 108, section 107 may still provide broader protection.[25] For example, Section 108(h) prohibits libraries from copying sheet music, but the fair use section permits copying of music on an "emergency" basis.[26]

According to the Register of Copyrights, library photocopying not exempt under section 108 may still be considered fair use under section 107 if the transaction is the type that could be fair use absent section 108 and if the fair use analysis of the transaction has already taken place. According to this view, courts deciding whether certain reproduction to distribute by a library qualifies as fair use must take into consideration whether the library has exhausted its privileges under section 108.[27] Libraries should be able to provide fair use privileges for patrons if 1) the reproduction occurs following a patron's request, 2) the library itself performs reproduction, and 3) the library does not profit.

Section 108 of the copyright law and the CONTU guidelines are the areas that pertain to ILL photocopying. Briefly what they mean is that a library is liable for a subscription charge or royalty fee for any periodical title from which it requested six or more article copies in any one year, with a limit that such items be published within the previous five years.

Copying limitations and copyright record-keeping are based on a calendar year. Unfilled ILL requests do not apply to the limitations on the number of copies made. Restrictions on copying apply only to periodical issues published in the most recent five years. The five-copies-per-year rule is waived if a library owns a work that is unavailable for copying or if the library places an order for the title.

A statement must be printed, typed, or stamped on the request form indicating that the request complies with section 108(g)(2) of the copyright guidelines. The revised ILL form of 1977 includes a checkoff box to indicate compliance with this requirement. The supplying library must reject a photocopy request if the request does not contain copyright compliance information.

The library placing requests for copies maintains records of all requests and the disposition of each request. Records must be retained for three years following the close of the calendar year.[28]

The words in subsection 108, "such aggregate quantities as to substitute for a subscription to or purchase of such work" shall mean:

1.  With respect to any given periodical (not issue of periodical), filled requests of a library or archives within any calendar year for a total of six or more copies of an article or articles published in such periodical within five years prior to the date of the request.

2.  Filled requests of a requesting entity (library, archives) within any calendar year for a total of six or more copies or phono-records of or from any given work during the period when such material shall be protected by copyright.

CONTU was prohibited from studying the reproduction of copy-righted works for use by professors in their classroom teaching.[29]

Drott and Griffith attempted to point out some potential inequities and uncertainties raised by the new copyright law. They determined that three areas needing investigation were 1) determining of the mathematical distribution of articles over journal titles for ILL requests, 2) obtaining estimates of the stability of such distributions (year-to-year fluctuations in requests for specific titles), and 3) analyzing the impact of the differential protection afforded to various subject fields due to the five-year limitation.

From a management point of view, the stability of the distribution of ILL requests over time is very important. An unstable distribution could mean that a library seeking to comply with the CONTU guidelines would be continually shifting subscriptions from one little-used journal to another in an essentially random pattern. If this were, indeed, true, there is a need to develop a concept of statistical compliance with the copyright law. For example, a library would not be expected to subscribe to specific titles thought to generate more than five users per year, but it would be expected to subscribe to a sufficient number of titles to ensure that titles requested in more than five ILL requests would be offset by titles in the library used fewer than five times per year. This statistical compliance would promote better collection development and reduce costs of placing and canceling subscriptions. It would also simplify ILL record keeping. The authors also suggested that the guidelines unfairly offer less protection to some journals and subject fields than to others. The "soft" sciences (social science) depend more heavily on older material than do the "hard" sciences. The authors foresaw an unenforceable law or chaos for major research collections.

The recommendation is made that research leading to a statistical model of copyright compliance would benefit both libraries and publishers. It would also advance our knowledge in this important class of probability functions as related to information, documents, and users.[30]

## Copyright Notice

Section 108 states that reproduction or distribution of a work includes a notice of copyright. If it is not printed on the pages being copied, the library must supply some form of notice. The ALA Reference and Adult Services Division's Interlibrary Loan Committee recommends placing the information "Notice: This material may be protected by copyright law" on all material copied. This may be done with a label or a rubber stamp, or the copyright page may be photocopied and sent along with the material.

Copyright warning signs must also be posted in prominent public areas where public copying is done and where people turn in ILL requests. Copyright warning must also appear on the ILL form that the patron submits. The law is explicit enough to indicate type, size of letters used on the warning, and the type of material on which to make the signs, as well as the exact wording placed on the sign.

The U.S. Copyright Office does not specify the wording that appears on the signs over unsupervised machines, so the following was recommended by the ALA Interlibrary Loan Committee: "Notice: The Copyright Law of the United

States governs the making of photocopies or other reproductions of copyrighted material. The person using this equipment is liable for any infringement." Individual libraries may vary the wording and remain in compliance.[31]

## Review of Copyright Law

At Cornell, Oakly reported that a journal for which there were four or more photocopy requests was considered "frequently ordered" and was considered for purchase. During the 1975-76 fiscal year, only 15 of 188 different journal titles involved copies of four or more articles from one journal. Of these 15, 9 were for more than five articles, usually requested by one individual working on a research project.[32]

In 1977, DeGennaro reported on the effect of the new copyright law on interlibrary loan at the University of Pennsylvania. During the year from July 1976 through June 1977, articles were requested from 247 different journal titles. Of these, 173, or 70 percent, had requests for only one article. Five had five requests, two had six requests, and one had seven requests. In every case where five or more articles were requested from the same journal, all were for one person working on a special project. Only two journals qualified for royalty payments; the others were nonprofit, scholarly journals. At the University of Pennsylvania, total ILL transactions amounted to about 1 percent of local use of materials.[33]

In May 1982, King Research Inc. published *Libraries, Publishers, and Photocopying*, a report of surveys conducted for the U.S. Copyright Office to satisfy section 108(g) of the Copyright Revision Act, which mandates "a report setting forth the extent to which this section has achieved the intended statutory balancing of the rights of creators and the needs of users." The King Research report projected more than 600 million copies being made yearly on library photocopying machines, but only 38 percent of public libraries posted copyright restrictions on their copies. Publishers' royalties from such large usage amounted to only $50 per publisher from all 1980 library photocopying revenues. The national total was over $170,000.

King Research also reported that librarians, with public librarians being the worst offenders, simply did not deny ILL requests when they appeared to violate copyright law. They refused to request permission to copy in quantities beyond fair use.

On the basis of this report, the Association of American Publishers (AAP) told the Copyright Office that the provisions intended to balance the needs of patrons and rights of publishers were not being observed as the law intended. The AAP asked librarians to become more involved, but librarians indicated they did not like to police patrons. Bailey suggested that perhaps a yearly restitution to publishers or a "copyright infringement" tax could be added to the purchase price of a photocopier.[34]

The King report followed efforts by library organizations to alert educators and libraries to their rights and responsibilities under the law. ALA promoted "Copyright Kit" hearings. Much discussion was held concerning the development of a standardized copyright stamp and the copyright compliance boxes printed on ALA interlibrary loan forms. The success of these educational efforts and data collected by librarians before the copyright review provide a solid statistical basis for the conclusion that the Copyright Act of 1976 is achieving the intended balance.[35]

## Enforcement of Copyright Law

Abramson points out contradictions, paradoxes, and inconsistencies in enforcement of the 1976 Copyright Act.[36] Application of the law is somewhat uneven. The law protects the expression of facts but not the facts themselves. It is also possible that a work may infringe on the original by lifting the "gist" of the work without copying anything from the original. The purpose of the Fair Use Doctrine should be judged first of all by whether the infringer will cause economic harm to the original by competing in the same marketplace, but emphasis is often placed by the courts on other factors. Because no clear line of demarcation exists between an idea and the expression of an idea, courts have had difficulty in determining the works that should be protected by copyright. Plots are protected, whereas themes, being broader than plots, are not protected. Characters, if well-developed, are also protected.[37] Courts have come to rely on idea and expression dichotomy in developing tests designed to show similarity between works—that is, copyright doesn't extend to the idea of a work but only to the expression of that idea.[38]

Court decisions have not done justice to parody. The interests of society in preserving parody as an art form, and the interests of copyright law, would be better served by addressing parody issues in light of the basic aim of copyright—the encouragement of new artistic creation.[39] Parody is the satirical imitation of a work. Courts and the Congress as well are committed to the principle that parodists are entitled to borrow more from an author's work than are other users. The parodist must satisfy two requirements—the work must contain some criticism of the original work and the work must not serve as a substitute for the original work. This does not necessarily mean, however, that fair use treatment for all parodies is warranted, as different types of parodies bring different benefits to the public.[40]

Authors, understandably, do not like to be ridiculed, so it is not surprising that authors refuse to grant copyright privileges for parody. Authors may also use copyright to hinder use of their writings by unsympathetic biographers, or they may simply want to enjoy their privacy. Money is not considered an adequate substitute for their copyright rights.[41]

Article 1, section 8 of the U.S. Constitution grants Congress the power to enact copyright and patent statutes. Until the Copyright Act of 1976, the United States, in effect, had a dual copyright system. Federal law protected published works and state law protected unpublished works. The new law covers both published and unpublished works, and section 301 of the Copyright Act provides for preemption of all equivalent state law, although assessment of cases would indicate that the extent of section 301's preemption effect has not been clarified.[42]

What if states themselves infringe on the law? The Eleventh Amendment to the U.S. Constitution renders states immune from suit. The amendment is intended to respect state autonomy and to facilitate governmental efficiency. When states infringe on a copyright by purchasing one copy of a work and distributing multiple copies, however, they take unfair advantage of the discretion the amendment has given them. Courts are, in fact, addressing whether states should be immune from suit for copyright infringement.[43]

The U.S. Ninth Circuit Court of Appeals rendered a decision in 1988 in *B.V. Engineering v. University of California at Los Angeles* that casts doubt over the ability of copyright owners to enforce their rights of ownership against the states.[44] In fact, in three different cases—*B.V. Engineering v. University of California at Los Angeles, Richard Anderson Photography v. Radford University,* and *Lane v. First National Bank of Boston*—three different federal circuit courts of appeals held that the Eleventh Amendment to the U.S. Constitution immunizes the states against monetary liability for copyright infringement.[45]

Eleventh Amendment immunity to monetary claims for copyright infringement permits the states, in principle, to set up their own production and publishing houses and to compete, free from royalty obligations, with private sector producers and publishers. Individuals, however, may be held liable for copyright infringement.

Producers and publishers asked Congress to restore their copyright remedies against the states, but the cases raised the question of whether the copyright law provides a balance between the needs of educators and encouraging creativity.[46] Under the law, control over an author's expression includes, besides copying, distribution, adaptation, public performance, and public display. It is difficult to teach without treading on some of these rights.

Sharing of ideas in scholarly publishing is also made difficult because of the copyright law. The law does not provide for broad copying of works created at public expense, and a large amount of academic and laboratory scientific research is so funded. The provision for systematic, collective ownership of publicly supported research is an omission from the Copyright Act, especially since the responsibility for maintaining publishers' warehouses falls on the publicly supported and not-for-profit institutions called libraries that are expected to reimburse the original publishers. Current copyright law also does not address the realities of the kind of scholarly communication increasingly available in the electronic information age—networked publications, electronic journals, CD-ROMs.[47]

CONTU recommended changes (that became effective in 1980) to address computer programs. The provisions for fair use seem to apply for downloaded data just as they do for printed copy. Limited use of a small part of a database unlikely to affect the database market should fall under the fair use provision. Copying large portions in order to develop a competitive product would constitute infringement, however. Section 117 provides a limited provision for fair use copying of computer programs. Microcomputers with software packages can now emulate terminals but can also record and store search results. These results could be altered and from them, copies of tailor-made reports could be made. A bibliography could likewise be compiled and even sold. In *Micro-Sparc, Inc. v. Amtype Corporation* (1984), the court found that the right to copy a program is limited to the possessor and does not extend to authorizing others to reproduce copies. The owner of a copy may make archival copies of his own copy but cannot authorize anyone else to do so.[48]

The Computer Software Act of 1980 amended sections 101 and 117 of the Copyright Act to define computer programs and extend the copyright protection to computer software. The courts have found that databases may be copyrighted because original compilation of the material is required in their creation. If files are built to create a personal database to avoid payment of connect and user fees, downloading is illegal.

Research downloading, if the material is deleted afterward, is considered fair use if the fair use criteria are applied. Computer software programs and databases do cause concern, however. At Texas A&M University Library notices were posted to inform users that library-owned computer software programs or programs used on the library terminals are covered by copyright law and that copying them is the same as photocopying printed material.[49]

In most cases, the use of fax for document delivery in ILL transactions requires the lending library to photocopy material twice—the copy made in preparation for transmission and the transmitted copy received by the borrower. Librarians are concerned that copyright liability might be affected by making two copies of material rather than the normal single copy. Law librarian David Ensign concluded, however, that making two reproductions is not an infringement of copyright when analyzed in terms of fair use, library reproduction, ILL guidelines, and technological considerations. Whether, in fact, fax or more conventional means of document delivery are used, the result is that one copy of the material is received at the borrowing institution. The CONTU guidelines also place responsibility for copyright compliance upon the requesting library.[50]

## Cases

The copyright law encourages copyright owners to bring suits for damages even when they are minimal or difficult to ascertain. The Copyright Act of 1976 provides for an increase in statutory damages where copyright infringement is willful. Because it is not defined in the act, the meaning of willfulness is left to judicial interpretation. Courts have not agreed on the proper definition of willfulness and have adopted tests that are vague and sometimes inconsistent with the statutory damages provision.[51]

Publishers have successfully sued copy shops, a university, faculty, and corporations. Two years after the Copyright Law of 1976 went into effect, two suits were initiated by publishers against businesses that did photocopying for the general public. In both, *Basic Books, Inc. v. Gnomon Corp.* and *Harper and Row, Publishers v. Tyco Copy Service*, enough copies of copyrighted material were being produced to make up a textbook for a faculty member's class. As a result of the suits, the copy shops were required to obtain copyright permission and to display the copyright guidelines in the business.

The first time a university and its faculty members were sued for copyright infringement under the Copyright Act of 1976 was in the case of *Addison-Wesley Publishing Company v. New York University*, settled in 1983. The publishers agreed to dismiss their claims against NYU and its nine faculty members in exchange for a new photocopying policy at the university. As a result, the faculty are unable to make more than minimal use of photocopies without permission from the copyright owners or university general counsel unless they are willing to risk personal liability. Because NYU's photocopying practices prior to settlement were representative of practices at colleges and universities generally, the publishers let it be known they were willing to challenge such photocopying.

Compliance with the NYU settlement threatens to restrict the flow of information made possible by inexpensive photocopying, and it is also contrary to copyright laws. The settlement is more restrictive than copyright law requires, and Brandfonbrener urged other colleges and universities not to follow the guidelines.[52]

A group of eight publishers successfully sued Kinko's Graphics Corporation, a national chain of photocopying stores, over copyright infringement. In a out-of-court settlement, Kinko's agreed to pay the publishers $510,000 in damages and $1,365,000 in legal fees. The suit, filed in 1989, claimed that the infringement resulted from the reproduction of excerpts from books without permission and selling them in anthologies to college students. The company's argument for fair use did not hold. The company is barred from copying and selling anthologies that contain more than one page from a work unless it has obtained the copyright owner's written permission. In the final analysis, Kinko's agreed that copyright protection is not harmful to education but is essential to it.[53]

Librarians tend to try to be law-abiding citizens. The literature reveals that lawsuits involving copyright infringement are usually not from ILL copying of scholarly writings but from the more lucrative markets involving videos or computer software. Infringement of the law has been brought to the campus by commercial copying establishments located on or near campuses. Kenneth Crews reported in his dissertation on copyright from the Library School at UCLA that librarians have an acute sensitivity to the possibility of liability.[54]

Nevertheless, ILL cases have been reported in the professional literature. The publisher Williams and Wilkins sued the National Institutes of Health and the National Library of Medicine for infringing on copyrights in six medical journals. Articles were copied for researchers at the National Institutes of Health in response to ILL requests. The U.S. Court of Claims voted 4-3 in favor of the National Institutes of Health and the National Library of Medicine. It was carried to the Supreme Court, where the 4-4 split vote sustained the decision of the lower court.[55]

Publishers were successful in two cases filed against corporate libraries— *Harper and Row, Publishers v. E.R. Squibb Company* and *Harper and Row, Publishers v. American Cyanamid Company*—for infringing on copyrights in journals registered with the Copyright Clearance Center. Six publishers sued Texaco for making only token payments to the Copyright Clearance Center for photocopies. The outcome of these cases will surely impact the extent to which libraries in for-profit organizations can qualify under section 108.[56]

Librarians and publishers had words over the fair use and photocopying provisions of the new copyright law that took effect January 1, 1978. Librarians were worried about the adverse effects sections 107 and 108(g) might have on their ability to serve their users as they were accustomed. Early proposed versions threatened to end, or severely limit, fair use and photocopying in interlibrary loan operations. The final version, however, was much less strict, and according to DeGennaro,[57] the impact of the new law was relatively slight in comparison to other library problems—escalating prices, theft, mutilation, budget problems, and so forth.

Perhaps publishers and librarians alike overreacted. Publishers feared that resource sharing would cut into their sales; librarians were looking to resource sharing to save them from decreasing budgets. In practical terms, however, the new law changed almost nothing for librarians. The most serious limitation appears in the CONTU guidelines, which prohibit libraries from copying for ILL purposes more than five articles a year from the previous five years of a periodical title. They also stipulate that libraries document their use, the burden of proof resting with the requesting library. Based on statistics gathered at the University of Pennsylvania and Cornell University, DeGennaro concluded that only a small fraction of ILL requests would be affected, and a library could decline to request more than five copies from any journal that required payment of royalties. Record keeping involved simply filing the third part of the ILL request form.

DeGennaro reported that one publisher misrepresented the provisions of the new law in a letter to librarians offering to sell copying privileges that the law already provided. He urged librarians not to enter into contractual agreements because section 108(f)(4) states that reproduction rights granted to libraries do not override any contractual obligations a library might have had when it obtained a work for its collections.

Time and experience will show that the publisher-librarian controversy over copyright, interlibrary loan, and photocopying was the result of fear and misunderstanding—largely on the part of the publishers. Further, librarians are cutting expenditures for books and journals because they do not have the funds, not because they can get items through interlibrary loans. Publishers, however, have clung to the idea that if they can discourage interlibrary loan and photocopying, libraries will be forced to spend more money to buy materials.[58]

*Obtaining Permission to Copy*

Permission to duplicate material in excess of fair use may be obtained in several ways. They are by transfer of ownership by will or by contract; by compulsory licenses, usually of a musical composition; or by voluntary licenses in which part of the copyright owner's rights are granted to others. The method most often used by libraries to obtain permission to copy is through a clearinghouse that collects royalty payments from users and sends them to the copyright owners. A journal article clearinghouse was established in 1977 by the AAP called the Copyright Clearance Center. Publishers participating in the clearinghouse place a notice on the first page of each article giving copying fee and identification code for the article and the journal. Some publishers charge a flat fee and others base their fees on length or importance of the articles.

Each participant is assigned an account number and may also be asked to open a deposit account. A record of charges is sent monthly to be applied against the deposit account. A simpler procedure requires the library to make an extra copy of the first page of each article made in excess of fair use. These pages and payment are sent to the center once a month.

One-time or single-use permission may be obtained by writing to the publisher explaining how the copies will be used. Some publishers charge a small fee.

Sometimes publishers will not respond. Miller suggests a good way around that is to send a letter stating that the copies will be made unless forbidden within a certain length of time. Or the ILL librarian may send a small check to cover copying fees and assume permission has been granted if the check is cashed. Another way to obtain permission is to include a requirement in a purchase order stipulating that copyrighted materials purchased through the order may be duplicated.[59]

On the author's survey, 40.9 percent of those responding indicated they purchased a title when they reached the legal borrowing limit. A surprising 19.5 percent borrow journals when they have reached their limit, 17.5 percent arrange for payment of royalties (11.5 percent require the patrons to pay the royalties), and 10.4 percent use other special means of obtaining copyrighted material.

# Public Domain

Works that are in the public domain may be copied freely. They include works that were either never copyrighted or that have lost their copyright protection because the copyright period terminated or the copyright was not renewed.

Some scholarly and professional journals do not copyright their material, so it can be photocopied. U.S. government publications are also in the public domain. Because of changes in the law concerning copyright duration, works copyrighted in the United States before September 19, 1906, are in the public domain.[60] To determine if a work has entered the public domain, one can search renewals and registrations through the Copyright Office or its publication *Catalog of Copyright Entries*.

## Notes

[1]Chuck Hamaker, "Costs of Scientific Journals Increase at Double of Research Costs," *ARL: A Bimonthly Newsletter of Research Library Issues and Activities* 153 (November 1990):1-2.

[2]Eric D. Brandfonbrener, "Fair Use and University Photocopying: *Addison-Wesley Publishing Co. v. New York University*," *Copyright Law Symposium* 36 (1989):42-43.

[3]Ann Okerson, "With Feathers: Effects of Copyright and Ownership on Scholarly Publishing," *College and Research Libraries* 52 (September 1991):427.

[4]Robert W. Dunaway and Michael A. Dillon, "*B.V. Engineering v. University of California, Los Angeles*: A License to Steal?" *Santa Clara Computer and High-Technology Law Journal* 5 (1989):349.

[5]Peter Prescott, "The Origins of Copyright: A Debunking View," *EIPR: European Intellectual Property Review* 11 (December 1989):453-546.

[6]John Corbin, *Find the Law in the Library: A Guide to Legal Research* (Chicago: ALA, 1989), 243.

[7]Ibid., 244.

[8]Randall Coyne, "Rights of Reproduction and the Provision of Library Services," *University of Arkansas at Little Rock Law Journal* 13 (Spring 1991):488.

[9]Jerome K. Miller, *Applying the New Copyright Law: A Guide for Educators and Librarians* (Chicago: ALA, 1979), 62-63.

[10]Ibid.

[11]*Berne Convention for the Protection of Literary and Artistic Work. 99th Congress, 2d Session, Senate Treaty Document 99-27.* (Washington, D.C.: United States Government Printing Office, 1986), 3.

[12]Graham P. Cornish, "Copyright Law and Document Supply: A Worldwide Review of Developments 1986-89," *Interlending and Document Supply: The Journal of the British Library Lending Division* 17 (October 1989):118.

[13]W. R. Cornish, "Moral Rights Under the 1988 Act," *EIPR: European Intellectual Property Review* 11 (December 1989):449-53.

[14]Ibid., 119-22.

[15]Lionel S. Sobel, "The Framework of International Copyright," *Cardozo Arts and Entertainment Law Journal* 8 (1989):1-27.

[16]Brandfonbrener, "Fair Use," 44-47.

[17]Patricia H. Penick, "Ownership of Copyright," in *Modern Copyright Fundamentals; Key Writings on Technological and Other Issues*, ed. Ben Weil and Barbara Friedman Polansky (Medford, N.J.:Learned Information, 1989), 67.

[18]Richard DeGennaro, "Copyright Resource Sharing and Hard Times: A View from the Field," *American Libraries* 8 (1977):430-35.

[19]Miller, *Applying the New Copyright Law*, 12-23.

[20]David Ensign, "Copyright Considerations for Telefacsimile Transmission of Documents in Interlibrary Loan Transactions," *Law Library Journal* 81 (1989):809.

[21]Joseph J. Mika and Bruce A. Shuman, "Legal Issues Affecting Libraries and Librarians," *American Libraries* 19 (February 1988):112.

[22]DeGennaro, "Copyright Resource Sharing," 431.

[23]Miller, *Applying the New Copyright Law*, 63-64.

[24]Coyne, "Rights of Reproduction," 503.

[25]Ibid., 511.

[26]Miller, *Applying the New Copyright Law*, 87.

[27]Coyne, "Rights of Reproduction," 512.

[28]Miller, *Applying the New Copyright Law*, 74-75.

[29]Brandfonbrener, "Fair Use," 47.

[30]M. C. Drott and B. C. Griffith, "Interlibrary Loans: Impact of the New Copyright Law," *American Society for Information Science Journal* 29 (September 1978):259.

[31]Miller, *Applying the New Copyright Law*, 66.

[32]Madeline Cohen Oakley, "The New Copyright Law: Implications for Libraries," *Cornell University Libraries Bulletin* 202 (October-December 1976):5.

[33]DeGennaro, "Copyright Resource Sharing," 431-32.

[34]Carl Bailey, "Photocopiers vs. Copyright: Round Two," *Wilson Library Bulletin* 57 (October 1982):144.

[35]N. Marshall, "Copyright—Major Challenges Ahead," *Wilson Library Bulletin* 57 (February 1983):481-84.

[36]Elliott M. Abramson, "How Much Copying Under Copyright? Contradictions, Paradoxes, Inconsistencies," *Temple Law Review* 61 (1988):133-96.

[37]Ibid., 187.

[38]Jamie Bushing, "*Shaw v. Lindheim*: The Ninth Circuit's Attempt to Equalize the Odds in Copyright Infringement," *Loyola Entertainment Law Journal* 11 (1991):71.

[39]Abramson, "How Much Copying Under Copyright?" 178.

[40]Alfred C. Yen, "When Authors Won't Sell: Parody, Fair Use, and Efficiency in Copyright Law," *University of Colorado Law Review* 62 (1991):91.

[41]Abramson, "How Much Copying Under Copyright?" 178.

[42]Deborah Kemp, "Preemption of State Law by Copyright Law," *Computer/Law Journal* 9 (1989):375-76.

[43]Gaelle Helene Gralnek, "The Forest for the Trees: Why States Should Not Be Immune from Suit for Copyright Infringement," *Arizona State Law Journal* 20 (1988):821-39.

[44]Dunaway and Dillon, "A License to Steal?" 349.

[45]Jay Dratler, "To Copy or Not to Copy: The Educator's Dilemma," *Journal of Law and Education* 19 (Winter 1990):1.

[46]Ibid., 3-4.

[47]Okerson, "With Feathers," 425-38.

[48]Pamela Reekes McKirdy, "Copyright Issues for Microcomputer Collections," in *The Library Microcomputer Environment: Management Issues*, ed. Sheila S. Intner and Jane Anne Hannigan (Phoenix, Ariz.: Oryx Press, 1988), 118.

[49]Mika and Shuman, "Legal Issues Affecting Libraries," 112.

[50]Ensign, "Copyright Considerations," 805-12.

[51]"Willful Copyright Infringement: In Search of a Standard," *Washington Law Review* 65 (October 1990):903-20.

[52]Brandfonbrener, "Fair Use," 33-40.

[53]"Photocopying Stores Agree to Pay Publishers Nearly $1.9 Million to End Copyright Case," *Chronicle of Higher Education* 38 (October 23, 1991):A13-A15.

[54]Kenneth Donald Crews, *Copyright Policies at American Research Universities: Balancing Information Needs and Legal Limits* (Los Angeles: University of California, 1990), 508.

[55]Miller, *Applying the New Copyright Law,* 63.

[56]Coyne, "Rights of Reproduction," 501.

[57]DeGennaro, "Copyright Resource Sharing," 430.

[58]Ibid., 433.

[59]Miller, *Applying the New Copyright Law,* 83.

[60]Ibid., 91-102.

# chapter 5

# Organization and Administration

## Organizational Structure

Interlibrary loan service is often considered a function of the reference department because verification and location tools are generally located there. It is also in this department that serious researchers would probably be working when they ascertained a need for the service or had the service recommended to them by the reference librarian assisting them in their work.

It was also in the Reference Division of the ALA that the ILL function was studied and standardized. Even though there appears to be some moving away from the organizational structure that places interlibrary loan in the reference department, it is still the ALA Reference and Adult Services Division that continues to monitor interlibrary loan in this country.

Lyle calls interlibrary loan a reference function.[1] Wilson and Tauber indicate that interlibrary loan may be in circulation as well as in reference.[2]

Actually, interlibrary loan fits well as an extension of the circulation department because, like circulation, it involves considerable record keeping, materials handling, and staff time. Circulation and interlibrary loan both are responsible for charging and discharging library materials, and both are involved in financial transactions with patrons.

Handling of materials is more of a problem for the ILL function than it is for circulation because loaned materials must be retrieved, checked out, wrapped and packaged, sent to the borrowing library, and, upon their return, unpacked, checked in, and returned to the stacks. Materials borrowed from other libraries must also be specially handled, wrapped, and so forth.

Where the ILL work is split between the circulation department and the reference department, the circulation department is ordinarily responsible for that part of the work having to do with circulating books to other libraries. In larger libraries the ILL unit is usually an appendage of circulation, reference, collection development, or even in a separate unit or department.

Library literature contains very little information on the organizational structure of interlibrary lending. In 1949 Carl Melinet from Syracuse University published the results of his research into the administration of interlibrary loans in American libraries. Thirty-four percent of the libraries surveyed handled all interlibrary loan work in the reference department; 31 percent handled it in the circulation department; 13 percent had reference handle borrowing and circulation handle lending.[3]

A survey of ILL staffing in college and university libraries, reported in 1965, found that (of 35 usable responses) in 17 libraries the ILL function was part of reference, in 8 it was part of circulation, and in 3 it was a separate unit. It was divided into separate divisions in 2 libraries and in miscellaneous arrangements in 5.[4]

In 1988 a survey of interlibrary loan in research libraries was conducted by LaGuardia and Dowell of the reference department at the University of California at Santa Barbara.[5] Results of the survey suggest that no clear pattern exists regarding the physical structures of interlibrary loan within a research library. It appears most often, however, in some combination of circulation or access services (36 percent). In 27 percent of the libraries surveyed, interlibrary loan is a separate unit. Interlibrary loan is part of the reference department in 30 percent of surveyed libraries, and within public services in 2 percent. The other 5 percent are included in collection development and microforms departments.

Interlibrary loan is, indeed, a strange phenomenon in libraries. It is a service specifically meant to serve the library's public, and yet it is sometimes housed in a technical service department for historical, technological, or staffing reasons. In a large operation, ILL requests may originate in reference and be referred to an ILL department. When the materials arrive they may be picked up in circulation. If ILL service is actually a part of reference service, it is more likely that reference librarians will be aware of the ramifications of suggesting this service to a patron. No matter where ILL service is located, a reference librarian or any other staff member, no matter how eager to provide good service, should not promise more than can be delivered.[6]

In the author's 1992 survey of multitype libraries, 18 percent of the respondents indicated that the reference department handles interlibrary loan. Twenty-three percent indicated that the circulation department handles it. Reference for borrowing and circulation for lending was reported by 8 percent, as was interlibrary loan as a separate department. Forty-one percent indicated that other arrangements were made for handling interlibrary loans. Many of the respondents in the latter category were from special libraries with very limited library staffs. The graphs in figures 5.1 to 5.5, on pages 94 to 98, illustrate the arrangement of the interlibrary loan function, as reported in the author's ILL survey.

According to the LaGuardia and Dowell survey, no clear pattern for centralized interlibrary operations within libraries seems to exist either.[7] Forty-seven percent of libraries surveyed had some decentralized ILL operations (for example, law, science and other libraries do their own interlibrary loans). No distinct pattern was seen in ILL staff reporting. Thirty-two percent reported directly to the associate director or director; the same percentage reported to the head of reference; 23 percent reported to access services; and 10 percent to circulation. In only 3 percent of the libraries did the head of ILL report to anyone else. The organizational charts in figures 5.6-5.11, on pages 99 to 104, illustrate the diversity of reporting patterns, even among libraries of the same type.

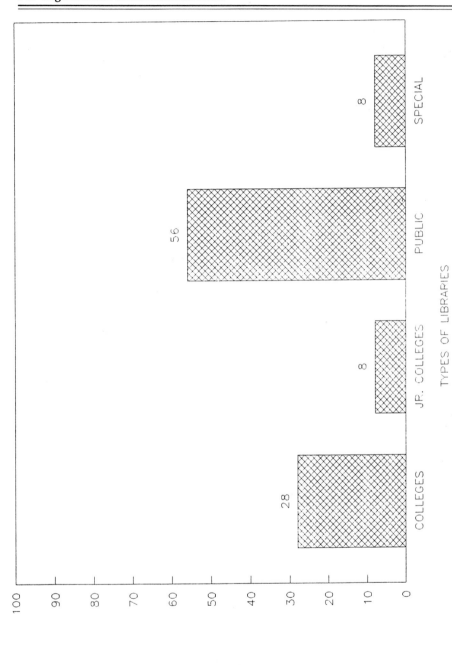

Fig. 5.1. Interlibrary loan located in reference department.

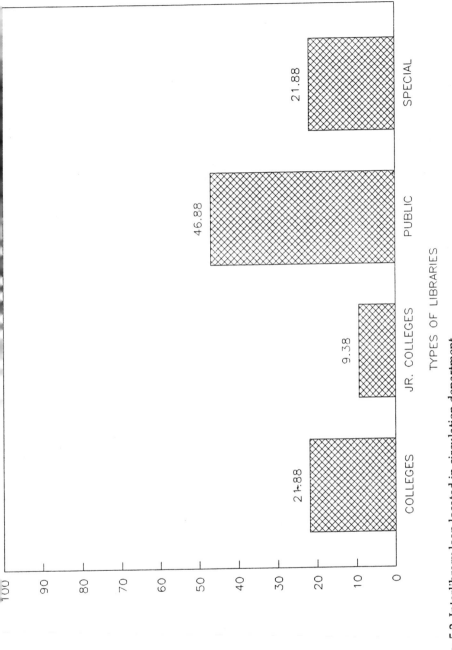

Fig. 5.2. Interlibrary loan located in circulation department.

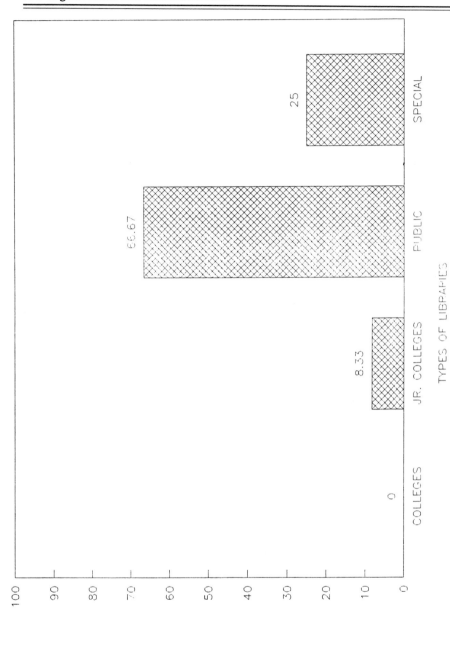

Fig. 5.3. Interlibrary loan located in reference/circulation department.

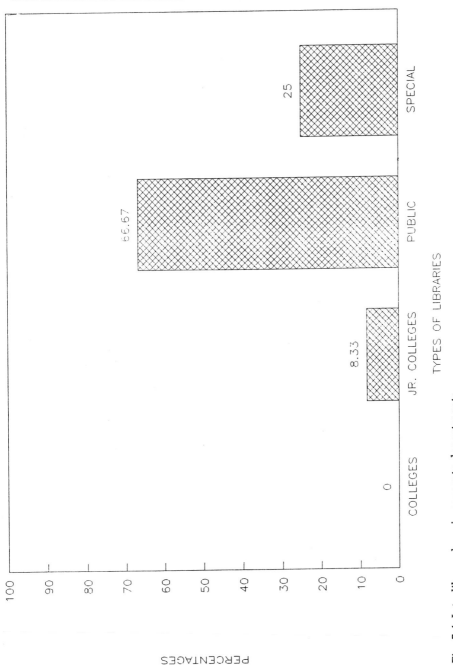

Fig. 5.4. Interlibrary loan in separate departments.

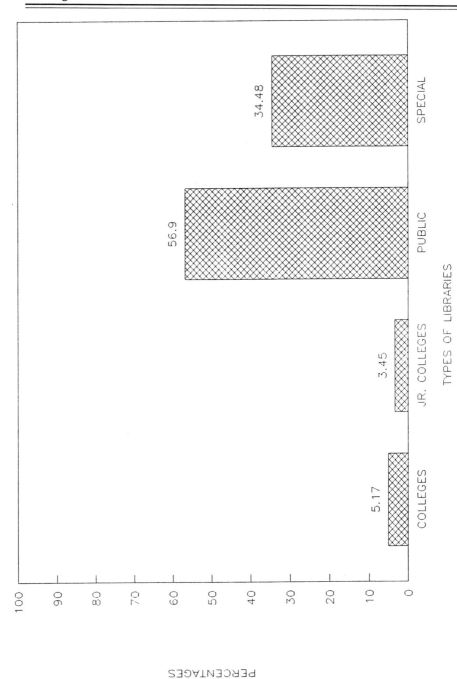

Fig. 5.5. Other arrangements made for interlibrary loan.

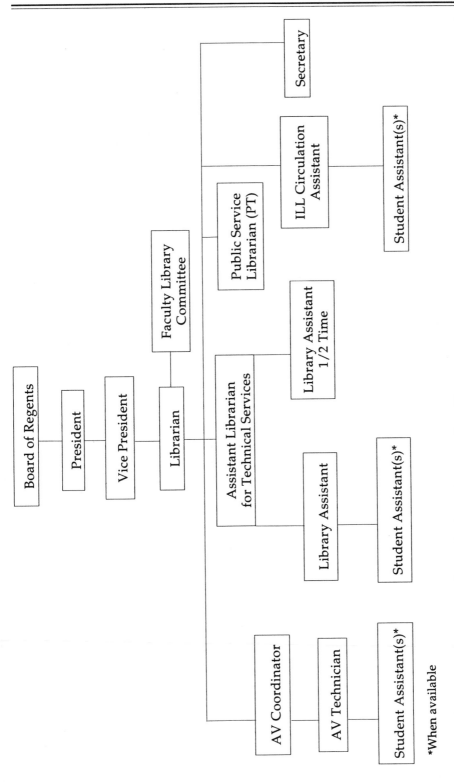

*When available

Fig. 5.6. Example of a reporting hierarchy in a two-year college library.

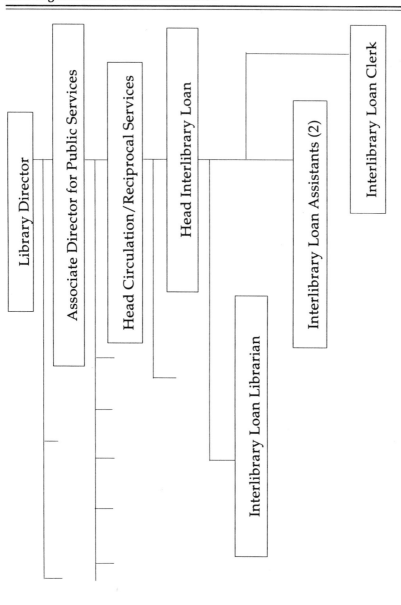

Fig. 5.7. Example of a reporting hierarchy in a public library.

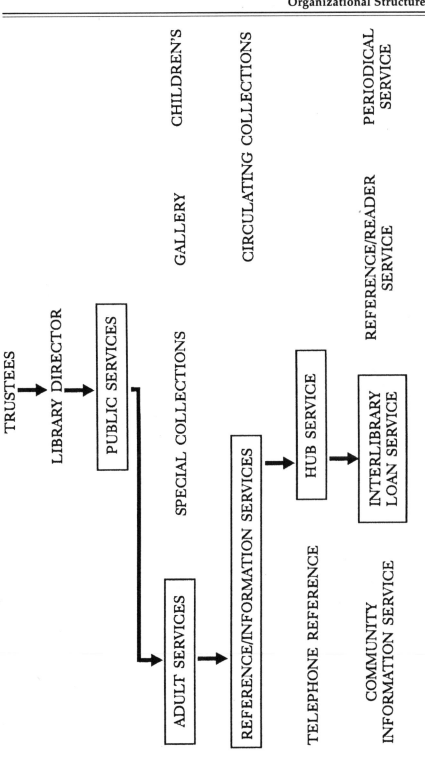

Fig. 5.8. Example of a reporting hierarchy in a public library.

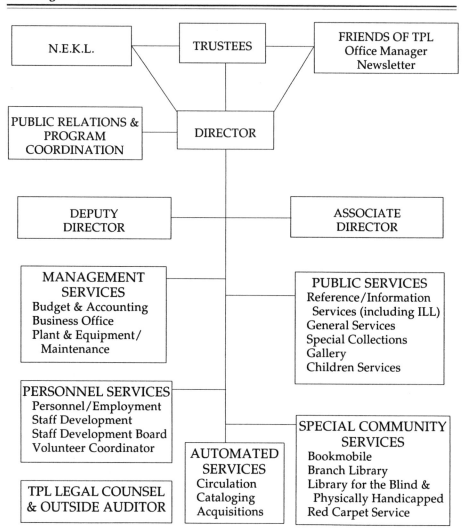

Fig. 5.9. Example of a reporting hierarchy in a public library.

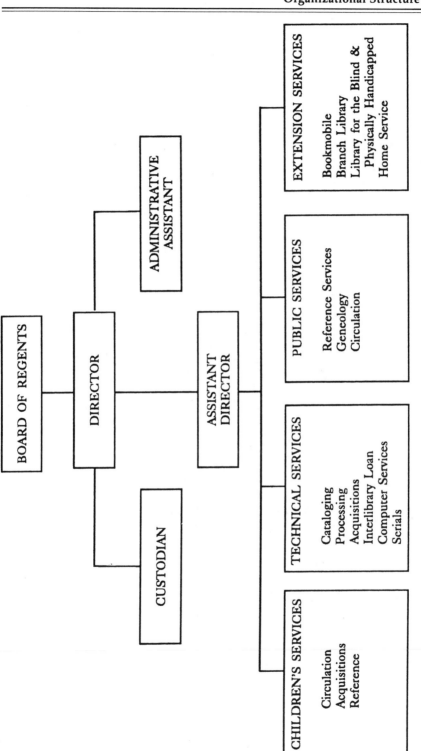

Fig. 5.10. Example of a reporting hierarchy in a public library.

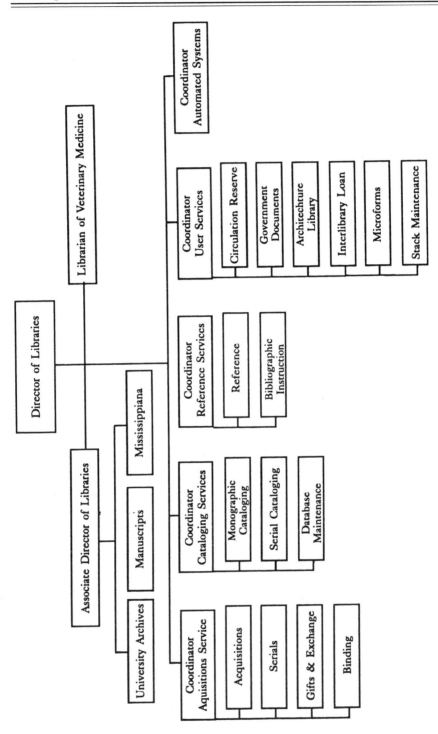

Fig. 5.11. Example of a reporting hierarchy in a university library.

# Staffing

Reser and Schuneman, in a content analysis study of the academic library job market, found that positions advertised in *American Libraries, College and Research Libraries News, Library Journal,* and *Chronicle of Higher Education* during the year 1988 included 698 public-service positions, only 17 (1.5 percent) of which were specified as ILL positions.[8]

In 65 percent of the libraries surveyed by LaGuardia and Dowell, a professional supervised interlibrary loan (53 full time; 12 part time). Nonlibrarians supervised the operation in 31 percent of the libraries. The number of staff members assigned to interlibrary loan varied greatly. Appendix C (p. 223) illustrates that job descriptions of ILL staff members also vary greatly.

With the new developments in bibliographic searching, transmission, and delivery, along with the attendant increase in volume, staffing is considered a serious problem.[9] An ACRL report published in 1989 suggested that the importance of professional librarians in ILL work may be underestimated and that increasing ILL activity may be causing a reduction in the quality of service in borrowing operations.[10]

Although still only a fraction of the total circulation activity in the County College of Morris, Randolph, New Jersey, interlibrary loan has expanded as a result of automated technology. It was reported in 1987 that it had become necessary to train as a backup someone other than the ILL assistant and that it might become necessary to add staff in order to keep up with demand. The 3,000-plus requests generated in 1985 were processed by the same number of staff as were the 351 in 1980, although from 1982 forward some redistribution of reference-related clerical duties was necessary to allow more time to be spent on ILL activities.[11] This example seems typical of other cases encountered through conversation or professional reading.

Interlibrary loan professional staffing, according to the author's survey, was almost equally divided between full-time and part-time professionals. Full-time library technical assistants were used by approximately 40 percent of the respondents, and part-time library technical assistants were used by approximately 60 percent of the respondents. Student assistants or pages are almost never used full time, but they were used part time.

When staffing is insufficient to handle the work load, as it often is, librarians cut down on the work load by processing only a given number of requests daily on a first-come, first-serve basis, or they may process only a given number of requests daily on a selective basis. Adjustments are made by some by pulling personnel from other areas of the library—library technical assistants, professional librarians, and student assistants or pages, in that order. Very few indicated on the author's survey that they would hire more help, either professional or nonprofessional. Librarians who responded to the survey indicated that if they could improve staffing they would hire—in order of number of responses given—more full-time library technical assistants, more part-time library technical assistants, more full-time student assistants or pages, more full-time professionals, and more part-time professionals.

In her 1991 ALA speech, Virginia Boucher, ILL librarian at the University of Colorado at Boulder, said that technology has not only increased access and workload but it has also made staffing the ILL office more difficult. The training program is longer, and more expertise is required. Staff now need training in computers, as well as in bibliography.

Further, she stated that the ILL staff is too small to handle present loads, and offices are too small to handle staff, computers, printers, bibliographic tools, and so forth. At the same time, the ILL office has been moved to a more visible area, causing more ILL traffic.

Interlibrary loan librarians need to be more highly visible professionals. They should be part of the team making any kind of decision affecting interlibrary loan. They should be able to articulate their needs and provide better management data for directors so the directors can support those needs.

## Work Load

Document delivery programs are sometimes associated with interlibrary loan and sometimes with circulation. Whoever is in charge is responsible for policy as well as for daily operational procedures. As with regular interlibrary loan, low-level staff members (preferably full time because of the routine nature of the work) can handle the detail. A high-level staff member is required for searching difficult requests and setting policy.

Some studies have been done on the actual amount of time spent on ILL work. Average time spent on each ILL transaction was 29.5 minutes in a 1972 study at Trent University Library in Peterborough, Ontario. The average borrowing request took 35.6 minutes—31.5 minutes of nonprofessional time and 4.9 minutes of professional time. It took an average of 11.1 minutes of nonprofessional time to fill a request from another library.[12]

Alternative methods of obtaining materials requested through interlibrary loans are being sought to improve service and to reduce cost. The Interlibrary Loan Center of the Corpus Christi Public Libraries, which serves as the major resource center for the South Texas Library System, began, in 1980, a purchase-on-demand, or fast-fill, method of filling ILL requests received from member libraries. Titles are checked in *Books in Print* and submitted to a jobber only if they are presently in stock. One jobber accepts phone calls and verifies availability, usually within two working days.

Titles selected for fast-fill must meet two other criteria besides availability. They must cost no more than a certain amount, and their appeal must be general, not specialized. The ILL librarian decides which titles to order, usually within one working day after receipt of the request. Books purchased in this way are generally received within two weeks—about the same amount of time it takes to fill an ILL request.[13]

There are certain definite steps that must be taken before a patron request can become an ILL order. First, the catalog of the patron's own library must be checked to make sure the material is not already owned. Then the title should be verified so that correct and complete bibliographic data can be supplied to the lending library. The responsibility for this rests with the borrowing library, according to the ILL code, so many librarians will not attempt to fill a request that requires additional bibliographic work. Then the most likely source for the borrowed material must be checked.

Whenever possible, the borrowing library should attempt to obtain photocopies or film so that the original material may remain in the lending library. The librarian, however, must be ever mindful of the restrictions of the copyright law and must also practice good management techniques in order to handle the many routine responsibilities and make the work flow smoothly.

In order to accomplish all this, librarians should keep on file ILL policies of the libraries from which loans are most frequently requested. Copies of the ILL librarians' own policies should be sent to other libraries with which they lend and borrow. Their own library patrons must also have a written set of policies. In the professional literature can be found copies of various policy and procedure manuals that can be used as models.[14, 15, 16]

A survey of multitype libraries in the Florida Library Information Network (FLIN), reported in 1982,[17] showed the average number of hours per week spent on the ILL operation:

College and university Libraries 52.2

Public libraries 15.6

State libraries 11.1

Government libraries 9.5

Corporation libraries 9.3

Community and junior college libraries 5.6

Military libraries 2.5

School libraries 1.3

Other 12.7

## The Professional Library

Copies of various ILL policies are maintained as a sort of professional library. The ILL librarian needs to also include in this library certain types of bibliographical tools such as union lists, manuals and directories from on-line ILL subsystems, directories of special collections, and regional surveys of materials. Lists of library symbols, directories of fax numbers, books on ILL practices, information on copyright, and other information should also be part of the library to which the ILL librarian has easy access. The bibliography in appendix D contains titles that have proved useful to the author and others who have worked with interlibrary loan. Different librarians will find different sources helpful in their own situations. Standard reference works available in most libraries, such as *Books in Print, Cumulative Book Index, Booklist,*

*Choice, Book Review Digest, Essay and General Literature Index, Standard Catalog,* and *United States Catalog* do not appear in the bibliography, but they are invaluable in bibliographic searching. The serials *Resource Sharing and Information Networks, Journal of Interlibrary Loan and Information Supply, Interlending and Document Supply, Copyright Society of the U.S.A. Journal,* and the "Library to Library" column of the *Wilson Library Bulletin* all contain current information relative to the subject of interlibrary loan.

## Interlibrary Loan Management

Whether the ILL unit is a department in its own right, or whether the ILL work is divided into two or more departments, management of the ILL office can be divided into borrowing activities and lending activities. The activities must be analyzed to determine what kind of forms will be needed, what kind of records or files should be kept, and how they should be arranged. Consideration must also be given to providing the training the staff will need to perform these tasks.

There are three distinct areas of work in an ILL unit—*record keeping, materials flow,* and *management.* Records must be kept on patrons, loans, overdues, charges, and statistics. Materials flow means the physical movement of materials back and forth between libraries, to and from patrons, and even within the library. Organization, personnel management and training, work flow and work load balancing, cost control, monitoring, reporting, synthesizing data and collection development issues all fall within the area of management in interlibrary loan.

Interlibrary loan is very labor intensive and requires an unusual amount of record keeping, as mentioned. Traditionally, manual files are kept and the data compiled into monthly and yearly reports. (See figs. 5.12-5.14, on pages 109-13 for examples of reports compiled in an ILL office.)

Automation has now come to the ILL office and has changed the way things are done. Work flow, however, remains pretty much the same. Janet Evans recommends that before deciding to automate record keeping involved in tracking or invoicing, one should write down the steps involved in doing the task manually. This helps to analyze, and perhaps streamline, the ways requests are processed.[18]

Perhaps the most important benefit of automation of the ILL office is the capability it provides the ILL librarian of detecting weaknesses in the collection and for detecting and handling problems related to transit, overdues, and other matters. Computer-based systems can provide the kind of statistics needed to monitor costs, staff performance, and output. Much of what is needed for automation support is a by-product of routine processing. Computer-based systems may be in-house systems, or they may be shared with other libraries through a consortium or through a bibliographic or commercial service.

| We lent to others | MONTH 1990 | # fr. LLC | # fr. others | unfilled | TOTAL | # frm. LLC | # fr. others | unfilled | TOTAL | for library | for patrons | TOTAL | RDY REF |
|---|---|---|---|---|---|---|---|---|---|---|---|---|---|
| | | TITLE | | | | PERIODICAL | | | | FILMS | | | |
| 61 | May | 113 | 11 | 13 | 137 | – | – | – | Ø | – | – | Ø | 4 |
| 74 | June | 139 | 18 | 12 | 169 | 6 | – | – | 6 | – | – | Ø | 3 |
| 97 | July | 106 | 12 | 18 | 136 | 1 | 1 | 0 | 2 | 0 | 0 | 0 | 2 |
| 92 | Aug | 125 | 25 | 14 | 164 | 1 | – | 1 | 2 | – | – | – | – |
| 120 | Sept | 113 | 16 | 6 | 135 | 1 | 1 | 0 | 2 | – | – | – | 6 |
| 101 | Oct | 185 | 24 | 7 | 185 | 5 | 5 | 0 | 10 | – | – | – | 2 |
| 84 | Nov | 147 | 17 | 14 | 178 | 17 | 1 | 0 | 18 | – | 1 | 1 | 1 |
| 65+ | Dec | 99 | 25 | 7 | 131 | 6 | 2 | 1 | 9 | – | – | – | – |
| 97 | Jan 1991 | 137 | 30 | 11 | 178 | 0 | 4 | 0 | 4 | 0 | 2 | 2 | 8 |
| 99 | Feb 91 | 124 | 39 | 7 | 170 | 8 | – | – | 8 | – | – | – | 5 |
| 80 | March 91 | 109 | 15 | 26 | 150 | 7 | 1 | 2 | 10 | – | – | – | 1 |
| 96 | April 91 | 151 | 22 | 6 | 179 | 6 | 0 | 0 | 6 | 0 | 2 | 2 | Ø |
| 102 | May 91 | 176 | 16 | 8 | 200 | 1 | 1 | 0 | 2 | 0 | 0 | 0 | 6 |
| 93 | June 91 | 128 | 11 | 10 | 149 | 0 | 3 | 0 | 3 | 0 | 0 | 0 | 3 |
| 99 | July 91 | 116 | 17 | 1 | 134 | 1 | 1 | 0 | 2 | 0 | 0 | 0 | 2 |
| 103 | Aug 91 | 157 | 19 | 3 | 157 | – | – | 2 | 2 | – | – | – | 6 |
| 121 | Sept 91 | 139 | 11 | 5 | 139 | 5 | – | – | 5 | 0 | 1 | 1 | 6 |
| 130 | Oct 91 | 131 | 21 | 4 | 156 | 13 | – | – | 13 | – | – | – | 4 |
| 103 | Nov 91 | 124 | 10 | 6 | 140 | 16 | – | – | 16 | – | – | – | 4 |
| 75 | Dec 91 | 106 | 6 | 6 | 118 | 2 | 2 | 0 | 4 | – | – | – | 1 |
| 128 | Jan 92 | 100 | 8 | 4 | 112 | 2 | 0 | 0 | 2 | 1 | 0 | 1 | 6 |

Fig. 5.12. Interlibrary loan transaction log.

TELEFAX MACHINE
MONTHLY RECORD OF TRANSACTIONS

LIBRARY_____          MONTH_____

| DATE | STUDENT / FACULTY REQUESTING | PERIODICAL TITLE | NO. OF PAGES | TOTAL CHAR( |
|------|------------------------------|------------------|--------------|-------------|
|      |                              |                  |              |             |
|      |                              |                  |              |             |
|      |                              |                  |              |             |
|      |                              |                  |              |             |
|      |                              |                  |              |             |
|      |                              |                  |              |             |
|      |                              |                  |              |             |
|      |                              |                  |              |             |
|      |                              |                  |              |             |
|      |                              |                  |              |             |
|      |                              |                  |              |             |
|      |                              |                  |              |             |
|      |                              |                  |              |             |
|      |                              |                  |              |             |
|      |                              |                  |              |             |
|      |                              |                  |              |             |
|      |                              |                  |              |             |
|      |                              |                  |              |             |
|      |                              |                  |              |             |
|      |                              |                  |              |             |
|      |                              |                  |              |             |
|      |                              |                  | TOTAL        |             |

Fig. 5.13. Telefax machine monthly record of transactions.

NATIONAL INTERLENDING STATISTICS

Name of library/institution:

1.  The statistics should not include requests to or from other countries.

2.  They should relate to a complete period of 12 months, preferably the last calender year: please state period covered by statistics:

3.  Please answer as many questions as possible: the most important are starred (*).

4.  Apart from questions A1 and B1, please give estimated percentages if exact figures are not known.

A.  Requests sent to other libraries ‡

                                                   Number

    *1.   How many requests were sent to other libraries (excluding reapplications for the same request)?

                                                             or   %

    1.1  How many requests were for books?

                         journals?

                         other?

    *2.   How many of the requests were satisfied altogether?

    2.1  How many requests were satisfied for books?

                         journals?

                         other?

    2.2  How many requests were satisfied by first library tried?

    2.3  How many requests were satisfied with one week?

                         two weeks?

                         four weeks?

---

‡   Throughout the questionnaire the term 'libraries' is taken to include union catalogue, document centres, archives, and other document supply centres or agencies.

(Fig. 5.14 continues on page 112.)

Fig. 5.14. Example of a national interlending statistics report.

Fig. 5.14—*Continued*

3.  To which five libraries were most
    requests sent?

Name of Library

1.

2.

3.

4

5.

B.  Requests received from other libraries

Number

*1. How many requests were received from
    other libraries?

Number        or  %

*2. How many of them were satisfied
    altogether?

2.1 How many were satisfied by loan?

photocopy?

microform?

3.  Which five libraries sent most
    requests to you?

Name of Library

1.

2.

3.

4

5.

C.   Additional information

Please give in the space below any further information that may be useful (eg categories of material that are difficult to obtain, relative speed of supply from different libraries, special factors, etc).

Name of person completing form:

Date:

Automated ILL record management and statistics projects reported in the professional literature combine a database management system such as dBase with a microcomputer and customized programming, or they have specialized software. Labor saved in the preparation of forms and compilation of statistics reports are reasons enough to implement a microcomputer program. Other applications for such a program are tracking of ILL requests, carrying out collection-development work, supplying the requesting patterns for groups of borrowers, and tracking cost factors. Other factors that could be monitored are user satisfaction in filling a request, reasons for unfilled requests, and turnaround time. This information can, of course, be gathered from manual files; but the data must be rearranged in the file, and the job is quite tedious.

The OCLC interlibrary loan subsystem has automated much of the daily borrowing and lending procedures. Throughout the process, both lender and borrower indicate on-line the availability of material, when shipped, when received, when returned, and so on. The monthly reports that are generated by OCLC, however, indicate only total lending and borrowing transactions by library, plus filled and unfilled requests. Additional statistics that are needed in an office, including the mandatory copyright statistics, must be captured in some other way.

## ILLFILE

Patterns of use by date, status of patron, department, type of material, or titles requested can be produced at the same time that an OCLC request is produced by using ILLFILE, a record-keeping software package. It can pick up information from any field of the OCLC interlibrary loan workform. Use of the program requires entering the data into the workform in a standard format and remembering to save, as well as send, each request; both functions can be easily integrated into the daily work flow.[19] The New Jersey Institute of Technology saves each outgoing OCLC request to a diskette to form an electronic archive of ILL requests.[20]

Kwan reports finding ILLFILE cumbersome for maintaining copyright files, because periodical issues older than five years cannot be omitted from the report. Other fields captured by ILLFILE are irrelevant for copyright compliance. Fields also cannot be reordered to sort by title. The University of Rhode Island combines ILLFILE and dBase III.[21]

## dBase III

At Texas Tech University, dBase III Plus was chosen to computerize interlibrary loans. The paper files were converted onto a database management system that maintains data, generates reports, and retrieves records. It is useful for storing, organizing, and sorting, as well as for generating reports and managing the daily paper flow. The database management system performs the following tasks: 1) adds new files to the database, 2) inserts new data into the files, 3) retrieves data from the files, 4) updates data in the files, and 5) generates reports.[22]

Since 1953, when it was established, the Medical Documentation Service (MDS) of the Library of the College of Physicians of Philadelphia has been meeting the information needs of the pharmaceutical industry. Document delivery service has always been an important aspect of the operation.

Because of good quality copies and 24-hour turnaround time, the document delivery service receives over 100 requests per day by phone, fax, E-mail, OCLC, and DOCLINE. Record keeping became so tedious that automation of several areas of the service seemed necessary. Daily processing of requests, invoicing, and generation of statistics were chosen to be automated. dBase III Plus was chosen as the software package. It was later replaced by dBase IV.

An invoicing system using dBase III was described by Evans. Names and addresses of libraries are stored in the LIBRARIES part of the system. The INVDBF database part of the system contains the fields necessary to post each photocopy order. Invoices can be issued using a number of programs and format files. Up to 10 items may be listed per invoice. The system is menu-driven.[23]

Invoices may be printed individually or batched for biweekly, monthly, or quarterly processing. When invoices have been printed, all records in the current Charges Table are moved to the Charge History Table, where they may be checked at any time for verification of charges or for statistical purposes. Statistical data are easily kept, and reports may be compiled through the use of the Library Statistics menu. Since the department changed from its previous "one request/one invoice" billing system using PFS:File to RBPHOTO, improvements have been seen in accuracy and time management. The problems encountered have been solved.

## F.I.L.L.S.

F.I.L.L.S.—Fast Interlibrary Loans and Statistics—software package for the IBM PC or PC/XT was developed by Macneal Hospital in Berwyn, Illinois. It is a library-specific software package developed by a librarian to be used by staff members with little or no computer experience. It cuts the time involved in processing loans to less than 50 percent of the manual time, and the statistics generated allow for improved analysis of the ILL service. Although it was created and is marketed by a health care institution, the program is designed to be used by all types of libraries.

Each loan is automatically assigned an identification number. Standard information such as borrowing library name and address, identification codes, and authorization data are entered and remain until typed over. Periodical titles are coded upon entry, and a list can be called up at any time. Names and addresses of lending libraries are done the same way. Reports are also generated on number of requests filled, referred, or outstanding in each lending institution. This helps to equalize the load among libraries. Reports are summarized and cumulate each month. F.I.L.L.S. can sort by discipline or department for loans filled and by patron for outstanding loans. It can also print mailing labels and document copyright compliance.[24]

## Interlibrary Loan Control

A program called Interlibrary Loan Control, available from Right On Programs for IBM and compatible machines, generates its own forms based on the standard ALA forms. Entering data on the forms requires answering on-screen prompts. One space on the form allows the request to be personalized by name or informational notes, such as "fill at no cost," and "do not refer." From the data input, the computer totals the number of requests per month and year and the number of times per month and year requests are sent to a particular library; it also stores names, addresses, and titles.

For requests that are transmitted by mail, fax, TWX, or other means, either statistics are compiled manually or another computerized system must be introduced. There are several database management systems applications packages for microcomputers on the market. These packages are not ready for use but are programming frameworks to assist in designing your own database. Most require creating a data-entering form, entering of the records, and setting up "report" formats.

A spreadsheet program on a microcomputer is another helpful way to capture statistics. In planning and organizing a spreadsheet, a computer operator may first make a rough design with paper and pencil. When complete, the spreadsheet model should be given a filename and saved on a disk for later retrieval.[25]

## ILLRKS

The need for improved file management in the ILL office and the need for more timely information for collection development caused the Colorado State University ILL librarian to review software packages capable of managing a large borrowing file so that ILL statistics and information for collection development can be generated. ILLRKS (Interlibrary Loan Record Keeping System), developed at the University of Wyoming, was chosen because even though it originally supported only OCLC, ALA, and E-mail requests, there was an interest in expanding its capacity to allow input of RLIN requests as well.[26]

ILLRKS is a menu-driven software for managing ILL borrowing records. It runs on an IBM PC/XT or compatible microcomputer. The ILLRKS database is maintained in three major files—active, inactive, and the CONTU file, containing photocopy requests in compliance with the CONTU guidelines and the copyright law of the United States (Title 17, U.S. code). ILLRKS allows full-screen editing in all of these files. ILLRKS's ability to capture requests sent through a multitude of systems into one file for managing copyright records and statistics and its complete and customized reporting features combine to make it a unique software package for ILL record management.[27]

## R:Base

The Interlibrary Loan Department of Southern Illinois University at Carbondale, one of the research and reference centers of ILLINET that borrows and lends worldwide, has found the microcomputer application software R:Base for DOS to be a product equal in quality and adaptability to dBase III. RBPHOTO, the library's ILL invoicing application, was developed with R:Base for DOS. It consists of six data tables that exist independently and can be accessed separately or in conjunction with one another. They are addresses, current charges, charge history, balance, payments, and statistics. The application is menu-driven, which makes it easy to search and manipulate.[28]

# Marketing the Interlibrary Loan Program

In her response to Thomas Ballard's "The Unfulfilled Promise of Resource Sharing," Jane English challenges public library staff members to market their program in order to encourage the growth of interlibrary loan and help fulfill the promise of resource sharing. She suggested making ILL more visible through signage and brochures and creating innovative ways to bring the public in to observe on-line transmission of ILL requests. She also recommended user-friendly policies and procedures and urged staff referrals to interlibrary loan. Her solution to overloads? Volunteers.

It is important not to promise more than can be delivered, however. Poorly handled ILL service can mean frustration and disappointment. Limitations must be communicated to patrons or they may come to believe that anything they want can be borrowed free and will arrive overnight.

# The Cost of Interlibrary Loan

On page 996 of the 1933 *Library Journal* appeared an announcement by Gilbert Doane, University of Nebraska librarian, concerning the adoption of ILL service charges "to offset the drain on a much reduced budget, and to curtail a rapidly growing tendency to ask for unnecessary loans." Transportation and service fees were charged for both incoming and outgoing loans. Libraries in Nebraska and certain alumni of the university did not have to pay the service fee.

In the 1970s, many large libraries that lent more books than they borrowed (net lenders) and that had not been charging for interlibrary loan began to charge fees. They did, however, make exceptions for other libraries in their geographic or subject area. Some also entered into reciprocal borrowing agreements.

With the availability of on-line access to holdings lists of smaller libraries, some of the ILL burden fell away from the larger institutions. Small libraries unaccustomed to participating were pleased to learn they had materials others were eager to borrow. For a large research library, the request from an Australian library that thrilled the American public librarian would have been just another request to fill.

Danuta Nitecki reported that in his 1974 survey, library users were willing to pay as much as five dollars just to obtain a book on loan for research. They were also willing to pay 10 to 20 cents per page for journal articles.[29] Scholars in colleges and universities, however, are afraid that their ability to do research required for promotion and tenure will suffer because of the fees charged for interlibrary loan.[30]

In three libraries or networks—Princeton University; Arizona Medical Library Network; and the Kentucky, Ohio, Michigan Regional Medical Library—it was found that ILL activity dropped when the fee was initiated, but gradually, especially if the turnaround time was faster, the number of requests received began to rise again.[31] A more recent study—a case study of the library of the State Historical Society of Wisconsin—found that only public libraries showed a decrease in interlibrary loans after fees were initiated.[32]

That there will be some charge associated with interlibrary loan has come to be expected. The absence of standardization and overpricing, including a cost for the service by some libraries, are very real problems, however.

Data from the 1975 and 1984 (1st and 2d) editions of the ALA *Interlibrary Loan Policies Directory* indicate that there was a large increase in prices from 1975 to 1984. Charges were considerably higher in private university libraries than they were in public university libraries. Fees were levied for not only the basic service fees but also for such things as unfilled requests, searches, and service to out-of-state libraries. Cline reports that the higher prices charged by private university libraries have succeeded in reducing lending by 38 percent.[33]

Several prominent librarians have, through the years, advocated standardization of fees.[34, 35, 36] This has been realized to some degree by members of local consortia. If long-term differences develop between lending and borrowing among consortium members, net borrowers have an obligation to reimburse institutions that are net lenders.[37]

A resource-sharing conference was held in 1987 for librarians in Washington, Oregon, and Montana. Several recommendations made at the conference concerned ILL funding: 1) users should not bear the costs of interlibrary loan; 2) research to discover the real costs of interlibrary loan should be funded by the Washington State Library; and 3) libraries should figure costs of interlibrary loan and build them into their materials budgets.[38]

# Notes

[1]Guy R. Lyle, *The Administration of the College Library*, 4th ed. (New York: Wilson, 1974), 102-4.

[2]Louis Round Wilson and Maurice F. Tauber, *The University Library*, 2d ed. (New York and London: Columbia University Press, 1956), 222.

[3]Carl H. Melinet, *The Administration of Interlibrary Loans in American Libraries*, (Syracuse, N.Y.: Syracuse University, 1949), 102.

[4]Genevieve Porterfield, "Staffing of Interlibrary Loan Service," *College and Research Libraries* 26 (July 1965):318-20.

[5]Cheryl LaGuardia and Connie V. Dowell, "The Structure of Resource Sharing in Academic Research Libraries," *RQ* 30 (Spring 1991):370-74.

[6]Elaine Zaremba Jennerich and Edward J. Jennerich, *The Reference Interview as a Creative Art* (Littleton, Colo.:Libraries Unlimited, 1987), 78.

[7]Herbert G. Canales and Karen K. Nichols, "Purchase on Demand for the South Texas Library System," *Texas Libraries* 43 (Fall 1981):113-18.

[8]David W. Reser and Anita P. Schuneman, "The Academic Library Job Market: A Content Analysis Comparing Public and Technical Services," *College and Research Libraries* 53 (January 1992):55.

[9]Ann L. Kelsey and John M. Cohn, "The Impact of Automation on Interlibrary Loan: One College Library's Experience," *Journal of Academic Librarianship* 13 (July 1987):165.

[10]Pat Weaver-Meyers, Shelly Clement, and Carolyn Mahin, *Interlibrary Loans in Academic and Research Libraries: Workload and Staffing*, ERIC Document 317 208 (Washington, D.C.: ACRL, 1989), 1-28.

[11]Bruce Cossar, "Interlibrary Loan Costs," *RQ* 12 (Spring 1973):243-46.

[12]Julie E. Wessling, "Benefits from Automated ILL Borrowing Records: Use of ILLRKS in an Academic Library," *RQ* 29 (Winter 1989):210.

[13]Ibid., 217.

[14]Alabama Public Library Service, *The ALIN Manual. The Alabama Public Library Service Interlibrary Loan Manual*, 2d ed., ERIC Document 325 133 (Montgomery: Alabama Public Library Service, 1990).

[15]Alaska State Department of Education, Division of State Libraries, *Interlibrary Loan, the Key to Resource Sharing: A Manual of Procedures and Protocols*, ERIC Document 311 936 (Juneau, Alaska: Division of State Libraries, 1989).

[16]Southeastern/Atlantic Regional Medical Library Services, *Document Delivery Policy, Region 2*, ERIC Document 324 015 (Baltimore, Md.: Southeastern/Atlantic Regional Medical Library Services, 1989).

[17]Wessling, "Automated ILL Borrowing Records," 211.

[18]Janet Evans, "Using dBase III to Create a Photocopy Invoicing System," *Library Software Review* 5 (September-October 1986):264-68.

[19]Carol Levin and Jim Nolte, "ILLFILE, ILLSORT, and ILLCOUNT Automate OCLC ILL Record Keeping," *OCLC MICRO* 4 (April 1988):9-11.

[20]Thomas H. Ballard, "The Unfulfilled Promise of Resource Sharing," *American Libraries* 21 (November 1990):990-93.

[21]Millie Kwan, "Monitoring 5-5 CONTU Compliance Using ILLFILE and dBASE III," *OCLC MICRO* 5 (June 1989):13-15.

[22]Amy Chang, "A Database Management System for Interlibrary Loan," *Information Technology and Libraries* 9 (June 1990):136.

[23]Evans, "Using dBase III," 264-68.

[24]Maryanne Witters, "Interlibrary Loans with a Micro ... Clean and Quick," *Online* 8 (November 1984):53-55.

[25]Philip M. Clark, *Microcomputer Spreadsheet Models for Libraries* (Chicago: ALA, 1985), 1-33.

[26]Wessling, "Automated ILL Borrowing Records," 210.

[27]Ibid., 211-17.

[28]Thomas L. Kilpatrick, David A. Brossart, and Raymond G. Einig, "A Photocopy Invoicing Application Using R:Base for DOS," *Library Software Review* 8 (May-June 1989):146.

[29]Danuta A. Nitecki, "Interlibrary Services: A Report on a Study of Measuring User Awareness and Satisfaction," *Tennessee Librarian* 28 (Summer 1976):85-94.

[30]J. Magarrel, "Fees for Interlibrary Loans Spread: Scholars Fear Work Will Suffer," *Chronicle of Higher Education* 27 (October 19, 1983):1.

[31]William A. Katz, *Introduction to Reference Work, V. II: Reference Services and Reference Processes*, 3d ed. (New York: McGraw-Hill, 1978), 229.

[32]James H. Sweetland and Darlene E. Weingand, "Interlibrary Loan Transaction Fees in a Major Research Library: They Don't Stop the Borrowers," *Library and Information Science Research* 12 (January-March 1990):87-101.

[33]Gloria S. Cline, "The High Price of Interlibrary Loan Service," *RQ* 27 (Fall 1987):81-83.

[34]David Kaser, "Whither Interlibrary Loan?" *College and Research Libraries* 33 (September 1972):401.

[35]John Berry, "Interlibrary Loan and the Network," *Library Journal* 103 (April 15, 1978):795.

[36]Cline, "High Price of Interlibrary Loan Service," 83.

[37]Richard M. Dougherty, "Research Libraries in an International Setting: Requirements for Expanded Resource Sharing," *College and Research Libraries* 46 (September 1985):387.

[38]Ernestine Kimbro, "Interlibrary Loan Funding: Some Recommendations," *PNLA Quarterly* 51 (1987):23.

# chapter 6

# Policies and Procedures

The results of the author's survey of multitype libraries paint an interesting picture of policies and practices or procedures in American libraries. As predicted, a great variety of networks and codes are in use, and practically everything is borrowed and loaned to practically everybody for generous loan periods and renewals. Most ILL librarians require materials borrowed from other libraries to be used by patrons in their own libraries only when requested to do so by the lending library. Some require that valuable or fragile items be used in the library even if this is not requested by the lending library. Conversely, the majority leave the decision of whether to place restrictions on materials loaned up to the borrowing library, some requiring only rare material to be used in the library building.

Most libraries do not charge overdue fines to libraries but are much more prone to impose fines on patrons. Most charge other libraries for damages or replacement costs, which are in turn passed along by the borrowing library to its patrons.

Interlibrary loan requests are verified in many different ways, but few libraries send them out unverified. Requests are transmitted by U.S. mail, fax, telephone, OCLC, van or courier, other bibliographic utility, other special ways, on-line to the commercial supplier, and by teletype—in that order.

Overwhelmingly, libraries reported on the survey that books were delivered by U.S. mail, usually by library rate. In descending order, books are also delivered by UPS, a courier serving a network, fax, overnight delivery service, in various other ways, and on-line. Photocopies are delivered— again in descending order—by U.S. mail, fax, courier serving a network, UPS, overnight delivery service, various other ways, and on-line.

Libraries that charge for interlibrary loan, the majority of the ones that responded to the survey, bill on an item-by-item basis, for the most part. Some use a formal invoice; others write the amount owed on the printed request form. Individual borrowers pay more often than do their institutions or companies. The library usually either does not pay insurance or absorbs the cost of insurance. The same is true for material received by mistake. An overwhelming majority keep paper files to keep up with materials loaned or borrowed. Back files are also kept for compiling statistical reports. Only five libraries reported keeping no paper files.

# Interlibrary Loan Patron Interview

Often librarians must use their greatest oral skills to extract from library patrons exactly what it is they wish to obtain through interlibrary loan and how they learned of the existence of the material in question. Many times patrons do not know the titles they need, but they may have very specific ideas on the subjects for which they need additional material. To obtain as much information as possible to help in filling the request, the ILL librarian must exercise the same kinds of interview skills as the reference librarian does in the traditional reference interview. Public relations may at this point be either enhanced or retarded.

Copyright restrictions, lending restrictions, fees for service, and delivery problems must be explained to patrons. Each library should have copies of the institutional ILL policies to hand out. The example in figure 6.1 from the Alabama Department of Archives and History answers most of the questions a patron might ask.

Whoever accepts ILL requests from patrons—whether he or she is the ILL librarian, reference librarian, or someone else the patron happens to encounter in the library—should explain the ILL service accurately or refer the request to the appropriate staff member. Referral is oftentimes the better part of valor. Some ILL requests are in reality reference questions, as was, for example, the request for the address of the Queen of England, which was turned in to one library, and the request for information on how elephants mate, which was turned in to another library. Or the patron may need reader advisory assistance, as did the one who turned in the request for information on how to make beef jerky. In short, the person accepting an ILL request should be able to ascertain if the request is a legitimate ILL request.

The interlibrary loan librarian needs to remember that the patron also will have many questions. Patrons may actually need reassurance that they can trust the librarian to fill their requests. They will also surely wonder how long it will take, how much it will cost, and how they will be notified when the material arrives. Librarians will need to know not only the aforementioned correct citation, but they also must determine if patrons are eligible for service, if they have already checked the library's holdings, how much they are willing to pay, and if they have time to wait for the material to come in. All of this is determined in the patron interview.

## INTERLIBRARY LOAN SERVICE
Reference Room                Department of Archives & History

Interlibrary Loan Services are offered to university scholars, NAAL members, public libraries, and patrons of the Department of Archives & History's reference room. The purpose of interlibrary loan is to obtain microfilmed copies produced by the Newspaper Project of newspapers which are not available at any other place within the state. The Ready Reference section is responsible for interlibrary loans. All copies of microfilmed newspapers must be borrowed on interlibrary loan through local libraries. While many newspapers are available on microfilm, some titles are only available in original format in the Archival Reference room. All interlibrary loan requests are coordinated through the interlibrary loan clerk or the head of Ready Reference.

## OTHER MATERIALS

State publications are loaned to NAAL members only. Only photocopies of state publications are loaned, never the originals. The following procedures apply also to state publications.

## REFERENCE ILL PROCEDURES

Interlibrary loan requests are generated through the ALA form or through the OCLC computer network. Loan newspapers on film only if not "First Generation." (This notation will be on the container.) See attachments for a complete explanation of each form.

## RECEIPT OF MATERIALS

It will normally take between two and four working days to fill an interlibrary loan request. For more difficult requests, it may take additional time to locate or photocopy. This is especially true for state publications.

Interlibrary loan patrons will be notified about the conditions of the loan. If unable to fill the request, the reasons should be stated on the interlibrary loan form.

## FINDING AIDS FOR MICROFILMED NEWSPAPERS

It will be necessary to look for references to microfilmed newspapers in the following areas: Archival Reference desk, red and black binders in the Archival Reference room, and the microfilm

(Fig. 6.1 continues on page 124.)

Fig. 6.1. Alabama Department of Archives and History interlibrary loan policy.

Fig. 6.1—*Continued*

room. Loaned microfilms are listed on a bulletin board in the microfilm room. Loaned state publications are designated by an "out slip."

**CHARGES**

There is a charge when copies are made except for NAAL
members. Fifty cents each for copies from film, $.25 each
for copies from books, and $.25 a foot for unfilmed news-
papers. Postage is paid by the department. No charge is
made for film loaned. NAAL reimburses the department
$7.50 for each item loaned to its members through OCLC.

**DURATION OF LOANS**

The loan period is determined by the lending institution and may vary from two to four weeks, including mailing time. Renewals of loans are not encouraged. If a
renewal is necessary, a request must be made by letter or
by phone to the person responsible for interlibrary loans.
Loans should be returned promptly. Failure to return materials on time jeopardizes the Archives' ability to deliver
to other institutions. Repeated failure to return loans
can result in suspension of interlibrary loan privileges.

**RESTRICTIONS ON USE**

The lending institution may impose restrictions on
the use of its materials. Such restrictions may include
"in library use only," "no photocopying permitted," or
"only two films sent at one time."

**COPYRIGHT RESTRICTIONS**

The copyright law of the United States governs the making
of photocopies or other reproductions of copyrighted materials. Photocopies or other reproductions can be furnished only
under certain conditions, if they will be used for private
study, scholarship, or research. Use of the reproduction for
other purposes may make the user liable for copyright infringement. This institution reserves the right to refuse to
accept a copying order if, in its judgment, fulfillment of the
request would involve violation of the copyright law.

ILLS/ft

# Interlibrary Loan Request Form

A primary ingredient of the ILL transaction is the ILL request. It must convey to the ILL librarian certain basic bibliographic elements necessary for the procurement of the needed item.

It is imperative, therefore, that all the information available be filled out on the ILL request form. Standardization of the ILL order form by the ALA takes the guesswork out of what bibliographic information should be provided, so the patron request form, if patterned after the order form, needs only to have the appropriate blanks filled in.

Information about the requester must be filled in as well: address and telephone number, patron status, library card number, account number or his social security number, the date the material is needed, and the amount the patron is willing to pay for the material may all be necessary for the successful completion of the request.

Printed ILL request forms come in all shapes and sizes, as shown in figures 6.2-6.4, on pages 126-28. Academic libraries tend to adopt forms very much like the standard ALA order form; public and special libraries are more likely to choose a nonstandard form.

Some colleges and universities are now accepting ILL requests through the campus network. Colorado College, for example, offers its faculty, staff, and administrators the opportunity of ordering materials either for purchase or for interlibrary loan through the campus network. An ISN (Information Systems Network) ties together the campus computers. An AT&T product, it works like a telephone-switching network, allowing the Vax Computer to be accessed from any remote location. The programs (BOOKORDER and LOANORDER) are written in Vax Pascal.

The system prompts the requester to fill in the needed information for books or periodical articles and to indicate whether the patron should be notified by E-mail when ILL materials arrive. Periodical articles are sent to the requester by campus mail.[1]

Library _____

(Please Print)

Periodical
Title _____

Date of issue _____

Vol. No. _____

Page(s) _____

Author _____

_____

Title of
article _____

_____

_____

Date _____

Patron's
Name _____

Address _____

_____ ZIP _____

Home Phone _____

Bus. Phone _____

Status: ( )Student ( )Faculty
( )Professional ( )Bus. or Ind.
( )Other: _____

Verified (Source): Author _____
Title _____
Page _____ Date of Pub. _____ Publisher _____

LLC SUBJECT FORM 6/86

| REQ.LIB. | REQ.DATE | MUST HAVE BY | | ☐ NO SPECIFIC DEADLINE. TRY ALL AVAILABLE SOURCES |

DATE

PATRON WILL ACCEPT ☐ BOOKS ☐ PARTS OF BOOKS ☐ ARTICLES/ PHOTOCOPIES ☐ ANYTHING

LEVEL ☐ ELEM ☐ JH ☐ HS ☐ COLLEGE ☐ ADULT ☐ BEGINNING ☐ ADVANCED

SUBJECT — STATE PURPOSE IF OTHER THAN GENERAL INTEREST, E.G. TRAVEL, SCHOOL, WORK. LIST ANY SOURCES ALREADY CHECKED. LIST ANY SPECIFIC TITLES REQUESTED THROUGH I.L.L.

LLC NOTES

REPORT
GRPL _____
KCL _____
OTHER _____

PHONE

PATRON NAME

Fig. 6.2. Interlibrary loan request forms appear in all shapes and sizes.

| INTERLIBRARY LOAN REQUEST | Staff initials taking request_____ |
|---|---|

Patron Name _____

Patron SS# _____  Phone: _____

Campus:
- ☐ Del Norte  ☐ Eureka  ☐ Mendocino Coast

Branch:
- ☐ Eel River  ☐ Klamath  ☐ McKinleyville  ☐ So. Humb.

Status:
- ☐ Student  ☐ Faculty  ☐ Classified  ☐ Resident

A fee is charged for the interlibrary loan of materials not owned by College of the Redwoods. CR staff members may borrow items not owned by CR without charge if the material is work related. Remit, as applicable:

☐ 25 cents  (Students)  ☐ $10.00  (Residents)

Author (of book or magazine article):

Title (of book or magazine article):

Book Publisher and Date of Publication:

Title of Magazine:

Location of Article in Magazine:
Vol # _____  No. _____  Date _____  Pages _____

| If owned by CR COM Catalog: | Call number: | Accession Number: |
|---|---|---|

Date after which this item will no longer be useful to you:
(you MUST enter this information)

If a charge is assessed for the loan or photocopies, how much are you willing to pay? Express in whole numbers only, such as 0, $1, $2, $5, etc.

$ _____  (Blank indicates you will pay any amount)

MAIN LIBRARY USE ONLY
CR Library Location of Book/Item    CA    CC    DN    EU    MC    PC

☐YES ☐NO  Patron on library computer. Number of overdues _____
_____ Initials of staff checking computer.
For OCLC Use Only  OCLC # _____  ILL # _____

Fig. 6.3. Example of an interlibrary loan request form from a college library.

## U OF PENN BIOMEDICAL LIBRARY DOCUMENT DELIVERY

☐ **BOOK REQUEST**   ☐ **PHOTOCOPY REQUEST:**   **PAYMENT:** *(If RUSH or Penn-M-Xpress)*
☐ Interlibrary Loan (5-10 days)   ☐ Deposit Acct./Journal Voucher:
☐ Interlibrary Loan (RUSH) (@ $5.00)   ☐ Cash   ☐ Check
☐ Penn-M-Xpress   ☐ Please Bill

Name _____   _____   Date _____
      last                        first

Dept./School _____   Bldg. Code _____

Receiving Address _____   Zip _____

Phone ( ___ ) _____   ( ___ ) _____   FAX _____
         home                      campus

Affiliation ☐ HUP ☐ CHOP ☐ MED ☐ NSG ☐ BIOL   Have you checked Franklin? ☐ yes
☐ Biomed Grad ☐ Faculty ☐ Staff ☐ Grad ☐ Undergrad                        ☐ no

**DELIVERY** ☐ Pick-up
☐ Please mail to above address   *(You will not be notified when photocopies are received)*

**JOURNAL ARTICLE**

Journal Title _____

Year _____ Volume _____ Issue No. _____ Month _____ Pages _____
                              *Above information must be completed to insure delivery*

Author(s) _____

Article Title _____

Source of Reference _____

Unique Identifier # _____   *(8 digit # on Grateful Med or NLM Searches)*

**BOOK**   notification sent upon arrival

Author or Editor _____

Book Title _____

Publisher _____   Place of Pub. _____

Pub. Date _____   Edition _____   If pages _____

Series (if any) _____   Source of Reference _____

**NOTICE — Warning Concerning Copyright Restrictions**
PLEASE READ & SIGN

The copyright law of the United States (Title 17, United States Code) governs the making of photocopies or other reproductions of copyright material. Under certain conditions specified in the law, libraries and archives are authorized to furnish a photocopy or other reproduction. One of these specified conditions is that the photocopy or reproduction is not to be "used for any purpose other than private study, scholarship, or research." If a user makes a request for, or later uses, a photocopy or reproduction for purposes in excess of "fair use," that user may be liable for copyright infringement. This institution reserves the right to refuse to accept a copying order if, in its judgement fulfillment of the order would involve violation of copyright law.

Signature _____

WHITE COPY  ILL        YELLOW COPY  Routing        PINK COPY  Patron

---

**Office Use Only**

Penn-M-Express _____  Date _____

Received _____
Completed _____

Fee _____

Notes

**Interlibrary Loan**
☐ RLIN
☐ Franklin
☐ OCLC
☐ CASSI
☐ UCMP
☐ LCCN
☐ ISBN
☐ MEDLINE

ISSN _____

**Status**
☐ Not Owned
☐ Bindery
☐ PGS MSG
☐ OWNED
☐ NOS
☐ LACK
☐ ON SHELF

Fig. 6.4. Example of an interlibrary loan request form from a university library.

# Verification and Location

Interlibrary loan requests are verified, that is, checked, to ensure that the citations are indeed correct before sending the request to be filled. The ILL code specifies that the sources of verification be given on the order form to inform the lending librarian that the citation was verified.

Verification can now be done on-line and the request initiated to holding libraries in the same exercise. Those who do not have access to an on-line database or who need materials unavailable through an on-line database should consult reference tools available in the library for verification as well as for location. It may even have to be ascertained in what language a request has been placed.

## Monographs

Different kinds of materials require different kinds of bibliographic information. For a book or monograph the author, title, edition, place, publisher, date, and series, if applicable, should be provided. This kind of information can be found through bibliographic utilities. It can also be found in such titles as *Books In Print, Cumulative Book Index, Library of Congress Catalog of Printed Cards* (LCPC) and the *National Union Catalog* (NUC), or for early imprints, in bibliographies like *A Checklist of American Imprints*. Small libraries with few bibliographic tools can verify through such titles as *Essay and General Literature Index, Book Review Digest, Booklist, Choice, Standard Catalog*, and *United States Catalog*. For special materials, large research libraries' printed catalogs or subject-specific catalogs such as the *University of Texas Catalog of the Latin American Collection* can be checked.

## Periodical Articles

Information needed for periodical articles includes the title of the periodical; its volume, number, and date; and the author and title of the article with the page numbers. Periodical titles are usually abbreviated in periodical indexes, so it may be necessary to check the appropriate periodical index to ascertain the title—most patrons write down exactly what they read—as well as to verify the article. That is why it is important to ask patrons the sources of their information. For further information on periodicals, *Ulrich's International Periodicals Directory, Union List of Serials* (ULS), and *New Serials Titles* (NST) may be checked. ULS and NST also contain holdings information. The ULS includes titles published before 1950. ULS is continued by NST. From these titles libraries can be located that own almost any periodical throughout its history. Any name changes and publication beginning and ending dates may be verified as well. Local, state, and regional serials lists should also be checked for holdings information. It is generally easier to borrow from libraries close to home than from distant libraries. Many union lists of serials may be accessed through on-line databases.

## Newspaper Articles

For newspapers, place of publication, date, author and title of article, and the page numbers of the articles are needed. Newspapers are not indexed as well as, or in as great numbers as, periodicals. Indexes are available for the *New York Times*, the *London Times,* and some large regional U.S. newspapers. In recent years there has been considerable interest in indexing state and local newspapers as well.

It may be necessary to request a newspaper article or a newspaper on microfilm from a library in the town where it is published. Places of publication may be verified through *Gale Directory of Publications*. For newspapers published before 1821, Brigham's *History and Bibliography of American Newspapers 1690-1820* should be checked. For newspapers published before 1936, *American Newspapers* is the title to consult.

The availability of newspapers in microform that might be sent out on loan may be checked in *Newspapers in Microform: U.S.* and *Newspapers in Microform: Foreign*. OCLC's microfiche version of the *United States Newspaper Program (USNP) National Union List* is a location tool for 77,000 newspapers published during the past three centuries.

## Theses and Dissertations

Theses and dissertations may sometimes be borrowed from the circulating collections of lending libraries. They may also be borrowed from the institutions at which they were written, so it is important to obtain that information, as well as the author, title, and year. Verification of these materials may be obtained in *Comprehensive Dissertation Index; Dissertation Abstracts International; American Doctoral Dissertations; National Union Catalog;* national, regional, state, or local on-line catalogs; or individual library catalogs. Theses and dissertations may be purchased in hard copy or on microfilm from University Microfilms International.

## Government Documents

Government documents may be verified in the *Monthly Catalog of U.S. Government Publications, Government Reports Announcements,* and numerous other government subject-oriented indexes. Government publications may also be found in the *National Union Catalog* and various other library catalogs. In addition to the usual bibliographical information, the superintendent of documents number, report numbers, and issuing agencies should be given.

## Subject Requests

Many libraries will neither borrow nor lend from subject requests, but small libraries with few verification tools may need to send subject requests. They should check first to be sure the proposed lending library is willing to honor them. Small public libraries may send their subject requests to the state library for verification or transmission or both. Special libraries that may be expected to have holdings in specific subject areas may be found in *Directory of Special Libraries and Information Centers*. Ash's *Subject Collections* is another tool that can be used in locating subject-specific materials. Library patrons should be informed that subject requests may take longer to fill than the normal request containing a specific citation.

In the early days, it was considered unethical to send out an unverified request unless the ILL librarian sent out with the request a letter of apology for not having the proper bibliographic tools or location devices. In fact, the model ILL code requires that all items requested be verified and the sources of verification cited. Union lists, union catalogs, and machine-stored databases make the verification and location process easier. As the number of these resources has increased over the past few years, so has the volume of use.

## Research Studies on Verification and Location

A survey in 1974 of the charter members of the OCLC network suggested that use of the OCLC database for ILL verification was successful 75 percent to 80 percent of the time in medium-to-small libraries. One large library indicated a verification success rate of 24 percent for pre-1950 imprints, 34 percent for 1950-1967 imprints, and 60 percent for post-1968 imprints. Forty-four percent of the ILL librarians indicated that use of the OCLC database resulted in slight, but noticeable, decreases in processing and receipt time for books.[2] Of all the requests generated in a month in multitype New England libraries in 1976, 28 percent were verified on the OCLC database.[3]

A 1980-1981 study of ILL requests generated through OCLC involving 254 serials requests and 255 monograph requests over a 7-month period showed that 95.3 percent of the serials requests (242) and 95.3 percent of the monograph requests (243) could be verified in the OCLC on-line union catalog. Of these items, holding institutions for 97.9 percent of the serials and 99.6 percent of the monographs could be found in the on-line union catalog.[4]

In three very special Canadian addictions libraries over a 10-month period, 70.2 percent of requests were found in OCLC. Most of the items were U.S. materials, causing the "hit rate" for U.S. materials to be 78.9 percent and the hit rate for Canadian materials to be 34.2 percent.[5]

A study reported in 1986 by the Southeastern Louisiana University Library found that the mean supply time for a document from the time the user made the request to the time the document arrived in the library was 19.13 days with a median of 17 days in a 2 to 95 day range. Of the 19.13 days, 6.46 days were required for the verification process.[6]

During a three-month study involving approximately 900 requests, the Health Sciences Library at East Carolina University examined the necessity and effectiveness of bibliographic verification of requests prior to the transmission of the request. They sought to determine the degree to which ILL requests were correct and complete when submitted. They also sought to determine if a trained verifier could identify incorrect or incomplete requests and limit verification to them.

It was found that among the requests with minimally complete citations, that is, citations without the issue number or month, only 8.9 percent of all the citations required verification. For that reason, and because verification is difficult for recent journal articles or articles not indexed, the researchers recommended sending requests unverified, with the lending library assuming no responsibility for verification.

Ethics should be considered, but based on mutual agreement, procedures for verification could be modified. The researchers have themselves followed this procedure with several medical libraries with no ill effects.[7]

## Transmission of Requests

After the bibliographic data are verified, the request must be transmitted to the lending library and a copy filed in the borrowing library. The earliest ILL requests were transmitted by mail and telephone. Mail is still used by libraries that cannot afford to automate or that need to borrow from other libraries that do not lend through an automated network, and the telephone as a transmission device is used mostly in local or emergency situations. The telephone cannot be beat for speed, ease of use, and immediate feedback, not to mention the fact that every library owns one. There are, at the same time, however, certain drawbacks that prevent it from being the transmission tool of choice. The interruption of daily ILL routine plus the fact that there is no written record either for the files or for citation verification are reasons enough not to rely on the telephone to either send or receive ILL requests.

The same kind of flexibility available with the telephone is provided by teletype transmission. Two parties who own the same type of instrument can "talk" back and forth, the teletype message being a printed telephone conversation. The teletype machine consists of a modified typewriter that prints at the same time a message at either end of a telephone circuit is sent at approximately 60 words per minute. The teletype, often referred to by the abbreviation TWX, offers certain advantages over the more traditional ways of transmitting ILL requests by mail or telephone. Speed is greater than sending by mail, and accuracy is greater than sending by telephone, because there is a printed message.

It is also inexpensive to send a TWX message. In the TWX heyday of the 1950s, a telephone call from Philadelphia to Denver cost $2.25; the same call by TWX cost $1.65.[8] At that time, TWX was used by the Philadelphia Union Catalog, which represented 149 cooperating libraries. There have been many, and there still are some, TWX networks across the country.

Libraries abroad provided the same type of teletype service as did the United States, through the Teleprinter Exchange Service, known as telex. The service, begun in 1957 by the Technological University in Delft, The Netherlands, was the first in any European library.[9]

Interlibrary loan requests (and the documents requested) may be transmitted by fax. This method rivals the speed of on-line requesting by computer. To save on the cost of transmission, the order form may be placed on the cover page, as illustrated by figure 6.5 on page 134.

## Transmission Speed Studies

The method used for transmitting requests is chosen according to speed, efficiency, and cost. Many studies have been conducted among the various methods of transmitting requests, especially since it became possible to send ILL requests on-line. In assessing the impact of OCLC's interlibrary loan subsystem on turnaround time, Memagaux reported that the use of the system by the New York South Central Research Council reduced the average turnaround time from the pre-OCLC 24 working days to 12 working days using OCLC for all types of requests.[10] Klapper reported in a 1982 study that using OCLC to request books on-line (both in-state and out-of-state) resulted in an average turnaround time of 16.3 calendar days. Requests for books using ALA order forms sent through the U.S. mail had a turnaround time of 22.1 calendar days.[11]

It is assumed that each new technology brings improvements. Shirley Baker sought to determine whether those improvements were considerable or marginal. She studied, also in 1982, the response time for requests submitted by an unnamed medium-sized library's ILL unit to other libraries by mail, by TWX, and by the OCLC interlibrary loan subsystem. Results indicated a mean response time from submission date to receipt date of 12 days for OCLC, 17 days for TWX, and 24 days for mailed requests. One question not answered by the Baker study is how the bibliographic utility affects costs. Another is how it affects work load.[12]

## Transmission Cost Studies

The determining factor in choosing a method of transmittal is more likely to be determined by cost than by speed. Harry and Ostvold indicated for what may be the first time in the professional literature that the cost problem—at that time, mostly transportation—must be faced. They indicated that ILL costs could no longer be charged to "expense."[13] During the same year—1949—Charles David called upon librarians to cut expenses by making direct loans to patrons. He estimated that an ILL transaction cost $3.50 at the University of Pennsylvania and if it cost the other library the same, a single ILL transaction would cost $7.00.[14] In their book on university library administration, published in 1945, Wilson and Tauber estimated the cost of an interlibrary loan at $4.00.[15] The average per-unit transaction cost was estimated in 1976 at Carnegie-Mellon University at $4.15-$5.28 for borrowing and $3.02 for lending.[16]

**ATTACHMENT A**
## ARKANSAS INTERLIBRARY LOAN REQUEST / TELEFACSIMLE TRANSMISSION
All telefacsimile requests should be made under the guidelines of the Arkansas Telefacsimile Libraries' Protocols

**Request Category:**          URGENT [1 hour]          RUSH [4 hrs.]          ROUTINE [24 hrs.]
(circle one)          NON-PRIORITY [normal ILL-Fax or Mail]          REGULAR [for schools-48 hrs.]

**Request for** _____ LOAN or _____ PHOTOCOPY; According to A.L.A. Interlibrary Loan Code

| Date of request: | Not needed after: | Requester's order no.: |
|---|---|---|

Call no.     [Lending library name & address]

**A**
**Request**
**[Modified]**

For use of          Status          Dept.
Book author: OR: periodical title, vol. and date

Book title, edition, place, year, series: OR periodical article, author, title, pages     This edition only?

Verified in: OR: item cited in
ISBN, or ISSN, or LC card, or OCLC or other number if known _____

If non-circulating, & cost does not exceed $_____, please supply   Microfilm   Hard copy:

[Borrowing library name & address]

Request complied with 108 (g)(2) guidelines (CCG)          AUTHORIZED BY:_____
other provisions of copyright law (CCL)          (Full Name)
          Title _____

Number of pages sent:

Additional Comments:

REPORTS:          Checked by

SENT BY:          Library rate;

Charges $          Insured for $
Date sent          DUE

RESTRICTIONS:
_____ for use in library only;
_____ copying not permitted

NOT SENT BECAUSE: _____ In use
_____ Not Owned: _____ Not circulating

Request of          Est. cost of:
          _____ Microfilm

BORROWING LIBRARY RECORD:

Date received:

Date returned:

By          Library rate

Postage
enclosed $          Insured for $

RENEWALS:          No renewals

Requested on  /  /  ; Renewed to
          (or period of renewal)

Fig. 6.5. Example of an interlibrary loan form for faxed requests.

In an attempt to determine comparative costs of sending requests several different ways, Gorin and Kanen in 1981 found that the average cost for a filled request was $4.21 for TWX, $2.82 for the mail, $1.60 for OCLC, and $.94 for a closed-circuit teletype system with the State Library of Florida.[17] Two cost studies were conducted the next year on the cost effectiveness of E-mail (OCLC). Givens found that use of E-mail reduced the cost from $1.25 per request using TWX to $.20.[18] DeJohn conducted a survey among northwest libraries that used E-mail and found that some libraries saved $1,200 to $2,500 per year by substituting electronic mail for TWX systems.[19]

Weaver carried his study a step further to include the cost of referring a request not filled by the first library to which the request was sent. For ILL requests filled on the first pass, the average transmission cost (including labor) was $1.13 for mail, $1.89 for TWX, and $2.63 for OCLC. When a sequential referral to three locations was needed to fill the request, the average cost of OCLC did not change, the cost of mail increased to $3.39, and the cost of TWX increased to $5.67 per filled request.[20] In light of these studies, it is not surprising that the TWX machine has largely been replaced by the computer; transmission of requests by computer is not only faster but is also less expensive.

Librarians are constantly striving to keep costs in check. In some instances, it is absolutely essential in order to maintain the ILL service.

In California, for example, Proposition 13 led to such loss of state funding that libraries, including the Metropolitan Library System in Pasadena, sought economical ways to process interlibrary loans. Their solution was E-mail batch messaging, in which each member library initiates, processes, and tracks its own requests and responds to requests from other libraries.

Costs for this method of transmission were $1.76 per loan and $.61 per request placed. Librarians were convinced that when kept within the system, this service was efficient and inexpensive.[21]

## Transmitting Requests On-line

To send an OCLC request, a workform is pulled up on the screen. Information pertaining to author, title, and the OCLC number automatically transfers from the OCLC record. The staff member then enters locations, citation of an article, patron name, and copyright information. Special messages for the lender may also be entered. The request is then sent electronically to assigned locations (up to five).

Each library has four working days to respond yes or no to the request before it is transferred automatically to the next location. If none of the libraries to which the request was sent can supply the material requested, an unfilled response is sent by the system to the borrower. Renewal requests, overdue notices, and shipping notices are also sent through the system.

Smaller libraries that do not catalog on-line may still benefit from OCLC services through group access, which is a structured arrangement provided by OCLC for resource sharing within defined groups of libraries. It allows for participation of "selective user" libraries that do not catalog on-line, as well as participation of full cataloging members.

OCLC access centers, or referral centers, have been developed in networks to assist with verification, location, and transmission of requests. The New Jersey access center is one example of the way state libraries provide for the opportunity for small libraries that don't participate in OCLC to take advantage of electronic interlibrary loan. A toll-free number is given, and staff members search the OCLC database, verify the request, check holdings, and send the request through the OCLC interlibrary loan subsystem first to any New Jersey library holding the material needed (68 percent of the requests are filled by New Jersey libraries) The material is sent by the supplying library directly to the requesting library. The access center is notified by the requesting library when the material is received and when it is returned to the lender. In addition to the system's providing increased service and faster delivery, growth in use of the system decreased the cost of a transaction from $8.58 in February 1986 to $3.57 a year later.[22]

ARL libraries send ILL requests on-line through RLIN. Bibliographic information can be copied from an existing record to expedite the creation of requests. Borrowers can be notified that a request is being filled. Unfilled requests can be forwarded to another library. Users may check status of requests, renew, recall, send overdue notices, and collect statistics.[23] In addition to the RLG member holdings, records are loaded into the database from the Library of Congress CONSER, the National Library of Medicine, the Government Printing Office, and the British Library. Special databases in this network are the On-Line Avery Index to Architectural Periodicals, SCIPIO (Sales Catalog Index Project Input On-Line), Eighteenth Century Short Title Catalogue, and the RLG Conspectus On-Line.

The WLN interlibrary loan subsystem began in July 1986. Bibliographic information is transferred to each ILL request linked to a record in the database. Libraries can also transfer bibliographic information to requests for items not in the database and route the requests through the system. All participating libraries have the ability to create referral requests on behalf of other libraries that do not use the system.

Each user of the system maintains an on-line profile including shipping address, costs, due dates, and other information. The system transfers this information to each request when it is created or when a library agrees to supply an item. Up to eight locations may be chosen, with routing from one to the other occurring every five working days.

A status summary screen for each user displays the number of requests in each status—request status, item status, and loan status—and allows the user to search and display requests according to status category. At least two printed reports are issued each month—a report on requests completed by borrower and lender and a journal title report. By now there are probably more.[24]

The LC database LOCIS can be searched to locate LC materials, and then a workform called FETCH can be generated. As with the OCLC interlibrary loan subsystem, elements from the bibliographic record are transferred from the database to the FETCH workform. For a book loan, the LC call number, the author, title, and publication date are also transferred. For serial requests, the borrowing library overrides the LC call number field so that complete information on call number, volume and issue number, date, pages, and last name of author will appear on the request.[25]

DOCLINE is the National Library of Medicine's automated ILL request and referral system. It is available to U.S. biomedical libraries.

## Bulletin Boards

A task force created by the Wisconsin Division for Library Services to find a replacement for an aging TWX system found that an electronic bulletin board could easily handle the traffic of 17 public library systems and three state-level resource centers serving as clearinghouses for their members. The bulletin-board system was inexpensive both for ILL librarians and for clearinghouses.

A microcomputer and word-processing or request-formatting software are used to type requests. Then a communications program and a modem connected to regular phone lines are used to send the request file to an IBM PC at the Wisconsin Interlibrary Services (WILS) interlibrary loan network.

Besides saving time and money, the bulletin-board system was found to have more potential than TWX or paper systems. Callers could store their requests in a database, replacing paper logs. Other advantages to the system were that newsletters and general announcements could be sent and that use of the microcomputer in libraries was promoted.

Some problems were experienced with printing requests, both because of the number received and because of inferior phone lines, but it was concluded that the advantages of storing requests electronically, under local control, more than compensated for the hassles of printing requests and dealing with the few problems encountered.[26]

Many electronic bulletin boards possess advanced mail features that allow them to be used to transmit ILL requests. Several library systems have taken advantage of this technology.

In 1986 the Delaware County, Pennsylvania, Library System began using a microcomputer-based bulletin board as an E-mail service to deliver ILL requests among member libraries. At first the computer software used was RBBS (Remote Bulletin Board System), a public domain software running under MS-DOS, but when it needed expanding, the software used by the area's OCLC broker, PALINET, was chosen. It allows access to multiple phone lines without major software or hardware modifications. It also allows sophisticated E-mail capabilities including message forwarding, sending messages to more than one mailbox, and listing of events.[27]

An ILL request is created off-line using the PC-Loan software package, then the connection is made to E-mail using a standard telecommunications package and the request is uploaded to a specific mailbox in the host computer. Users can read and print the messages in their mailboxes. The receiving library notifies the requesting library through E-mail of material that can be supplied. If material cannot be supplied, the ILL message is forwarded to the next potential lender.[28]

Prior to E-mail, ILL requests were sent by van. A survey taken to compare that service with E-mail showed that the average time to receive a book using paper forms delivered by van was 7.1 days. The survey did not include requests transmitted through OCLC.[29]

As an increasingly common application, communication software packages such as SMARTCOM from Hayes Microcomputer Products, CROSSTALK from Digital Communications Associates; MITE from Mycroft Labs, and PC-TALK from Headlands Press give microcomputers access to electronic bulletin boards and similar message systems maintained by other microcomputers. In addition to accessing computers, a few software packages support communications between a personal computer and a TWX or telex terminal. They are consequently suitable for ILL applications that utilize the TWX or telex networks for message transmissions.[30]

### Commercial Database Vendors

Interlibrary loan requests can also be transmitted through commercial database vendors. With DIALOG, for example, when the CREATE option is entered from the DIALMAIL main menu, two of the options available are FORMS and interlibrary loan. FORMS allows a form with empty fields (to be filled in later) to be created and stored on DIALMAIL for later use. Interlibrary loan is a form permanently set up within DIALMAIL for use in ILL applications.

## Office Routines and Records

In her book *Introduction to Reference Work*, published by the ALA in 1944, Margaret Hutchins wrote that the librarian who works with interlibrary loans needs to establish a routine and records for the requests so that anyone who has to take over the work will understand what has been done and when books are due. One record card for each book may be used, she said, to keep track of the whole process and later for statistics and a permanent record. Such a card may at first be filed alphabetically by last name of the patron; then when the loan has been secured, in a date file. When the publication is returned, the card can be filed in an alphabetical file of libraries, and finally, in an alphabetical author file for a permanent record in case the book is wanted again.[31]

### Borrowing

The basic concept of the procedure described by Hutchins continues to be sound today, for each request must be noted and updated several times as it passes through the ILL pipeline. Files must be accessible to check the status of a request and to provide data for various statistical reports. Usually either the ILL request form or the ILL order form or both are updated and kept in the office files. Most libraries still use paper files, many use paper files plus a transaction log, and still others maintain on-line paperless files, accessing the request by a transaction number.

Whatever type of file is kept following transmission of the request, some record should be made of it so that the request can be identified when the material is received. The borrowing library and library patron must then wait for a response from the library to which the request was sent. It may send the material or send a response indicating why it is unable to send the material, or it may send no response at all. The request may need to be followed up with a query, or it may have to be sent to another library or group of libraries on a lender string if the patron has time to wait. The librarian may have to get back in touch with the patron in order to determine this.

When the material requested has been received, some sort of record must be processed to indicate receipt and to make a note of when the material is due and the charges that apply. Then the patron must be notified, usually by telephone or through the mail. Obviously the quickest method is preferred because of the time constraints on materials that must be returned and in the interest of getting the material to the requester in the shortest time possible.

Borrowers should be notified a few days before materials are to be returned to lending libraries if that is possible. They should be reminded that prompt return is necessary to prevent imposing on the lending library. The patron may request a renewal in which case the librarian must contact the lending library again unless it is already known that the library will not renew.

Fines may or may not be charged for ILL items kept overdue. It is not likely, but possible, that patrons could owe overdue fines to both their own library and to the lending library if they keep an ILL item past the due date. At any rate, if fines are assessed, librarians must see to it that they are paid. They must also process the records, indicating the return date, sending a copy to the lending library, and keeping a copy to show that the transaction has been completed.

The material should be wrapped and packaged to prevent damage and then should be returned to the lending library in the manner requested. If no preference is given, the material should be returned as it was sent. Then comes the question of whether to insure and, if so, for how much. The answer may or may not have been provided by the lender. The flow chart presented in figure 6.6, page 140, outlines the basic steps involved in the ILL borrowing routine.

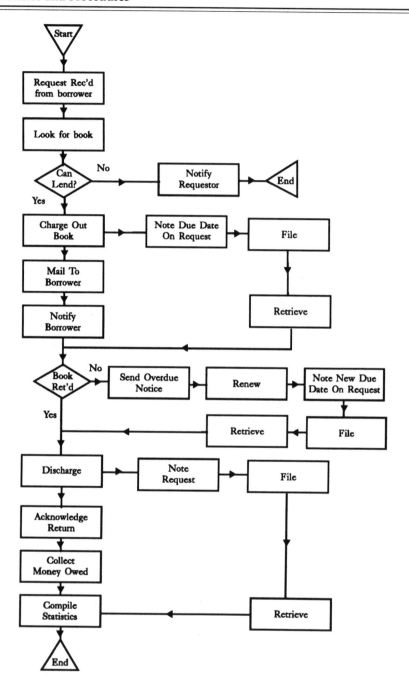

Fig. 6.6. Interlibrary loan lending procedures.

## Lending

The lending library must determine if the item requested can be lent, if it is available to be lent, and what charges are to be made. Each item loaned requires a request record and an appropriate borrowing library to identify the patron, the item requested, the status of the request, whether the item has been received, when it is due, and whether special charges apply. If an ALA request form is used, appropriate parts of the form are filled in. In such a manual system, these records, like those for borrowing, are filed, updated, and refiled several times during an ILL transaction. The files must also be reviewed on a regular basis to identify overdues and other problems. Status checks should be a weekly routine. Most of these routine matters can be handled by clerical assistants. Decisions on what can be lent can best be made by professionals.

When a request is received, it should be dated. It should also be examined to determine if it is a rush request or if it requires any other special handling.

The library catalog should be searched to determine availability and the call number noted. Material should then be located in the collection and picked up quickly. It is both interesting and informative to keep notes on the reason that materials may not be supplied. Either a check mark on a pre-printed form or a one-word explanation written on the request form, such as "out," "bindery," "reserve," "missing," are quickly applied and may point out weaknesses in service.[32] The brief explanation will also inform the borrower that an attempt was made to supply. If the publication cannot be borrowed from other libraries, the borrower might want to resubmit the request.

Loans to other libraries are charged the same way loans are charged to local library patrons unless the length of the loan period is different. A copy of the request, or perhaps a slip of paper containing a transaction number, should be placed inside the book or with other materials on which is written the due date, statement of charges, instructions for insuring and returning materials, and so forth. Most libraries also include a mailing label to be used to return the borrowed material. It is also helpful to include a copy of the institution's lending policy both to ensure that there is mutual understanding of the conditions placed upon the loan and to encourage reciprocal borrowing.

Some libraries place a paper band around the loaned book on which has been written patron name, charges, and due date. (See fig. 6.7, p. 142.) A copy of the information sent with the material to the borrower should also be accessible to the lender, either in a paper file under the name of the library to which it was sent or in a paperless file. The average periodical request (because the material is photocopied) takes 2.9 days longer to fill than does a monograph request.[33]

The University of
# West Florida
Library
Fort Walton Beach
Campus

## INTERLIBRARY LOANS

This book was borrowed
for you from the

_____

Library.

Charge: $ _____

Return to the FWB Campus
by _____
(Renew at the FWB Campus
only.)

Fig. 6.7. Some libraries place a paper band around a loaned book.

There are advantages to supplying photocopies or microform copies instead of the original. The patron may keep the copy, which can be packaged and mailed more easily and cheaply than the original. Perhaps most important, the lending-library copy remains in the library for use by that library's patrons. The same procedure is followed for photocopied materials as for loans except for the copying and the absence of instructions for returning.

There are various ways to send and receive documents other than through the U.S. mail, as has been thus far implied. Document delivery is covered in some detail in chapter 7.

When materials are returned, they should be unwrapped and inspected. The request records should be changed and filed in the complete file. The complete file may later be subdivided into files by library, state, or in some other way. Materials should then be discharged and reshelved.

## Insuring Interlibrary Loans

Practices on the insuring of interlibrary loans vary widely, leading to confusion for all, even those who have a well-established policy on the matter; for the policy in the national code is inconsistent. Michael Moran felt this to be a significant enough problem to try to define a reasonable policy and to recommend appropriate practice.

First of all, there are several possible types of insurance connected with an ILL transaction, and borrowers and lenders may not know what type the other has used or wishes to have them use. The ALA request form contains a small blank that says simply, "Insured for $____."

The ILL material may be insured by the lender through common carriers such as the U.S. Postal Service, United Parcel Service (UPS), Federal Express, Emery Express, and trucking firms from the premises of the lender to the premises of the borrower. This charge may be passed on to the borrower.

There are three other ways by which the lender may insure. With a commercial insurance agent, premiums are often based on total annual transactions, so charges may not be known at the time of shipment. Estimates based on prior experience may be made and passed on. The library's parent institution may have self-insurance with some agreed-upon figure passed on to borrowers. The most efficient kind of insurance protects materials both to and from the lender and while on the premises of the borrower, again with an estimated cost figure passed on to the borrower.

There is hardly ever agreement on when—for the purpose of insurance—ownership of material is passed from lender to borrower. That is why lenders insure and pass the cost along to borrowers even though the ILL code holds the borrower responsible for materials from the time they are mailed. And what about the lender insuring materials that were never intended to be returned? Moran suggests that lenders wastes their money by assuming the responsibility assigned by the code to the borrower.

If the borrower, then, is charged with the responsibility of protecting materials borrowed, does the lender have the right to ask that materials being returned be insured? Moran suggests that lenders should assume that borrowers will fulfill their obligations until experience has proved otherwise. He further suggests that insuring all transactions would probably cost more in staff time and premiums than the volumes lost in ILL transactions are worth. Determining the value itself would be a sizable task, but if rare books are loaned, this should be done and the books insured. Theses and dissertations should be insured, according to the code but perhaps requiring in-house use would protect them more than would insuring them, Moran says.

The international lending code recommends the uniform policy of assigning responsibility for safety of borrowed materials to the borrower as well. The risk of loss is greater because of greater distances and methods of delivery in different countries, but if requests are received on International Federation of Library Associations (IFLA) request forms, the lender knows that the borrower follows the international code. Refused service is about the only way to enforce the codes, national or international.[34]

## International Borrowing and Lending

Discussion among ILL librarians at a 1990 meeting of the Southeastern Library Association isolated four major barriers to international interlibrary loan. They are 1) bibliographic access (union lists, etc.), 2) physical access (getting material through the mail), 3) language barriers (IFLA request forms are written in several—not all—languages), and 4) payment (besides the problem of monetary exchange is the question of who pays the postage). It was agreed by the American librarians present that the British Library Document Supply Center serves the cause of international lending best, followed by the Bibliothèque Nationale.

## Notes

[1] Jan Keder, "Using the Campus Network for Interlibrary Loan and Book Orders," *Library Software Review* 8 (September-October 1989):250-51.

[2] Joe A. Hewitt, "The Impact of OCLC," *American Libraries* 7 (May 1976):268-75.

[3] Libby Trudell and James Wolper, "Interlibrary Loan in New England," *College and Research Libraries* 39 (September 1978):365-71.

[4] Ann T. Dodson, Paul P. Philbin, and Kunj B. Rastogi, "Electronic Interlibrary Loan in the OCLC Library: A Study of Its Effectiveness," *Special Libraries* 73 (January 1982):12-20.

[5] Susan Dingle-Cliff and Charles H. David, "Comparison of Recent Acquisitions and OCLC Find Rates for Three Canadian Special Libraries," *Journal of the American Society for Information Science* 32 (January 1981):65-69.

[6]J. Budd, "Interlibrary Loan Service: A Study of Turnaround Time," *RQ* 26 (1986):75-80.

[7]J. A. Bell and S. C. Speer, "Bibliographic Verification for Interlibrary Loan: Is It Necessary?" *College and Research Libraries* 49 (November 1988):494-500.

[8]James D. Mack, "Teletype Speeds Interlibrary Loans and References," *Library Journal* 83 (May 1, 1958):1326.

[9]Ibid., 1329.

[10]E. A. Memagaux, "Effectiveness of Automated Interlibrary Loan: Papers from a 1980 ALA Preconference, New York, New York, June 27 and 28, 1980. Co-chairmen Neal K. Kaske and William G. Jones. Foreword by Bruce A. Miller," in *Library Effectiveness: A State-of-the-Art* (Chicago: ALA, 1980), 161-71.

[11]I. Taler and P. Klapper, "Automated and Manual ILL: Time Effectiveness and Success Rate," *Information Technology and Libraries* 1 (1982):277-80.

[12]Shirley K. Baker, "The Efficacy of Interlibrary Loan: A Study of Response Time for Interlibrary Loans Submitted by Mail, TWX, and an Automated System," in *Options for the 80's: Proceedings of the Second National Conference of the Association of College and Research Libraries*, ed. Michael D. Kathman and Virgil F. Massman (Greenwich, Conn.: JAI Press, 1982), 259-64.

[13]Ruth Harry and Harold Ostvold, "Interlibrary Loan Service and National Research," *College and Research Libraries* 10 (April 1949):145.

[14]Charles W. David, "Remarks upon Interlibrary Loans Mid-20th Century Style," *College and Research Libraries* 10 (1949):431-32.

[15]Louis R. Wilson and Maurice F. Tauber, *The University Library* (Chicago: University of Chicago Press, 1945), 411.

[16]Dorothea M. Thompson, "The Correct Uses of Library Data Bases Can Improve Interlibrary Loan Efficiency," *Journal of Academic Librarianship* 6 (May 1980):83-86.

[17]R. S. Gorin and R. A. Kanen, *Florida Library Information Network Project: A Comparative Study of OCLC, TWX, U.S. Mail, and Closed-Circuit Teletype*, ERIC Document 211 076 (Tallahassee: Florida State University, 1981).

[18]B. Givens, "Montana's Use of Microcomputers for Interlibrary Loan Communication," *Information Technology and Libraries* 1 (1982):260-64.

[19]W. DeJohn, "Use of Electronic Mail for ILL," *Information Technology and Libraries* 1 (1982):48-51.

[20]C. G. Weaver, "Electronic Document Delivery: Directing Interlibrary Loan Traffic Through Multiple Electronic Networks," *Bulletin of the Medical Library Association* 72 (1984):187-92.

[21]"Intrasystem ILL Cost-Effective for Pasadena-Based Co-op System," *Library Journal* 108 (November 1, 1983):2004.

[22]Nita Dean, "The New Jersey State Library Provides ILL Access," *OCLC Newsletter* (July-August 1987):13.

[23]Sally H. McCallum, "Standards and Linked Online Information Systems," *LRTS* 34 (July 1990):360-66.

[24]Jeanne Otten Lipscomb, "The WLN Interlibrary Loan Subsystem: Progress Report," *PNLA Quarterly* 51 (1987):17-18.

[25]Sandra McAninch, Bradley D. Carrington, and Barbara S. Hale, "Online to the Nation's Library: Kentucky's Experience with the Library of Congress Information System," *Online* 14 (November 1990):74.

[26]Cathy Moore, "Do-It-Yourself Automation: Interloan Bulletin Boards," *Library Journal* 112 (November 1, 1987):66-68.

[27]David Belanger, "Interlibrary Loan Via Electronic Mail: Improving the Process," *Wilson Library Bulletin* 63 (March 1989):62.

[28]Ibid., 63.

[29]Ibid.

[30]William Saffady, *Introduction to Automation for Librarians*, 2d ed. (Chicago: ALA, 1989), 104.

[31]Margaret Hutchins, *Introduction to Reference Work* (Chicago: ALA, 1944), 192.

[32]Guy R. Lyle, *The Administration of the College Library* (New York: Wilson, 1944), 146.

[33]Budd, "Interlibrary Loan Service," 75-80.

[34]Michael L. Moran, "Insuring Interlibrary Loans," *RQ* 22 (Summer 1982):395-99.

# chapter 7

# Document Delivery

Depending upon circumstances, 20 percent to 60 percent of the total turnaround time for an ILL request can be attributed to the actual delivery of the requested material.[1] Average delivery time for books sent library rate through the U.S. Postal Service is five days; delivery time for photocopies sent first class through the U.S. Postal Service is two days, according to a study by Kaya and Harlebas.[2]

The closest competitor of the U.S. Postal Service is UPS, but it is not as accessible as the postal service. Other special delivery systems, for example, Federal Express, are even less accessible and are more expensive. Average delivery time for UPS is two days, and when documents are insured at the same rate, the costs of the U.S. Postal Service and UPS are essentially the same. For photocopies, which do not need to be insured, the U.S. Postal Service is far more economical than UPS as a document carrier.[3]

Boss and McQueen noted in 1983 that 95 percent of the time materials requested through interlibrary loan are sent through the U.S. Postal Service.[4] The most important reasons for using this type of mail delivery are availability and cost. Everybody has easy access to the U.S. mail, and special library rates make this method of delivery the least expensive.

Courier systems of a formal or informal nature exist between parent and branch libraries, or if a library belongs to a regional or statewide network, it may be able to participate in a broader-based courier service. Nitecki reports that Illinois, Pennsylvania, and Connecticut library-sponsored document delivery services have one to three days' delivery time with a high degree of reliability.[5]

Library-sponsored delivery services seem to be the least expensive, the fastest, and the most reliable when there is a high volume of activities within a limited geographical area, when a large part of the ILL traffic consists of books rather than photocopies, and when a high degree of reliability in delivery is needed.[6] Turlock reported that in 1986, 73 percent of national multitype library networks had delivery systems linking libraries of the same type and of different types.[7]

Deekle's 1990 article in the *Wilson Library Bulletin* presents an interesting description of the Interlibrary Delivery Service (IDS) of Pennsylvania. It was established in 1969 for delivery of interlibrary loans and other educational materials among its members (academic, public, and school libraries).[8]

## Commercial Suppliers

Commercial database suppliers, such as BRS and DIALOG have developed end-user services. DIALOG started in 1972 with two databases. DIALORDER was initiated in 1979 (at about the time OCLC introduced the ILL subsystem) with 14 suppliers. It now has many times that number. BRS began in 1976 with just a few databases. Likewise, it also now has many times that number. Quick ORDER, an on-line, on demand, document delivery service for National Technical Information Service (NTIS) documents has been used, especially by special libraries, for many years.

ERIC (Educational Resources Information Center), NTIS, and several other producers offer for sale in microform their document collections accessed through machine-readable databases. CD-ROM disks containing full-text articles may also be purchased.

For a long time database producers have supplied copies of their materials cited in printed indexes and bibliographies. The Institute for Scientific Information, one of the oldest and best known, was the first to be accessible through on-line search services. Deposit accounts are established, and on-line searchers place orders for documents through their terminals. The orders are sent to the database producer, which mails copies to the requesters. DIALOG searchers have access to many database producers and document supply centers, including the British Library Lending Division.[9]

Various document delivery services are accessible through the OCLC interlibrary loan subsystem. An appendix to the OCLC manual gives special instructions for ordering through the interlibrary loan subsystem. Some of the services available are

1. British Library Document Supply Service.

2. Center for Research Libraries, Chicago. Primarily for members, but loans are sometimes made to nonmember libraries. Interlibrary loan librarians should write in advance for information on policies, procedures, and costs.

3. Chemical Abstracts Service. Either documents or photocopies may be obtained. Shipping costs other than first class mail have to be paid.

4. University Microfilms International Article Clearinghouse. The clearinghouse provides copies of articles and conference papers. Copyright clearance and shipment within 48 hours are guaranteed. Payment may be made by institutional deposit account or by credit card. Extra charges are assessed for special handling.

Dissertations, on-demand books, and serials in microform are also available through the ILL subsystem. Policies and prices are different from clearinghouse items. University Microfilms International has developed a prototype information delivery module; it supports local and remote document retrieval and integrates information searching, ordering, and delivery.[10]

Arthur D. Little's study in 1979 estimated that commercial document suppliers were responsible for about 10 percent of the total document delivery activity and that this percentage was growing at a larger rate than was interlibrary lending among libraries as a whole.[11] In their 1980 report to the Council on Library Resources, Boss and McQueen indicated that 34 percent of special libraries, and more than 10 percent of the nation's academic and public libraries, used nonlibrary document suppliers.[12]

It was assumed by Miller and Tegler that document suppliers must be able to fill a void and supply documents more quickly than libraries were supplying them to one another. To test their hypothesis, they did an analysis of interlibrary loan and commercial document-supply performance.

They compared the performance of commercial document suppliers with the performance of traditional interlibrary loan at the University of Illinois at Chicago. They found that 1) commercial document suppliers are not faster than ILL suppliers; 2) higher charges do not mean faster document supply; 3) local commercial suppliers are no faster than commercial suppliers located at a distance; 4) foreign-language materials, items published before 1970, technical reports, and proceedings do not arrive more slowly or cost more and are not more difficult to supply than current English-language journal articles; and 5) except for engineering, cost, speed, and success rate do not vary by subject area.[13]

Industrial chemistry libraries report that they make heavier use of commercial services during peak load periods or when the ILL clerks are backlogged.[14] By 1982 there were 1,000 electronic newsletters and journals available with BRS, offering 18 American Chemical Society journals on-line.[15]

## Downloading

Downloading from full-text databases offered by BRS, DIALOG, and other commercial systems is another option to consider in document delivery. There are currently more than 1,500 full-text databases available that allow downloading. They are listed in a publication titled *Directory of Online Databases*, which began publication in 1979.[16]

Reintjes found that it is technologically and economically feasible to move the contents of documents electronically among library networks rather than photocopies or the documents themselves. Comparisons were made on response-to-request time, quality of reproduced copy, and cost factors.[17]

Colbert pointed out that disadvantages of full-text on-line retrieval were subscription fees, membership dues, and monthly premiums that must be paid to utilize the on-line services needed for broad coverage, even though she indicated that in many cases, full-text on-line retrieval can be cheaper than hard copy. On the plus side, access to hard-to-find information sources such as newsletters may be obtained on-line. Another advantage is early access. Current information is sometimes accessible on-line before the hard copy is available. On-line is also, in some cases, offering exclusive availability to some publications, because they do not appear in print form.[18] Colbert warns in her "Document Delivery" column in *Online* that in some DIALOG business databases "full-text" can mean an abstracted version of an article or pieces of data abstracted from an article.

A pilot project at the University of Tennessee, Knoxville, January-March, 1989 measured the usage of on-line systems and the cost of obtaining full-text articles electronically. Ninety-one articles were searched for and 83 retrieved for 26 patrons at an average cost of $3.03 per citation with a turnaround time of one to two days.

The procedure of building the search strategy in a less expensive database, saving the search strategy, executing it in the desired database, and then ordering the results through DIALMAIL (from DIALOG) consistently provided less expensive searches than searching and ordering through BRS. Based on this study, the University of Tennessee at Knoxville obtains journal articles from electronic sources as a regular ILL function.

There are several advantages to obtaining full-text journal articles electronically:

1.  A large number of articles may be obtained from one journal without copyright infringement because the articles are purchased with a royalty charge included in the transaction.

2.  Electronic retrieval provides faster service than does traditional interlibrary loan.

3.  This procedure involves the staff of one library instead of two or more libraries.

There are also some disadvantages in obtaining full-text articles on-line. They are the high cost of searching for incorrect citations and the inability to obtain illustrations electronically.[19]

Downloading requires considerable expertise. In her *Online* column Susan Bjorner discussed ways to minimize the cost of producing full-text output from on-line files when the bibliographic source is known. For each title, the publication *Fulltext Sources Online* lists the systems and databases that contain the source, including dates of coverage. Her own research and research conducted by others indicate that on-line retrieval and printing can be even less costly than commercial document delivery and traditional interlibrary loan because much of the cost associated with the latter two is for retrieval and reproduction labor.[20]

BiblioData has recently made available three publications regarding on-line, full-text searches. *Online Business Sourcebook*, published in the United Kingdom, also contains some U.S. material. *Newspapers Online* is a directory of daily newspapers. *Fulltext Sources Online* also contains listings of newspapers, as well as newsletters, newswires, journals, and magazines made available by various vendors.

# Telefacsimile

The technology of transmitting documents over ordinary phone lines has the potential of revolutionizing ILL document delivery. Telefacsimile, or fax, as it is commonly called, is presently being used for delivery of journal articles. Fax equipment is operated much like a photocopier except that it is also hooked up to a telephone jack.

Fax operates by scanning a page and translating it into tones to be transmitted by the phone, and the tones are, in turn, translated back to dots on a page. Lindberg estimated in 1986 that transmission of a fax took about 20 seconds per page.[21] Many improvements have been made in the technology since that time. One of them is the ability to copy directly from the pages of a book. University of California, Berkeley, library staff, however, expressed disappointment with the direct book-copying feature of the fax machine. The machine performed so slowly that articles continue to be photocopied first and then faxed.[22]

From October 1, 1985, through March 31, 1986, the Lending Division of the National Library of Canada worked on a project with interlibrary loan and document delivery using fax. The three purposes they had in mind were 1) to assess the quality of the documents transmitted, 2) to gather comparative statistics for this and other types of document delivery services, and 3) to assess costs and efficiency of the system.

General findings of the study were that 99 percent of the material transmitted was acceptable, with 70 percent considered good quality and 25 percent considered very good quality. Average turnaround time was 2.34 days compared to 10.9 days for postal delivery. Fax per-item charges ran approximately $26.46 compared to $.75 for priority post.

Obviously, document delivery by fax is expensive compared to other types of document delivery. It was pointed out that improvements in machines that prevent having to photocopy articles before they are transmitted and that allow for storing documents in memory and transmitting at a later time would cut down on the greatest barrier to fax delivery. Other advantages and disadvantages pointed out by the Canadian study were 1) document delivery via fax is instantaneous; 2) fax transmission is ideal for a large network of participants, a high volume of transactions, usage over a lengthy period of time, and when immediate delivery is required; 3) savings in human resources can be realized only if sophisticated enhancements are added to the unit; and 4) E-mail is more effective and efficient than fax for sending messages.[23]

Fax boards installed within a computer are another option for fax transmission. The computer sends and receives the transmissions. The problem that once existed, the inability to run other applications on the computer while faxing, has been overcome.[24]

Images are stored on the computer hard disk until the librarian is ready to print them. Some of the better fax boards, which also cost more money, answer incoming calls and receive and store incoming boxes without interrupting computer work that may be going on at the time.

Using the fax board for document delivery is more complicated. Before an article from a journal can be faxed, it must be scanned into the computer, which calls for extra equipment, extra software, and extra time.[25] A disadvantage to the fax board is that unless a scanner is attached to the computer, information must be keyed in to be transmitted.[26]

Anyone interested in setting up a fax network would benefit from an article written by Wilson in the 1988 volume of *Online*. He reported on the experience of Pennsylvania libraries in setting up a fax network. His article also explains how to estimate the cost of fax transmission. He includes the long-distance phone call, personnel costs, and costs of supplies.[27]

## Campus Delivery

In order to enhance faculty research, a number of college and university libraries have begun campus delivery of library documents. The professional literature contains descriptions of the campus document delivery systems developed by several large universities.

After 18 months of the campus book delivery operation at the University of Colorado, 43 percent of the respondents to a 1970 survey (the majority of whom were resident teaching faculty) assessed the service as important or essential to their pattern of use. Sixty-eight percent of the respondents rated the service as excellent; 23 percent rated it as good.[28]

A comparison study of spring quarter 1971 and spring quarter 1972 circulation statistics at Georgia Tech before and after the installation of microfiche catalogs in 35 academic and research departments and the institution of a twice-daily book delivery service showed a statistically significant difference in faculty book circulation.[29] Faculty members use the message module of the library's local on-line system to request delivery service to their offices. It has been reported that 90 percent of their requests are delivered within two days.[30]

At the University of Minnesota Twin Cities campus, a document delivery system was considered by those with departmental libraries as helpful by 79 percent and as essential by 15 percent. Those without independent departmental libraries considered the service helpful (66 percent) or essential (17 percent).[31]

A study reported in 1978 at Indiana University, Bloomington, involving 39 political scientists, 14 economists, and 5,478 articles from 620 different journals and newspapers, showed that most articles were supplied by their own library through its delivery service. Nine percent were available through interlibrary loan.[32]

The circulation department of the University of California at Irvine (UCI) began document delivery service in 1986. Circulation staff worked with the campus computing facility to develop an on-line service. A computer program named MELDOC allows users of E-mail to generate requests for delivery of library material, interlibrary loans, MEDLINE materials, and pickup of materials to be returned to the library.

At first only books were delivered, and then photocopy delivery was added. The price of $.20 per exposure was charged. Soon afterward, faculty began to ask for electronic interlibrary loan as well. In 1988 the ILL Electronic

Mail Request Service was put into operation. The service was extended to graduate students, librarians, and administrative staff with E-mail accounts. If documents are unavailable at UCI, they are provided through interlibrary loan. Document delivery requests take 24 hours to process; interlibrary loan requests take 3-10 working days.[33]

The University of California at Berkeley has developed a fee-based document delivery and bibliographic verification service called Baker. It is available to faculty, graduate students, and staff. Four types of services are offered: delivery of materials to the patron's campus mailbox; verification of citations using local and national catalogs and standard bibliographic works; provision of bibliographic information necessary for requesting through interlibrary loan; and placement of the request with the ILL office, including subsequent delivery of material to the patron. Requests for Baker service are made through E-mail, through campus mail, and by telephone.[34]

Researchers at North Carolina State University can receive journal articles and other library materials via the computers located in their offices, jobs, and research facilities. The Electronic Document Delivery Service (EDDS) automates the entire process of requesting and receiving research materials retrieved from other libraries' collections. There is also investigation under way into the feasibility of delivering library materials electronically between research libraries and across campus networks to the individual researchers. The EDDS includes a mechanism that automatically notifies the researcher through the campus network and retrieves the document. Requests are placed through E-mail. Any type of library information that can be captured in digital form can be delivered over Internet (an international network of networks) and across campus networks to the researcher.[35]

The University of California system, which is composed of nine campuses, is building a prototype system for automating delivery requests that will serve as a model for other systems around the country. A library user will be able to access any document delivery system on the campuses either through the local campus catalog or through the MELVYL (union catalog) system. In addition to setting up standards, the university system is exploring links to commercial document delivery services.[36]

ARIEL, the document transmission workstation (DTW) being pioneered by the Research Libraries Group (RLG), has the potential of streamlining interlibrary loans. ARIEL uses RLG application software with a personal computer, document scanner, and laser printer. Articles from bound journals are scanned into the personal computer, transmitted over Internet to the borrower's workstation, and printed.

ARIEL is similar to the fax machine, but it has several advantages: 1) high-quality, high-resolution images printed on regular paper (including fine print, photographs, Chinese scripts); 2) its use of Internet. Many libraries are not being charged for access to Internet, eliminating communication costs; 3) it can store entire documents, which only the most sophisticated Group III fax machines can do; 4) stand-alone fax machines are single-application machines. The ARIEL components can be used for desktop publishing, word processing, scanning, printing, and other ILL operations.

The DTW can be used as a sending and receiving station. When the copyright issues related to electronic storage have been addressed, ARIEL can be used as a scan-and-send workstation for storage facilities or branch libraries, as a print-only station in a branch library or a professor's office, or as a complete scan-send-print workstation in an ILL office.

After several months of testing, the librarians involved were impressed with ARIEL document quality, with how easy it is to use, and with its potential of reducing turnaround time. With RLG's ILL manager, the entire ILL process—from verification through document delivery—will be achieved with one workstation. After testing is complete and changes have been made to the software, RLG plans to make the software available to other libraries.[37]

## Home Delivery

Marketing both to the end user and to libraries, Faxon Research Service's Faxon Finder, CARL System's UnCover 2, the RLG's CitaDel, and Lonesome Doc couple journal-citation-level searching with rapid document delivery. Linking citation databases to library holdings streamlines the search process.

The Faxon Finder databases contain more than 11,000 journals covering many subjects. Patrons who search it can then order their articles using Faxon Xpress, Faxon Research Service's delivery service. Faxon Finder may also be searched through OCLC by ILL staff. Faxon Finder promises 24-hour delivery service through fax.

Requests from 12,000 journals can be placed and delivered by fax within 24 hours through CARL's UnCover 2. UnCover 2 is associated with the British Library Document Supply Centre (BLDSC), and in the future, users may be able to order directly from BLDSC.

RLG, which developed the document transmission station called ARIEL, has also developed CitaDel to combine access to commercial and special databases with document delivery direct to the patron. Fax or ARIEL is used for fast delivery.

Lonesome Doc was developed for use in the field of medicine. It also targets the end user by offering citation searching and document delivery. Articles are supplied by participating medical libraries.[38]

## Alternative Methods of Delivery

Offprints of articles, especially in the scientific field, are easily obtained from the publishers. Securing offprints for patrons has been an ILL practice for a long time. Issues of periodicals may also be purchased, perhaps eliminating the need for a subscription as well as avoiding the question of copyright.

Herbert White, a library consultant, writes that ILL librarians can do more than simply send a request and then wait, for however long it takes, for a response. He suggests that a quick check of OCLC will sometimes reveal a nearby library as owning material needed quickly; a phone call will determine whether the material is on the shelf and whether it can be held for an ILL patron, until the proper paperwork arrives. He even suggests the material might be hand-delivered by a colleague.[39] In fairness to ILL librarians, I have known many to go that extra mile for their patrons, actually in much the same fashion as he described it.

Libraries of institutions participating in distance education are faced with special difficulties in providing all types of library services, including document delivery. The electronic library is being utilized heavily in distance education.

# Notes

[1]T. J. Waldhart, "Performance Evaluation of Interlibrary Loan in the United States: A Review of Research," *Library and Information Science Research* 7 (1985):313-31.

[2]B. Kaya and A. Hurlebaus, "Comparison of United Parcel Service and United States Postal Service Delivery Speed and Cost for Interlibrary Loan," *Bulletin of the Medical Library Association* 66 (1978):345-46.

[3]Ibid.

[4]Richard W. Boss and Judy McQueen, *Document Delivery in the United States; A Report to the Council on Library Resources by Information Systems Consultants, Inc.*, ERIC Document 244 626 (Washington, D.C.: Council on Library Resources, 1983).

[5]D. Nitecki, "Document Delivery and the Rise of the Automated Midwife," *Resource Sharing and Information Networks* 1 (1984):83-101.

[6]Waldhart, "Performance Evaluation of Interlibrary Loan," 313-31.

[7]B. J. Turlock, "Organization Factors in Multitype Library Networking: A National Test of the Model," *Library and Information Science Research* 8 (1986):117-54.

[8]Peterm Deekle, "Document Delivery Comes of Age in Pennsylvania," *Wilson Library Bulletin* 65 (1990):31-33.

[9]William Saffady, *Introduction to Automation for Librarians*, 2d ed. (Chicago: ALA, 1989), 321.

[10]S. Kennedy, "The Role of Commercial Document Delivery Services in Interlibrary Loan," *Interlending and Document Supply* 15 (1987):67-73.

[11]Arthur Little, *A Comparative Evaluation of Alternative Systems for the Provision of Access to Periodical Literature* (Washington, D.C.: National Commission on Libraries and Information Science, 1979).

[12]Boss and McQueen, *Document Delivery in the United States*, 7.

[13]Connie Miller and Patricia Tegler, "An Analysis of Interlibrary Loan and Commercial Document Supply Performance," *Library Quarterly* 58 (October 1988):352.

[14]Herbert S. White, *Librarians and the Awakening from Innocence* (Boston: G. K. Hall, 1989).

[15]Roy Adams, *Communication and Delivery Systems for Librarians* (Brookfield, Vt: Gower, 1990).

[16]*Directory of Online Databases* (Santa Monica, Calif.: Cuadra Associates, 1979- ).

[17]J. Francis Reintjes, "Application of Modern Technologies to Interlibrary Resource-Sharing Networks," *Journal of the American Society for Information Science* 35 (January 1984):45-52.

[18]Antoinette W. Colbert, "Document Delivery," *Online* 12 (May 1986):91.

[19]David P. Gillikin, "Document Delivery from Full-Text Online Files: A Pilot Project," *Online* 14 (May 1990):27-31.

[20]Susan N. Bjorner, "Full-Text Document Delivery Online—It Makes Sense," *Online* 14 (September 1990):109-12.

[21]Dennis L. Lindberg, "Why Automation? Getting Information Technology Off-Campus," in *The Off-Campus Library Services Conference Proceedings, Reno, Nevada, October 23-24, 1986*, ed. B. M. Lessin (Mount Pleasant, Mich.: Central Michigan University Press, 1986), 194-99.

[22]Dennis E. Smith and Clifford A. Lynch, "An Overview of Document Delivery Systems at the University of California," *Journal of Interlibrary Loan and Information Supply* 2 (1991):24.

[23]Havelin Anand, "Interlibrary Loan and Document Delivery Using Telefacsimile Transmissions: Part II, Telefacsimile Project," *Electronic Library* 5 (April 1987):100-107.

[24]T. J. Byers, "Fax Boards for Fast Times," *PC World* 8 (January 1990):118-29.

[25]Steven J. Schmidt, "PC/Fax Boards," *Journal of Interlibrary Loan and Information Supply* 2 (1991):7.

[26]Robert Swisher, Kathleen L. Spitzer, Barbara Spriestersbach, Tim Markus, and Jerry M. Burris, "Telecommunications for School Library Media Centers," *School Library Media Quarterly* 19 (Spring 1991):155.

[27]M. Wilson, "How to Set Up a Telefacsimile Network—The Pennsylvania Libraries' Experience," *Online* 12 (1988):15-19.

[28]Richard M. Dougherty, "The Evaluation of Campus Library Document Delivery Service," *College and Research Libraries* 34 (January 1973):29-39.

[29]Robert J. Greene, "LENDS: An Approach to the Centralization/Decentralization Dilemma," *College and Research Libraries* 36 (May 1975):201-7.

[30]Miriam A. Drake, "From Crystal Ball to Electronic Library," *Online* 14 (January 1990):6-8.

[31]David C. Genaway and Edward B. Stanford, "Quasi-Departmental Libraries," *College and Research Libraries* 38 (May 1977):187-94.

[32]Robert Goehlert, "Periodical Use in an Academic Library: A Study of Economists and Political Scientists," *Special Libraries* 69 (February 1978):51-60.

[33]Sara Eichhorn, "The Making of MELDOC," *College and Research Libraries News* 51 (May 1990):441-43.

[34]Smith and Lynch, "Document Delivery Systems," 23.

[35]Tracy Casorso, "Research Materials: Now Only Keystrokes Away," *College and Research Libraries News* 53 (February 1992):128.

[36]Smith and Lynch, "Document Delivery Systems," 29.

[37]Mary E. Jackson, "Library to Library," *Wilson Library Bulletin* 65 (April 1991):84-87.

[38]Mary E. Jackson, "Stand and Deliver," *Wilson Library Bulletin* 66 (April 1992):860-88.

[39]White, "The Awakening from Innocence," 275.

# chapter 8
# Issues and Trends

The Association of College and Research Libraries (ACRL) recently commissioned Research USA to conduct a survey among 600 members of ACRL. Members returned 468 questionnaires (79 percent). The data captured from the survey identified five issues as the most significant problems facing members. They are 1) rising journal prices, 2) provision of access to information, 3) preservation of library materials, 4) recruitment and retention of library staff, and 5) security for collections and users. Members also ranked the activities in which the ACRL was engaged. In descending order of perceived importance, the activities were developing standards and guidelines, job information, opportunities to discuss issues, research, collection of statistics, education, publications, awards, advisory services, and liaison activities.[1]

The issues raised by the survey pertain to college and research libraries as a whole, but some clearly can be associated with the ILL function in college and university libraries and in other types of libraries as well. Rising journal prices, for example, and providing access to information both impact on interlibrary loan, because higher prices not only prevent a library from subscribing to new journals but may also cause journal subscriptions to be canceled. At a time when more sophisticated ways of retrieving bibliographic citations are causing an increase in ILL traffic, fewer or even the same number of journals held in the home library means that an even larger number of articles must be retrieved through interlibrary loan.

Interlibrary loan staffing has not kept apace with patron demands, so any addition to the work load can be a burden. An increase in work load, however, is only one of the results of the problem of more journal articles being requested through interlibrary loan. Increased borrowing of articles is hampered by the 1976 copyright guidelines, which restrict a library from borrowing more than five articles from the same title within the most recent five years without buying a subscription. The 1976 Copyright Act also does not fully address on-line document retrieval.

To help relieve the problems of subscription costs, copyright violations, and slow document delivery, innovative methods of retrieving journal articles are being devised. Pat Molholt, associate director of libraries at Rensselaer Institute, speaking at an ILL session at the 1991 Conference of the ALA, indicated that interlibrary loan librarians need to expand upon technology already available. Patrons should be encouraged to request materials electronically. When patrons move from an on-line catalog to an actual digital article, it will change how people access information and the cost of same, she said. She further suggested that interlibrary loan librarians should ask for part of the acquisitions budget and spend it for resources patrons have indicated they need.

Although it is not uncommon for books borrowed through interlibrary loan to be recommended for purchasing "after the fact," there appears to be a trend toward purchase on a rush basis instead of requesting the book through interlibrary loan. This does reduce the ILL work load and cuts down on cost. Purchasing journal articles as offprints or purchasing single issues of journals has been done for years through the serials budget. Purchasing journal aricles from the acquisitions budget is a newer idea, but an idea whose time has probably come.

## Access to Information

Interlibrary loan has changed rapidly in the past few years, of that there can be no doubt. Perhaps the single most important factor or trend is greater access to information. As patrons learn more about what is available and how it can be obtained quickly, they borrow in greater numbers and become more demanding. On-line searching is shifting the burden of cost from the patron to the institution. The institution, in turn, is shifting the cost of acquiring materials on a temporary basis to the acquisition budget. The technology—networking, computers, fax machines—that makes greater access and faster delivery possible has also increased the stature of the ILL office and its occupants. Updated management techniques have also added a dimension of professionalism.

### The Electronic Library

On-line database searching of commercial systems, such as DIALOG or BRS through voice-grade telephone lines gave librarians and patrons alike a taste of on-line services and a vision for changing the way people obtain information. Improvements in networking, the use of personal computers in libraries, and the increased demand for on-line information set the stage for the next step, the installation of databases in on-line local systems.[2] Libraries that use local on-line, however, don't necessarily reduce spending on traditional remote searching but instead do more searching of databases not held locally.[3]

Local on-line use is heaviest at the college and university level and among large public library systems. These libraries have large numbers of users with a strong need for information. Special and corporate libraries have not widely embraced local on-line, except for a few products. These libraries rely more heavily on remote on-line. Because they lack large numbers of users, they often need to use numerous databases, and they often demand more current information than is available on local products. High costs are likely less of a problem than in academic and public libraries.[4] To justify the cost and added work load that local on-line generates, a library must have

large numbers of people seriously seeking information, or for small popula-
tions, there must be intensive need for certain databases.

Local on-line is the first step in the creation of an electronic library and
the first stage of shifting the cost of finding information from the user to the
institution. The costs of computer and network facilities, software, and
databases will be sustained by the institution, not by the user.[5]

The OCLC FirstSearch catalog is a new low-cost, easy-to-use reference
system that allows patrons to search the on-line union catalog and other
databases—ERIC, GPO Monthly Catalog, Consumers Index to Product
Evaluations, BIOSIS/FS, Mini Geo-Ref, and various Wilson databases.

FirstSearch is priced by the search based on the number of searches
made. Access may be made through an OCLC terminal, either dedicated or
dial-access; the Internet; or through an on-line catalog or local area network
linked to OCLC in Ohio.[6]

Libraries providing the OCLC FirstSearch catalog have the option of
allowing patrons to enter ILL requests into an on-line review file to be processed
later by the library staff. Because bibliographic information transfers automatically, this procedure ensures accurate, verified citations, and probably a
larger volume of ILL requests. Consequently, some libraries may opt not to
make the service available to the end user, but rather choose to make it available
to selected users through separate FirstSearch authorizations.

Electronic libraries are in place in a number of large universities. Miriam
Drake, dean and director of libraries at Georgia Institute of Technology,
reports a high degree of satisfaction with the Georgia Tech Electronic Library
(GTEL). Students and faculty use it at all hours of the day and night from
their offices, homes, and dormitories.

Faculty use the message module to request delivery of materials to their
offices. Some ask the system to alert them to research opportunities. Their
interest profiles are run against the full text of the *Commerce Business Daily*
every night, and their mail file is downloaded with the results.

Users are finding, through the electronic library, resources they didn't know
existed. Students are reading more from journals, conference proceedings, and
technical reports because citations and abstracts are easy and quick to find.
In-house use of journals doubled in one year at Georgia Institute of Technology.
Faculty requests for delivery of materials increased 36 percent in the year 1989.

Adding databases to the GTEL is limited by lack of funds, disk space,
and the reluctance of some publishers to lease their data for use on the
system. Nevertheless, Drake predicts that user demand (perhaps because
cost is absorbed by the institution); the increasing value of time; the need to
improve productivity; and the value of information to business, industry,
and education will be among the forces causing the installation of electronic
libraries. The on-line version of the *Commerce Business Daily* at Georgia
Institute of Technology has eliminated the need to buy almost 100 paper
copies and has also increased faculty awareness of research opportunities.[7]

Site database networks are on the verge of a tremendous expansion.
State libraries, state universities, and library consortia are using database
site licenses to provide local on-line at no cost to an entire region or state.

The Colorado Alliance of Research Libraries (CARL) offers several Information Access Corporation databases to academic and public libraries statewide. The Florida Center for Library Automation, using the NOTIS software, provides local on-line searching of ERIC, Information Access Corporation databases, and some H. W. Wilson databases.

The widely used NOTIS library management system can accept several databases, including MEDLINE and some WILSONLINE files. Several Information Access Corporation databases are compatible with the UTLAS public access catalog system.[8]

A library user at a local NOTIS on-line public access catalog (OPAC) is able to connect, using the software package PACLink, to a NOTIS OPAC at a remote library, searching and displaying in exactly the same way as the local OPAC. It is expected that PACLink will provide the ability to search several remote NOTIS catalogs simultaneously and to conduct ILL activity. Future releases will address the need to search non-NOTIS sites from the local NOTIS OPAC.[9]

Off-campus libraries are heavy users of the electronic library. For example, in spring 1986, Indiana University's Bloomington Academic Computing Services put together a number of information services including connections to off-campus computing services, on-line databases, E-mail, a campus telephone book, audiovisual and library services, and gateways to other large networks. Full-time faculty and graduate students were given accounts to use for the services.[10]

## Networking and Internetworking

In the mid 1980s, Avram described four issues that needed to be dealt with regarding networks. They are local systems, linking, linking standards, and database ownership. Their resolution will affect the future of networking nationwide, she said.[11] She was right.

The automated ILL systems of OCLC and RLG use records from databases containing millions of titles. They provide information about library holdings, reduce turnaround time, reduce paper files, and allow librarians to monitor and evaluate ILL performance. This has caused a rapid rise in the volume of ILL traffic—more than some libraries can bear. Fearing they could never keep up with their requests, many large libraries have never been suppliers through OCLC, for example. So, even though verification may be accomplished faster, transmission of the request may actually be slower than it has been in the past because many libraries will not honor requests unless they are mailed on the standard ILL order form. Many other libraries require potential borrowers to input their symbol twice in the lender string, giving them more time in which to respond to their many requests.

These same libraries, and others, also charge to lend materials, and the costs keep going up. One wonders if there might be a twofold purpose involved—recouping some of the costs of lending and borrowing as well as detering would-be borrowers. Dougherty also suggested that deteriorating library collections is an added problem connected to increased ILL borrowing.[12]

## OCLC

OCLC offers computer-based services to more than 11,000 libraries in 40 countries and adds 2 million records to its database each year. Its telecommunications system includes some 280,000 miles of wire.[13]

OCLC has just installed its new packet-switched telecommunications network, which supports the open systems interconnection standard. It provides new links to other networks in the educational and scientific communities, accommodates longer messages and faster speeds. It is also said to be more reliable than the original nertwork.[14]

## RLIN

In June 1991, RLG announced changes affecting membership, dues, and governance. The purpose of the changes was to build a broader alliance of institutions to meet research needs in a cost-effective manner for its RLIN.

RLG has added Arabic to the collection of non-Roman scripts available on its on-line network. Records may now be searched in Arabic, Chinese, Cyrillic, Hebraic, Japanese, Korean, Persian, and Yiddish. The system, which also includes characters for other languages written in Arabic script, allows users to read from right to left, the natural order of that language. It also supplies the correct form of characters, which vary in shape depending on their location in a word.[15]

### Microcomputer Networks

In the early 1980s, microcomputers brought the advantages of word processing, spreadsheets, and database applications into the office. In order to use this technology and share resources on large computers, users employed communications software or terminal emulation programs to allow the microcomputer to act as a terminal on a mainframe.

Microcomputers could then communicate with mainframes and each other to obtain more data from other computers. This required additional technological development so that computers with dissimilar hardware and software could communicate.

The history of this development involves governmental networking. ARPANET (Advanced Research Projects Agency Network), also called DARPA (Defense Advanced Research Projects Agency), was formed in the late 1960s and early to mid-1970s. ARPANET split in 1984 to form MILNET for military use, and ARPANET became a research component. These networks fostered the technology of packet-switching and communications protocols, allowing dissimilar networks to communicate using gateways. Thus internetworking was born.

## Internetworks

Internet is a network of networks. It is international in scope and is composed of 400-500 other networks. Many regional networks belong to Internet. Through Internet, librarians exchange E-mail, subscribe to bulletin boards, and internationally access library catalogs such as CARL and the University of California's MELVYL.

Internet provides only the basics. In the mid-1980s the network situation came under study of the U.S. government. Librarians became involved through ARLCAUSE (the professional association for the management of information technology in higher education), and EDUCOM (a nonprofit consortium of colleges, universities, and other institutions involved with campus information networking). Librarians realized that a national information network will allow libraries of all types to provide faculty, students, and the community with access to resources that was never before possible.[16]

ARPANET and Internet are open only to educational institutions doing government-sponsored research. As a result BITNET (Because It's Time NETwork) was formed in 1981. Although BITNET and Internet use different protocols within the two networks, E-mail is possible through a gateway.[17]

BITNET merged with NSFNET (National Science Foundation Network), a general purpose research network that is a part of Internet. NSFNET and Internet are to provide the backbone and foundation for the National Research and Education Network (NREN).[18]

BITNET and Internet can serve as an international forum for librarians in an electronic network. They are able to send messages back and forth, or they can search each other's on-line catalog without telephone charges. In addition, Internet contains local databases, regional newsletters, hypercards, public domain educational software, and other information.

BITNET is a research network for E-mail and file transfers. Its communications capability is less than is Internet's, but many more colleges and universities access it. On BITNET are electronic journals, interest group forums, and file servers. File servers automatically respond to mail requests. Most campus computing centers can provide the hardware and the documentation needed to search Internet and BITNET.[19] NREN, which became a reality in December 1991, will offer tremendous information-generating and -distributing opportunities to universities, colleges, and research laboratories.

NREN will serve to develop access to databases, services, and knowledge banks at a very high speed (100,000 typed pages per second).[20] The original idea for NREN was to connect supercomputer centers, allowing them to share massive amounts of data produced by high-performance computer projects. Along the way, librarians became involved in designing the network and acting as suppliers of information for the network.

NREN is to expand and upgrade Internet. It is expected that 1,500 college, university, and research libraries will be linked to NREN.[21]

Libraries will be able to share expensive serial publications through digital document delivery. Researchers of all kinds in geographically remote locations can gain immediate access to remote databases. Because the network will be interactive in nature, E-mail, file transfers, and mailing lists will allow researchers with similar interests to communicate with each other.[22]

## State Networks

Networks on the statewide level have also made great progress toward on-line interlibrary loan. ILLINET, for example, is a statewide union catalog and resource-sharing network enabling libraries of all types to initiate ILL transactions from among approximately 5 million bibliographic records in the ILLINET on-line database. The libraries access the database through dial access in metropolitan areas across the state.[23]

OhioLINK, the Ohio Library and Information Network, has linked 17 institutions of higher education and the state library for shared database searching, checkout, and delivery across the network. Another phase of the project will link community colleges and other colleges. Eventually more than 2,500 concurrent users will be connected to the network in 18 cities.[24]

The University of Michigan has linked its library to a network of eight community libraries, offering patrons in small towns the opportunity to tap into the resources of a research institution. The pilot project, called M-Link, began in 1988. The university supplies personal computers, modems, printers, and fax machines. The university and community libraries communicate by E-mail on a regional computer network linked to Internet. Patrons may also do research through Internet.[25]

## Journal Costs Versus On-line Usage

In his April 12, 1989, article in the *Chronicle of Higher Education*, Richard Dougherty stated that universities should regain control over their own sizable scholarly work—targeting rising journal costs in particular— through their own electronic publishing.[26] Later the same year Sharon Rogers and Charlene Hurt, in the same publication, proposed a university-based publishing system into which scholars from all disciplines would place their works to be reviewed by their peers for six months before being entered permanently into the system.[27] Others have called for research and educational institutions to control electronic publishing to their advantage and to print knowledge on demand. There exists, in fact, an ARL directory (first published in the summer of 1991) of scholarly networked publications available through BITNET and Internet. The directory includes descriptions of services and instructions on how to obtain them. The first edition contained 27 academic electronic journals, 67 electronic newsletters, and hundreds of academic discussion lists.[28]

The day is approaching when publications will be available only on-line. Many U.S. government information products will no longer be published in paper.

The growing body of electronic publications presents both philosophical and practical issues. Librarians are concerned about the impact of electronic delivery of information on scholarship and about their own roles in providing access. If they are to be intermediaries, they must develop ways of receiving, storing, and making available to present and future users the journals in the electronic format.[29]

*Personal Computers*

Personal computers are now being used extensively to electronically mail messages from one library to another and also to send ILL requests. Messages can even be sent to fax machines. With Western Union's software package and Easy Link service, personal computers can also access databases.

The Delaware County Library System in Pennsylvania expanded upon an existing bulletin board in order to send ILL requests on-line within the system. The cost to implement this full-scale multiline bulletin board was $2,700, excluding the host computer and installation of telephone lines, but the improved ILL turnaround time was considered worth the cost.[30]

Illinois academic library patrons borrow from other libraries through their IBM personal computers by using user-friendly ILL commands. Other libraries allow home computer users to access their on-line catalogs. *Dial In, 1990-91: An Annual Guide to Library Online Public Access Catalogs in North America*, edited by Michael Schugler, is a directory of more than 150 libraries supporting on-line access to their catalogs by modem from a microcomputer. Entries vary from small public libraries to large research libraries. The publication is to be updated annually.

The Maggie computer system in the Pikes Peak Library Service in Colorado was used in an attempt by a public library to deliver services to end users in their homes. Another experiment carried out by the Columbus Public Library, the Franklin County Library, and OCLC, all in Ohio, did not enjoy as much success as the Colorado experiment. It offered sophisticated on-line access to the library and to commercial databases.[31]

It is likely that most, if not all, libraries will depend on electronic information in the future. Costs for traditional acquisitions, storage, and retrieval will decline; costs for databases, computers, printers, and other tools will increase, resulting in no net savings. The quality of users' work will increase; librarians will spend more time training users and selecting appropriate on-line sources.[32]

The on-line catalog of the next century will include as a new feature software designed to provide an access guide for automated search systems based on library database directories. It will analyze a local system to establish a profile of the library's holdings. By updating the information and reporting it regularly to a central index, participating libraries can access the stored data using their own search software.

Individual information seekers will have software that allows them to access the database from within the structure of their own search environment. The software will give access to an artificial intelligence environment to assist with searching and location of information and with controlling delivery of information for inclusion in the user's own processing systems. The software will assist in establishing the best database to search and in setting up the system for retrieval, but it will also establish the preferred method of material delivery to the user, taking into consideration cost, speed, storage, and final form of presentation. The greatly increased computing power available and its low cost will enable such systems to be available to many end users who will then be able to manage their own information retrieval in a manner not now possible.[33]

# Document Delivery

Some libraries report an increase in ILL activity due to database searching. To ease the burden of document delivery, some are increasingly using fax and ordering more on-line from information brokers. Others realize that patrons are settling for far fewer articles than a search might identify because of the time involved in obtaining obscure articles.

Library systems are becoming interconnected in a far greater way than they were by the gateways of the past. Even the databases that can be searched through these systems have changed from including simple bibliographic citations to providing full-text document delivery. Document delivery can cross international boundaries or can take place in the privacy of one's own home.

The CD-ROMs, microcomputer-based databases searched through text-management software, and local databases being searched by end users as well as by librarians, are adding complexity not only to networking in general but to interlibrary loan in particular. Access to on-line catalogs and databases through Internet not only has the potential of adding to the interlibrary loan work load but raises the question of whether requests may be accepted directly from the user on a far broader scale than that of the direct or branch borrowing presently taking place.

Commercial database suppliers such as BRS and DIALOG have also been busy developing end-user services. When asked in 1986 what he expected to see in the next decade, the founder and president of Dynamic Information Corporation, Randy Marcinko, replied that 1) the average document will routinely be supplied within 24 hours, 2) paper copies will continue to account for well over half of the documents delivered, and 3) the cost of an article, relative to other products and services in the industry, will probably be the same or become lower. Sue Rugge, founder of Information on Demand, stated that the information industry continues to suffer because of the "Carnegie syndrome"—that is, access to information should be free and publicly available to every citizen. She is unable to see the information industry overcoming that philosophy.[34]

The rapidly developing trend of the delivery of materials to library patrons on a campus has also become an issue. A dimension of service is added, but complications connected with staffing and funding may also be added.

Costs may be absorbed from the regular budget, a library may receive a subsidy from its administrative body, or user fees may be charged to the patrons. It must also be decided who will be served. Faculty? Graduate students? Undergraduates? Staff? In large institutions, it must also be determined if delivery will be made from all libraries or just from the central library. Policy decisions concerning subject searches and requesting materials not owned must also be made. Stevenson, University of Notre Dame, provides advice about issues to resolve before beginning a document delivery service.[35]

Several producers of CD-ROM products are trying to provide better document delivery solutions, such as microform collections, image files on CD-ROM, and ASCII files of document text bundled with the CD-ROM index.[36] Information Access Company has three microform products that provide access to many articles referenced in the CD-ROM InfoTrac or in microfilm indexes such as Magazine Collection and Business Collection. A Text on Microfiche (TOM) product for school libraries includes microfiche copies of articles referenced in the TOM index.

University Microfilms has taken a different approach. Its Business Periodicals Ondisc and General Periodicals Ondisc, for example, include scanned articles. EBSCO has a CD-ROM product called Magazine Article Summaries, which contains general-reference magazines and subject magazines in full text.[37]

As stated previously, OCLC has also been involved in developing services for end users. FirstSearch, the computerized system for reference searches, which was initiated in October 1991, is aimed directly to library patrons and may change the way research is performed. The cost is expected to be lower than for research done through commercial databases.

FirstSearch will allow for searching of OCLC's bibliographic database for books and other materials by subject. Users will then be able to obtain journal articles through the mail or through fax machines. OCLC's president, K. Wayne Smith, predicted in 1991 that "in five years you will look up a journal through OCLC databases, punch a button on the computer, and get the document in your hand."[38]

The Integrated Services Digital Network (ISDN) allows existing telephone lines to carry digital information. It is available in large cities like Chicago, Houston, Atlanta, and Washington, D.C. International in scope, it converts telephone circuits from analog signaling to digital signaling, allowing users to connect personal computers or other digital equipment to a data outlet. The ISDN will simplify the process of linking personal computers to each other and to mainframes. Such links could open the world of databases, E-mail, and shared resources to most personal computer users.[39]

When prices fall to a suitable level, individuals will own their own fax machines as they now own their own personal computers, providing a tremendous opportunity to make information readily available to consumers. A voice-activated fax machine has been announced in which users can follow a series of menus to retrieve information from a database and receive it on their fax machines.[40]

The similarity between PCs and fax machines in their internal workings and in their use of modems to communicate with each other has led to the creation of the technology for the working together of the two. A "fax card," which plugs into a PC, allows the PC to communicate with any fax machine so messages can be sent between the two.

At the heart of the fax card is a fax modem. The cards usually come with software that allows the user to type the phone number of a fax machine to be called, then send or receive fax transmissions through the fax cards. Faxes received by the PC can be printed on the printer; files of spreadsheets and other documents can be sent to other fax machines.

There are several problems in using the PC as a fax machine. The fax card's software must be running all the time. Faxes must be printed with the printer operating in the "graphics mode," which is very slow. A scanner is also needed to feed the original document to be transmitted.

The best use of the fax card is for sending documents from your other PC software directly to someone else's fax machine. For example, a letter written on your word processor or a graph created on your graphics program can be sent directly from your PC to a remote fax machine. The real potential is in on-line database and information-retrieval systems. Today, storage is cheap. Fax machines are capable of communicating the contents of the printed page. The need and technology are both here for widespread use of fax machines.[41]

Fax is replacing E-mail for communication because the output is in paper form, and users do not have to sign on to a system and download their messages or enter them from a keyboard. No special instructions, classes, or lengthy user manuals are needed to send a fax.

Insofar as document delivery is concerned, Herbert White indicated that the sky is, indeed, the limit when he told how in 1975 he and other members of a consultant team made plans for what was to have been a new national library in Iran. Interlibrary loans were to be delivered from the British Museum and the LC to Teheran via satellite, with local delivery (because of poor roads) via helicopter.[42]

## Copyright Concerns

The present copyright law does not treat new technological advances, and there is much talk of amending the law or doing away with it altogether. In electronic communications, it is not possible to distinguish between ideas and the expression of those ideas as it is in the print medium. Copying becomes indispensable to reading the idea, and a copy can be easily counted only the first time it is made.

Several suggestions have been made by various experts in response to problems in the copyright law. Amending the law, realizing that there will be lag time between development of the technology and amendment of the law, is one option. The law might be supplemented with contracts or licenses granting permission to use (as in the case of CD-ROMs) but limiting sharing of information that is rented, not owned. Or the Copyright Clearance Center (CCC) could be authorized to collect fees to send to the owners. New laws that meet the requirements of each type of technology could be made as needed, or the present law could be thrown out or revised completely.[43]

Bruce Flanders predicts that what he calls the intellectual property crisis will cause librarians fits of soul-searching. The "intellectual property crisis" is the loss of control over the flow of information as new technologies change the way people access, store, manipulate, and reuse information. High-speed telecommunications networks allow individuals and organizations that own computers and modems to download hundreds of documents in seconds and to build personal databases if they so desire. They can even modify the information for resale, totally ignoring the copyright law.

Librarians are unable to solve the problem of the intellectual property crisis, but Flanders believes they may be able to bring it to public awareness. They may even advocate legislation strengthening governmental enforcement of intellectual property rights. Librarians must also respond if new methods for collecting royalties limit access to information by the economically disadvantaged.[44]

On March 28, 1991, a group of major New York publishers won a landmark case against a corporation of 300 nationwide copy shops (*Basic Books, Inc. v. Kinko's Graphics Corp.*). Excerpts from copyrighted books were photocopied, compiled into course packets, and sold to New York University and Columbia University students. Kinko's claimed it should be insulated from liability by section 107 (fair use) because the copying was requested by college professors and sold to college students.

The fact that the judge did not agree is likely to cause an increase in copyright litigation against copy shops. It could also impact upon libraries that leave themselves open to liability.[45]

## Organization and Administration

Automation of ILL record management and statistics is quite widespread in the United States and elsewhere. A.I.M. (Automation of Interlending by Microcomputer project), developed by the British Library and Leicester Polytechnic, integrates transmission of requests and processing of requests. The system called ACUILLA, designed in Canada by the University of Calgary, handles both borrowing and lending activity.

Systems developed in this country include F.I.L.L.S. developed at Macneal Hospital in Berwyn, Illinois; BASIS, a software management system developed by Battelle, with one component being devoted to ILL management; and ILLRKS developed at the University of Wyoming, among others.

Further development of the software to allow it to go beyond separate systems into a workstation is being developed. For the workstation, Wessling called for total integration of ILL activity into a local library system and into regional and national networks.

She says that the software should support local file management; printing of ALA forms, transmission of E-mail requests; transfer of data from union databases such as those of OCLC, RLIN, and WLN; and integration with local or regional databases. Optical scanning of incoming requests would eliminate paper files. Standards to ensure uniformity and compatibility are necessary.[46] We are seeing his dreams become reality.

Are ILL librarians actively seeking a different organizational or physical location for the ILL operation? A 1988 survey of 100 ARL heads of interlibrary loan found widely varied patterns of organizational structure. The operation is frequently placed within access services/circulation, reference, or on its own, but almost half of those who responded to the survey said their operations were not centrally located. The ratio of librarian to nonlibrarian supervisors was almost two to one, but levels of staffing ranged from 1.5 FTE to 24.5 FTE. Fax is used widely, and document delivery is offered by 37 percent of the institutions surveyed.[47]

To meet the explosive growth of ILL activity, many libraries have had to expand and upgrade their ILL facilities. The University of Montana expanded from a library office with no technology to one with the most advanced technologies. The original ILL office held one person who accomplished about one-fourth of the current work load. By 1990, the ILL staff—full time staff and student help—had to be scheduled in shifts because staff, desks, and machines competing for space spilled out into the hallway and around the corner.[48]

Virginia Boucher suggests that reaching the goal of successful borrowing and lending may be made easier by following the advice of outside consultants. Automation, for example, has brought about many changes in the ILL process, forcing changes in procedures. She says that consultants may be able to help in crisis situations or in long-range planning, but careful planning must be done to prevent the employees from feeling threatened. A recent advertisement for an academic librarian, however, indicates that professionals with considerable expertise are being sought also. (See fig. 8.1.)

---

AUTOMATION/INTERLIBRARY LOAN LIBRARIAN. Completes plans for implementation of integrated library system in 1993; coordinates library automation and networking activities; serves as liaison with campus computer center; trains staff in automation applications. Responsible for interlibrary loan service, supervising one staff member and student assistants. Qualifications: MLS from ALA accredited institution; at least two years' experience with library automation, including integrated library systems, OCLC, and CD-ROM applications. Evidence of successful implementation of library technology projects. Evidence of successful implementation of library technology projects. Interlibrary loan experience preferred. Faculty rank, 12-month appointment. Salary commensurate with qualifications.

---

Fig. 8.1. Advertisement for an ILL librarian.

Consultants may be chosen from several areas within and outside the library. An experienced ILL librarian would make a good consultant. A reference librarian would make a good consultant. For example, a reference librarian who conducts good reference interviews would be able to give advice on the ILL interview. Librarians with public relations experience could advise on printed materials to project a library's image. Subject specialists may advise on bibliographic verification. Outside consultation may be needed in the areas of copyright law, telecommunications and automation, and management of the ILL operation.[49]

On the author's survey, respondents were asked to rank ILL problems as they have experienced them. On the borrowing side of the operation, the following were considered problems: verification (33.3 percent), location (10.5 percent), insufficient staff (27.5 percent), time spent excessive for service rendered (2.3 percent), money spent excessive for service rendered (5 percent), regulations abused or not followed (4.8 percent), unfilled requests (16.1 percent), copyright restrictions (15.9 percent), insufficient loan period (4.5 percent), document delivery too slow (18.9 percent), excessive work load (17.8 percent), loss or deterioration (5.6 percent), burden on resources (2.7 percent), and others (8.7 percent).

The picture was quite different on the lending side of the operation. The following were considered lending problems: verification (23.7 percent), location (18.4 percent), noncirculating materials (12.1 percent), insufficient staff (36.7 percent), time spent excessive for service rendered (11.1 percent), regulations abused or not followed (3.7 percent), unfilled requests (3.8 percent), copyright restrictions (22.2 percent), insufficient loan period (8 percent), document delivery too slow (18.5 percent), excessive work load (16.1 percent), and burden on resources (7.1 percent).

Respondents were asked to agree or disagree with statements reflecting issues and trends in ILL work as reported in the professional literature. Yes responses were received for the following statements:

1. The ILL office is becoming more visible to the public (37.4 percent).

2. There is increased involvement of professional librarians in the ILL process (50.5 percent).

3. Staffing patterns have changed in the ILL operation in recent years (53.8 percent).

4. Interlibrary loan staff require more training than just a few years ago (69.1 percent).

5. There is interest in a different organizational placement of interlibrary loan (17.4 percent).

6. The document delivery unit is separate from the ILL unit (12.6 percent).

7. Interlibrary loan is decentralized (each branch, department library, etc. handles its own (13.1 percent).

8. Interlibrary loan receives part of the acquisition budget for "temporary acquisition" (7.8 percent).

9. We design our own request forms to capture statistical information (29.8 percent).

10. Expanded bibliographic access has increased our participation in interlibrary loan (72.1 percent).

11. We are experiencing a need for standardization of codes, protocols, etc. (32.6 percent).

12. There is increased international borrowing (11 percent).

13. Requests are transmitted by library patrons from home computers (4.1 percent).

14. We have our own in-house automation program (5.3 percent).

Philosophically, survey respondents believe that interlibrary loan has gone beyond the original intent of being a tool for research (54.2 percent) and that there should be no user fees for interlibrary loan (57 percent). Interlibrary loan should be considered as just another way to obtain materials patrons need to have purchased from the acquisitions budget (44.4 percent). Shared collection development is a natural outgrowth of interlibrary loan (87.4 percent). Because of technological advancements, the copyright law should be rewritten (79.1 percent). User expectations of 24-hour turnaround are reasonable (11.3 percent). Global interlibrary loan is feasible (75.3 percent) and global interlibrary loan is desirable (58.1 percent).

## International Trends

The growth of interlibrary loan seems consistent, yet ILL systems vary greatly from country to country. Resource sharing is largely decentralized in the United States; internationally centralization is more common. The trend is, however, toward more direct borrowing in some countries. The Universal Availability of Publications program of the IFLA has sharpened the understanding of international agencies, library officials, and users of libraries to both the potential and the limitations of resource sharing. Richard Dougherty writes that to the extent that university libraries in the United States and Western European countries enhance shared collection development, expand bibliographic access, and provide efficient, affordable delivery of documents, we can gauge the library profession's success at fulfilling the IFLA ideals of universal bibliographic control and availability of publications.[50]

Networking has changed librarianship throughout the world. The challenge of a technological approach to American librarianship has been accepted by European librarians. The professional literature devoted to networking and automated systems has resulted in the publication *European Library Networks*, edited by Karl Neubauer and Esther Dyer.

The capability of libraries to share information determines the success of interlibrary loan. The OCLC database has become international in scope. Japanese libraries using UTLAS have access to Western bibliographic data and to location data of other UTLAS users.[51]

The first international conference geared toward interlibrary loan librarians was held in London, November 14-16, 1988. It was sponsored by IFLA and the journal *Interlending and Document Supply*. The IFLA Office for International Lending is based at the British Library Document Supply Centre (BLDSC) in Boston Spa, England.

In her "Library to Library" column in the February 1989 issue of *Wilson Library Bulletin*, Mary Jackson describes the conference in some detail. It is, likewise, reported here in some detail to emphasize that national issues and international issues are much the same. Among the issues addressed were electronic document delivery, union lists, access to difficult-to-locate material, and copyright.

Speaker Maurice Line estimated international ILL activity at that time to be approximately 1.5 million requests per year, about half of which may be sent to the BLDSC. Areas that needed attention, according to Line, were alternative modes of publication, standards and protocols, measurement of performance systems, and the ability to anticipate rather than react to patron needs.

Problems of interlibrary loan and other resource sharing are very similar in many parts of the world and in many different types of libraries. Nancy Fjallbrandt of Sweden spoke on access strategies for document delivery. Barrie Stern reported on a project called ADONIS (Automatic Digital On-Line Instrumentation System) which was tested by the British Lending Division and the University College in London. At that time ADONIS was storing images of 219 biomedical journals from 1987 and 1988 and published by 10 different publishers. The images were scanned onto CD-ROM disks.

American presenters at the conference spoke of the fax revolution (Group IV fax machines were just emerging). The librarian of the Royal Library, The Hague, questioned whether the new technologies being installed in libraries will increase the availability of materials.

On-line catalogs were discussed by the president of OCLC, Rowland Brown, and Jean Plaister, director of LASER (London and South Eastern Library Region). Plaister described technology as a friend and an enemy to libraries in the London and in the South Eastern Library Region. They view the on-line catalog as an alternative approach to the centralized BLDSC concept.

Concerning copyright, Georgia Finnigan, president of The Information Store, claimed that traditional ILL operations were not properly adhering to copyright laws. Graham Cornish maintained that copyright is about protecting the physical item, not the information. He noted that the queen signed a new British law permitting everyone, not just educators, to make a copy. How the information can be controlled is probably the real question. Finnigan stated that the private sector has established the value of information. This led to speculation as to whether libraries should continue to provide documentation delivery or whether private companies will take over that market.[52]

Several papers from the 1990 IFLA Annual Conference, which was held in Stockholm, Sweden, were published in the journal *Resource Sharing and Information Networks* for 1991. Like the first conference, it was filled with issues that were of global interest and concern. It dealt with such varied topics as cooperation among national libraries, cooperation between public and school libraries, interlending audio books for the blind, and mobile libraries made possible by the use of new technologies to serve as extensions of the modern library.

United States and foreign consortia were described, as was the Commission of the European Communities program to investigate the potential of CD-ROM products. Document delivery was the theme of several papers.

Interlibrary loan is now going into places where it dared not go before, or where there is distrust over events of the past. Some of the difficulties experienced by American libraries in lending materials to other countries were addressed when libraries in the southwestern United States and Mexico conducted a pilot program to explore the possibility of establishing a permanent system of interlibrary loans between the two countries, with materials being exchanged through the U.S. Embassy courier.[53]

Ononogbo makes a plea for interlibrary loans to be performed between libraries in the free world and those in South Africa. In withholding information, the population we seek to protect could be harmed, as information from the rest of the world could effect positive changes in South Africa, he says.[54] There are some U.S. libraries performing interlibrary loans with South African libraries.[55]

The Open Systems Interconnection (OSI) is an international standard set of rules or protocols that allow computers of different manufacturers, using different types of internal programs, to communicate with each other as equals with minimal prior negotiation. Because these are general standards, not library standards, librarians must work with computing-center personnel and others to implement this protocol.[56]

There are seven layers of OSI. A layer communicates with its peer, or equivalent, layer. Layer 7, the application layer, is the one that controls application interfaces. It is in this layer that library-specific programs such as information retrieval, file transfer, and interlibrary loan are found. The creation of effective, efficient application programs will be the focus of OSI efforts within the library community over the next few years.[57]

The 12 members of the European Community—Portugal, Spain, Denmark, Belgium, France, Greece, Italy, Ireland, Luxembourg, Germany, The Netherlands, and the United Kingdom—are removing technical and economic barriers that exist between them, and they are becoming a single European market. Librarians of the countries involved expect a gradual move toward greater integration of services and resource sharing. This integration is expected to also have an effect on the international level.

Heretofore, most computer databases have been located in the United States, and Japan has led the way in technology. Now the European Community is convinced that information is the most important thing needed by business to become efficient and competitive.

A proposed plan of action for libraries—the European Library Plan—has been funded, at least in part. Proposals have also been initiated to deal with the areas of copyright, book prices, taxes, and cooperation in automation and networking. The laws controlling electronic information in Europe will be simplified to make it easier for its libraries to transfer information internationally. American libraries will also have easier access to European databases in Europe because they won't have to meet so many separate protocols.[58]

With the advent of computerized document delivery, transfer of information across international borders will be the final barrier to be overcome. This will mean access to a wider base of data and to more comprehensive information sources than are possible at present. International cooperation and the flow of information across borders will bring the global village into reality.[59]

# Notes

[1]"ACRL Survey Identifies Five Major Problems," *American Libraries* 22 (January 1991):108.

[2]Miriam A. Drake, "From Crystal Ball to Electronic Library," *Online* 14 (January 1990):6.

[3]Mick O'Leary, "Local Online: The Genie Is Out of the Bottle, Part 1," *Online* 14 (January 1990):17.

[4]Ibid., 18.

[5]Drake, "From Crystal Ball to Electronic Library," 7.

[6]"Dedicated Line," *American Libraries* 23 (January 1992):90.

[7]Drake, "From Crystal Ball to Electronic Library," 7.

[8]Mick O'Leary, "Local Online: The Genie Is Out of the Bottle, Part 2," *Online* 14 (March 1990):29.

[9]"Dedicated Line," 90.

[10]Judith A. Copler, "Reaching Remote Users—Library Services Through a System-wide Computing Network," in *The Off-Campus Library Services Conference Proceedings, Charleston, South Carolina, October 21-22, 1988.* ed. Barton M. Lessin (Mount Pleasant: Central Michigan University, 1988), 79.

[11]Henriette D. Avram, "Current Issues in Networking," *Journal of Academic Librarianship* 12 (September 1986):205-9.

[12]Richard M. Dougherty, "Research Libraries in an International Setting: Requirements for Expanded Resource Sharing," *College and Research Libraries* 46 (September 1985):383.

[13]Tom Gaughan, "The Corporate Culture of OCLC," *American Libraries* 22 (October 1991):894.

[14]Bruce Flanders, "OCLC Telecom Network Complete," *American Libraries* 23 (March 1992):242.

[15]"On Line," *Chronicle of Higher Education* 38 (October 16, 1991):A25.

[16]Roberta A. Corbin, "The Development of the National Research and Education Network," *Information Technology and Libraries* 10 (September 1991):214-19.

[17]Ibid., 213-14.

[18]Ibid., 215.

[19]William A. Britten, "BITNET and the Internet: Scholarly Networks for Librarians," *College and Research Libraries News* 51 (February 1990):103-7.

[20]Ibid., 103.

[21]Bruce Flanders, "NREN: The Big Issues Aren't Technical," *American Libraries* 22 (June 1991):572.

[22]Ibid., 574.

[23]"ILLINET Awarded Grant," *Wilson Library Bulletin* 64 (January 1990):10.

[24]Bruce Flanders, "Dedicated Line," *American Libraries* 23 (February 1992):174.

[25]David L. Wilson, "Libraries," *Chronicle of Higher Education* 38 (October 23, 1991):A21.

[26]Richard M. Dougherty, "To Meet the Crisis in Journal Costs Universities Must Reassert Their Role in Scholarly Publishing," *Chronicle of Higher Education* 35 (April 12, 1989):A52.

[27]Sharon J. Rogers and Charlene S. Hurt, "How Scholarly Communication Should Work in the 21st Century," *Chronicle of Higher Education* 35 (October 18, 1989):A56.

[28]"Netting E-Journals," *American Libraries* 22 (November 1991):980.

[29]Michael E. Stoller, "Electronic Journals in the Humanities: A Survey and Critique," *Library Trends* 40 (Spring 1992):647-66.

[30]David Belanger, "Interlibrary Loan via Electronic Mail: Improving the Process," *Wilson Library Bulletin* 63 (March 1989):62-63.

[31]Roy Adams, *Communication and Delivery Systems for Librarians* (Brookfield, Vt.: Gower, 1990), 81.

[32]Drake, "From Crystal Ball to Electronic Library," 8.

[33]Adams, *Communication and Delivery Systems for Librarians*, 226-27.

[34]Antoinette W. Colbert, "Document Delivery," *Online* 11 (January 1987):122.

[35]Marsha Stevenson, "Design Options for an On-Campus Document Delivery Program," *College and Research Libraries News* 51 (May 1990):437-40.

[36]Carol Tenopir, "Article Delivery Solutions," *Library Journal* 115 (June 1990):91.

[37]Ibid., 91-92.

[38]David L. Wilson, "Researchers Get Direct Access to Huge Data Base," *Chronicle of Higher Education* 38 (October 9, 1991):A24-A25.

[39]Robert Swisher, Kathleen L. Spitzer, Barbara Spriestersbach, Tim Markus, and Jerry M. Burris, "Telecommunications for School Library Media Centers," *School Library Media Quarterly* 19 (Spring 1991):158.

[40]"Spectra FAX Introduces Special Request Fax Information Retrieval Service," *IDP Report* 10 (October 6, 1989):9.

[41]Robert Rindfuss, "Information Delivery and Fax Technology," *Online* 14 (July 1990):100-101.

[42]Herbert S. White, *Librarians and the Awakening from Innocence* (Boston: G. K. Hall, 1989), 274.

[43]Ann Okerson, "With Feathers: Effects of Copyright and Ownership on Scholarly Publishing," *College and Research Libraries* 52 (September 1991):430.

[44]Bruce Flanders, "Barbarians at the Gate," *American Libraries* 22 (July-August 1991):668-69.

[45]Randall Coyne, "Rights of Reproduction and the Provision of Library Services," *University of Arkansas at Little Rock Law Journal* 13 (Spring 1991):516.

[46]Julie E. Wessling, "Benefits from Automated ILL Borrowing Records: Use of ILLRKS in an Academic Library," *RQ* 29 (Winter 1989):210.

[47]Cheryl La Guardia and Connie V. Dowell, "The Structure of Resource Sharing in Academic Research Libraries," *RQ* 30 (Spring 1991):370.

[48]Marianne Farr and Barry Brown, "Explosive ILL Growth at the University of Montana: A Case Study," *Journal of Interlibrary Loan and Information Supply* 2 (1991):52.

[49]Virginia Boucher, "Consultants for Interlibrary Loan," in *Information Brokers and Reference Services*, ed. Robin Kinder and Bill Katz (New York: Haworth Press, 1988), 233-38.

[50]Dougherty, "Research Libraries in an International Setting," 389.

[51]Susan K. Martin, "Library Networks: Trends and Issues," *Journal of Library Administration* 8 (Summer 1987):28.

[52]Mary E. Jackson, "Library to Library," *Wilson Library Bulletin* 63 (February 1989):78-79.

[53]"U.S. and Mexican Libraries Test Interlibrary Loan Programs," *Library Journal* 114 (November 1989):28.

[54]Raphael U. Ononogbo, "Performing Interlibrary Loans with Libraries in South Africa," *Journal of Interlibrary Loan and Information Supply* 2 (1991):17.

[55]Corinne Nyquist, "Interlibrary Loan and the ALA/SRRT Guidelines," *Journal of Interlibrary Loan and Information Supply* 1 (1990):45-46.

[56]David Bishop, "The Open Systems Interconnection: An Introduction," *Resource Sharing and Information Networks* 7 (1991):7.

[57]Ibid., 11.

[58]Ron Chepesiuk, "The Dawn of European Economic Unity: What It Means for Libraries," *American Libraries* 23 (March 1992):212-14.

[59]Sheila S. Intner and Jane Anne Hannigan, *The Library Microcomputer Environment: Management Issues* (Phoenix and New York: Oryx Press, 1988), 57.

# Appendix A
## Interlibrary Loan Codes

### National and Model Interlibrary Loan Codes*
*Reprinted with permission of the American Library Association

*National Interlibrary Loan Code, 1980*[1]

Adopted by Reference and Adult Services Division
Board of Directors, New York, 1980[1]

**INTRODUCTION**

Interlibrary loan is essential to the vitality of libraries of all types and sizes and is a means by which a wide range of material can be made available to users. This code is designed primarily to regulate lending relations between research libraries and between libraries operating outside networks or consortia. It is recognized that through specific agreements, libraries organized geographically, by mutual subject interest, or other bases will have developed codes of their own. It is not the intent of this code to prescribe the nature of interlibrary lending under such arrangements. (See "Model Interlibrary Loan Code for Regional, State, Local, or Other Special Groups of Libraries.")[2]

The effectiveness of a national system of interlibrary lending is directly related to the equitable distribution of costs among all the libraries involved. Interlibrary loan is an adjunct to, not a substitute for, collection development in individual libraries. Requests to national and research libraries or requests beyond networks and consortia should only be made after local, state, and regional sources have been exhausted. It is understood that every library must maintain an appropriate balance between resource sharing and responsibility to its primary clientele.

This national code contains general guidelines for the borrowing and lending of library material. Details of procedures to be used in implementing the code will be found in the *Interlibrary Loan Procedure Manual* published by the American Library Association.[3] All libraries participating in interlibrary loan should have copies of this publication and should follow these recommendations. The manual also provides information on international interlibrary loan.

The Reference and Adult Services Division, acting for the American Library Association in its adoption of this code, recognizes that the exchange of material between libraries is an important element in the provision of library service and believes it to be in the public interest to encourage such an exchange.

179

I. Definition

An interlibrary loan is a transaction in which library material, or a copy of the material, is made available by one library to another upon request.

II. Purpose

The purpose of interlibrary loan as defined in this code is to obtain, for research and serious study, library material not available through local, state, or regional libraries.

III. Scope

A. A loan or a copy of any material may be requested from another library in accordance with the published lending policy of that library. The lending library will decide in each case whether a particular item can be provided.

B. Most libraries will not ordinarily lend the following types of materials:
1. Rare or valuable material, including manuscripts;
2. Bulky or fragile items that are difficult or expensive to ship;
3. Material in high demand at the lending library;
4. Material with local circulation restrictions;
5. Unique material that would be difficult or impossible to replaces.

IV. Responsibilities of Borrowing Libraries

A. Each library should provide the resources to meet the study, instructional, informational, and normal research needs of its primary clientele. This can be accomplished through its own collection or through local, state, or regional cooperative resource-sharing agreements. Material requested from another library under this code should generally be limited to those items that do not conform to the library's collection development policy and for which there is no recurring demand.

B. The interlibrary loan staff of each library should be familiar with, and use, relevant interlibrary loan documents and aids. These include this code, the *Interlibrary Loan Procedure Manual*, lending policies of the major research libraries, and standard bibliographic tools and services.

C. Each library should inform its users of the purpose of interlibrary loan and of the library's interlibrary borrowing policy.

D. The borrowing library is responsible for compliance with the copyright law (Title 17, *U.S. Code*) and its accompanying guidelines, and should inform its users of the applicable portions of the law. An indication of compliance must be provided with all copy requests.

E. Requested material must be described completely and accurately following accepted bibliographic practice as outlined in the current *Interlibrary Loan Procedure Manual*. If the item cannot be verified, the statement "cannot verify" should be included along with complete information as to the original source of the citation.

F. The borrowing library should carefully screen all requests for loans and reject any that do not conform to this code.

G. Standard bibliographic tools, such as union catalogs, computerized data bases, and other listing services, should be used in determining the location of material. Care should be taken to avoid concentrating the burden of requests on a few libraries.

H. Standard interlibrary loan formats should be used for all requests, regardless of the means of transmission.

I. The safety of borrowed material is the responsibility of the borrowing library from the time the material leaves the lending library until it is received by the lending library. The borrowing library is responsible for packaging the material so as to ensure its return in good condition. If damage or loss occurs, the borrowing library must meet all costs of repair or replacement, in accordance with the preference of the lending library.

J. The borrowing library and its users must comply with the conditions of loan established by the lending library. Unless specifically forbidden by the lending library, copying by the borrowing library is permitted provided that it is in accordance with the copyright law and no damage to the original material will result.

K. The borrowing library should encourage library users to travel to other libraries for on-site access to material when extensive use of a collection is required or the nature of the material requires special handling. The borrowing library should assist the user in making the necessary arrangements.

V. Responsibilities of Lending Libraries

A. The decision to lend material is at the discretion of the lending library. Each library is encouraged, however, to interpret as generously as possible its own lending policy with due consideration to the interests of its primary clientele.

B. A statement of interlibrary loan policy and charges should be made available upon request.

C. The lending library should process requests promptly. Conditions of loan should be stated clearly and material should be packaged carefully. The lending library should notify the borrowing library when unable to fill a request, stating the reason for not filling the request.

D. A lending library is responsible for informing any borrowing library of its apparent failure to follow the provisions of this code.

VI. Expenses

A. The borrowing library assumes responsibility for all costs charged by the lending library, including transportation, insurance, copying, and any service charges. The borrowing library should try to anticipate charges and authorize them on the original request.

B. It is recommended that nominal costs, such as postage, be absorbed by the lending library.

C. If the charges are more than nominal and not authorized by the borrowing library, the lending library should inform the requesting library and ask for authorization to proceed.

VII. Duration of Loan

A. The duration of loan, unless otherwise specified by the lending library, is the period of time the item may remain with the borrowing library disregarding the time spent in transit.

B. Interlibrary loan material should be returned promptly.

C. The borrowing library should ask for renewals only in unusual circumstances. The renewal request should be sent in time to reach the lending library no later than the date due. If the lending library does not respond, it will be assumed that renewal, for the same period as the original loan, is granted.

D. All material on loan is subject to immediate recall, and the borrowing library should comply promptly.

VIII. Violation of Code

Continued disregard of any provision of this code is sufficient reason for suspension of borrowing privileges.

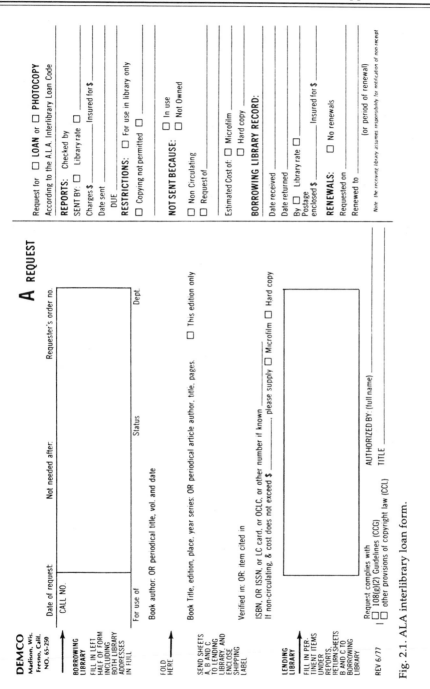

Fig. 2.1. ALA interlibrary loan form.

The loan request form, as reproduced above, was revised and approved by the Reference and Adult Services Division Board of ALA at the Annual Conference, June 1977. It is available from library supply houses. Reprinted by permission of the American Library Association.

## NOTES

[1]Endorsed by the boards of directors of the Association for Library Service to Children and of the Young Adults Services Division, both divisions of the American Library Association, June 1980, New York, and by the membership of the Association of Research Libraries, May 15, 1980, Salt Lake City.

[2]"Model Interlibrary Loan Code for Regional, State, Local, or Other Special Groups of Libraries" appears on pages 185-88.

[3]This manual (Chicago: American Library Association, 1970), prepared by Sarah Katharine Thomson, has been superseded by *Interlibrary Loan Practices Handbook.*—Ed.

## Model Interlibrary Loan Code for Regional, State, Local or Other Special Groups of Libraries

Endorsed by Reference and Adult Services Division
Board of Directors, New York, June 1980.[1]

### PREFACE

The "Model Interlibrary Loan Code for Regional, State, Local or Other Special Groups of Libraries" is intended to provide guidelines for any group of libraries interested in developing an interlibrary loan code to meet special needs. The Model Code, while complementing the *National Interlibrary Loan Code, 1980,*[2] allows libraries more flexibility and creativity in satisfying interlibrary loan needs in a specific situation.

The Model Code is designed to provide a framework for cooperation. Since it is recognized that most networks and consortia can be more liberal in loaning materials, the Model Code has fewer restrictions than the National Code. All libraries in a network or consortium should participate in developing an interlibrary loan code. Each section of the code should be discussed and should be expanded or modified, if necessary, for local use. The bracketed sections of the Model Code indicate specific areas where local information may be necessary. Libraries are encouraged to put as few restrictions as possible on the exchange of materials.

The use of interlibrary loan service is becoming increasingly important to libraries committed to providing a high level of service to their clientele. In *A Commitment to Information Services: Developmental Guidelines, 1979,* the Reference and Adult Services Division emphasizes the importance of considering "the needs and interests of all users, including children, young adults, adults...." Interlibrary loan is a service that should be publicized and provided to all members of the library's clientele.

A strong interlibrary loan network within a local, state, or regional jurisdiction should be the primary source of interlibrary loan materials for all libraries. Only after all of these resources have been exhausted should a library request material outside of these arrangements. In making outside requests, the *National Interlibrary Loan Code, 1980,* and the *Interlibrary Loan Procedure Manual*[3] should be followed. This approach will distribute the burden of requests more equitably and provide better service for all libraries.

This code is a voluntary agreement adopted by_____
_____[system, consortium, network, etc.]
on_____[date] to govern interlibrary lending among
libraries in _____[metropolitan area, region, state, system, network, consortium, etc.].

## INTRODUCTION

Interlibrary loan service is essential to the vitality of libraries of all types and sizes as a means of greatly expanding the range of materials available to users. Lending between libraries is in the public interest and should be encouraged. This code is intended to make interlibrary loan policies among those libraries adopting it as liberal and as easy to apply as possible. Interlibrary loan should serve as an adjunct to, not a substitute for, collection development. When resources within the region have been exhausted, loan requests to more distant libraries should then conform to the provisions of the *National Interlibrary Loan Code, 1980*.

I. Definition

An interlibrary loan is a transaction in which library material, or a copy of the material, is made available by one library to another upon request.

II. Purpose

The purpose of interlibrary loan as defined in this code is to obtain library material not available in the local library.

III. Scope

Under the terms of this agreement, it is permissible to request on interlibrary loan any type of library material [except ...].

IV. Responsibilities of Borrowing Libraries

A. Each library should provide the resources to meet the ordinary needs and interest of its primary clientele. Material requested from another library under this code should generally be limited to those items that do not conform to the library's collection development policy or for which there is no recurring demand.

B. Borrowing libraries should make every effort to exhaust their own resources before resorting to interlibrary loans.

C. The interlibrary loan staff of each library should be familiar with, and use, relevant interlibrary loan documents and aids including _____. [List here pertinent interlibrary loan codes, interlibrary loan procedure manuals, and bibliographic tools and services.]

D. Each library should inform its users of the purpose of interlibrary loan and of the library's interlibrary borrowing policy. Any member of the borrowing library's clientele should be eligible for interlibrary loan.

E. The borrowing library is responsible for compliance with the copyright law (Title 17, U.S. Code) and its accompanying guidelines, and should inform its users of the applicable portions of the law. An indication of compliance must be provided with all copy requests.

F. Requested material must be described as completely and accurately as possible following accepted bibliographic practice. If an item cannot be verified, the statement "cannot verify" should be included along with information about the original source of citation. [Variations in accepted bibliographic practice may be referred to here.]

G. Requests should be routed through channels established by libraries participating in this agreement. These channels are outlined in _____. [List here specific documents outlining agreed upon channels.]

H. Standard interlibrary loan formats should be used for all requests, regardless of the means of transmission. [Variations from standard interlibrary loan formats may be referred to here.]

I. The safety of borrowed materials is the responsibility of the borrowing library from the time the material leaves the lending library until it is received by the lending library. The borrowing library is responsible for packaging the material so as to ensure its return in good condition. If damage or loss occurs, the borrowing library must meet all costs of repairs or replacement, in accordance with the preferences of the lending library.

J. The borrowing library and its users must comply with the conditions of loan established by the lending library. Unless specifically forbidden by the lending library, copying by the borrowing library is permitted provided that it is in accordance with the copyright law and no damage to the original volume will result.

K. The borrowing library should encourage library users to travel to other libraries for on-site access to material when extensive use of a collection is required or the nature of the material requires special handling. The borrowing library should assist the user in making the necessary arrangements.

V. Responsibilities of Lending Libraries

A. The decision to loan material is at the discretion of the lending library. Each library is encouraged, however, to interpret as generously as possible its own lending policy with due consideration to the interests of its primary clientele.

B. A statement of interlibrary loan policy should be made available upon request and should be on file in the state library [or other appropriate agency].

C. The lending library should process requests promptly. [A specific number of days for processing may be inserted here.] Conditions of loan should be stated clearly and material should be packaged carefully. The lending library should notify the borrowing library when unable to fill a request, stating the reason for not filling the request.

D. A lending library is responsible for informing any borrowing library of its apparent failure to follow the provisions of this code.

VI. Expenses

    A. The borrowing library should be prepared to assume any costs charged by the lending library and should attempt to anticipate charges and authorize them on the initial request. [List here any documents referring to charging policies.]

    B. If the charges are more than nominal and not authorized by the borrowing library, the lending library should inform the requesting library and ask for authorization to proceed.

VII. Duration of Loan

    A. The duration of loan unless otherwise specified by the lending library, is the period of time the item may remain with the borrowing library disregarding the time spent in transit.

    B. Interlibrary loan material should be returned promptly.

    C. A renewal request should be sent in time to reach the lending library no later than the due date. If the lending library does not respond, it will be assumed that renewal, for the same period as the original loan, is granted.

    D. All material on loan is subject to immediate recall, and the borrowing library should comply promptly.

VIII. Violation of the Code

Each library is responsible for maintaining the provisions of this code in good faith.

## NOTES

[1]Also endorsed by the boards of directors of the Association for Library Service to Children and of the Young Adult Services Division, both divisions of the American Library Association, June 1980, New York.

[2]This manual (Chicago: American Library Association, 1970), prepared by Sarah Katharine Thomson, has been superseded by *Interlibrary Loan Practices Handbook.*—Ed.

# Code Used by Regional Network AMIGOS

### AMIGOS Interlibrary Loan Code
### May 15, 1981
### (Revised March 27, 1992)

This Code is a voluntary agreement to govern all interlibrary lending among libraries in the AMIGOS Bibliographic Council, Inc., and is intended to promote a more liberal interlibrary loan policy among the libraries adopting it than that of the ALA National Interlibrary Loan Code. It is based on the premise that lending among libraries for the use of an individual served by an AMIGOS member library is in the public interest and should be encouraged. Interlibrary borrowing and lending is regarded by the library subscribing to this agreement as essential to library service since it is evident that it is impossible for any one library to be self-sufficient and that the furtherance of knowledge is in the general interest. However, interlibrary lending should be no substitute for the development of adequate collections based on the needs of the service areas represented in libraries and library systems.

I.  Definition

Interlibrary loans are transactions in which library materials or copies of library materials are made available by one library to another upon request.

II.  Scope

Under the terms of this agreement, any type of library material may be requested on loan or in photocopy from another library. The lending library retains the right of deciding in each case whether a particular item should or should not be provided, and whether the original or a copy should be sent.

III.  Responsibility of Borrowing Libraries

A.  It is recognized that interlibrary lending does not relieve any library of the responsibility of developing its own collection. Each library will provide the resources to meet the ordinary study, educational, instructional, informational and research needs of its users. No library should depend upon another to supply the normal needs of its clients except under special agreement for such service.

B.  AMIGOS members will, where feasible and cost effective following state network protocols, or in the absence of state protocols, exhaust local resources before requesting materials from other members and will route requests to the closest libraries first, taking care to avoid concentrating the burden of requests on a few libraries.

C.  The borrowing library is responsible for compliance with the copyright law (Title 17, U.S. Code) and its accompanying guidelines, and should inform its users of the applicability of the law. An indication of compliance must be provided with all copy requests.

D. The safety of borrowed material is the responsibility of the borrowing library from the time the material leaves the lending library until it is returned to the lending library. The borrowing library is responsible for packaging the material so as to insure its return in good condition. If damage or loss occurs, the borrowing library must meet all costs of repair or replacement, in accordance with the preference of the lending library.

E. The borrowing library and its users must comply with the conditions of loan established by the lending library. All material on loan is subject to immediate recall, and the borrowing library shall comply promptly.

F. Unless specifically forbidden by the lending library, copying by the borrowing library is permitted provided that it is accordance with the copyright law and no damage to the original volume will result.

G. The borrowing library agreeing to abide by this code should place this data on the request form in these locations:

OCLC - BORROWING NOTES
ALA - Cost area

IV. Responsibility of Lending Libraries

A. The decision to loan material is at the discretion of the lending library. AMIGOS members are encouraged, however, to interpret as generously as possible their own lending policy with due consideration to the interest of their primary clientele.

B. A statement of interlibrary loan policy and charges will be provided to other AMIGOS members upon request. *Members will input and regularly update a statement of their policies in the appropriate Name Address Directory records.*

C. A lending library is responsible for informing any borrowing library of its apparent failure to follow the provision of this code.

D. AMIGOS members will not require information about the status of the individual for whom material is being requested.

E. All libraries that list themselves as supplies on OCLC and have signed this code will lend to any other OCLC supplier in the AMIGOS Network through the OCLC ILL Subsystem.

F. *Libraries will mail photocopies via First Class Mail. Members are strongly urged to utilize telefacsimile to transmit photocopies for interlibrary loan.*

V. Expenses

   A.  The borrowing library should be prepared to assume costs for lost and damaged materials and any other costs not excluded by this Code.

   B.  AMIGOS members will not charge each other for the following: (except charges may be made to nonsuppliers)

      1.  Fees for handling interlibrary loan requests
      2.  Postage or other transportation charges, *including telefacsimile transmission costs*
      3.  Photocopying (up to 50 pages per request)
      4.  Insurance

   C.  Telephone communications costs will be paid by the telephoning library.

VI.  Violation of the Code

Each library is responsible for maintaining the provisions of this code in good faith.

Guidelines for Use with the
AMIGOS Interlibrary Loan Code
May 15, 1981
(Revised March 27, 1992)

These guidelines were prepared by the AMIGOS Task Force to Prepare Guidelines for Use with the AMIGOS Interlibrary Loan Code during the summer and fall of 1981. Revisions to the guidelines will be issued by AMIGOS as deemed appropriate in the future.

Users of the OCLC ILL Subsystem are encouraged to refer to *OCLC Guidelines for Using the OCLC Interlibrary Loan Subsystem* issued as an Appendix to OCLC's *Interlibrary Loan: User Manual*.

| Section | Guidelines |
| --- | --- |
| Introduction | Covers all interlibrary loan requests among AMIGOS members who sign the Code regardless of the method of transmission, e.g. ALA form, TWX, mail, telephone, OCLC Subsystem. |
| I.  Definition | None |
| II.  Scope | The borrower should make every effort within reason to identify serial holdings in the online OCLC Union List of Serials or other tools, rather than simply using the OCLC 3-letter symbol holdings displays. The request should also be verified and include the following information: (1) correct title of periodical in full, (2) correct volume number, part number and year of periodical in full, (3) full author and title of article, (4) page numbers of article, and (5) the source of verification, e.g. *Reader's Guide 1978*, p. 43, or "bibliographic citation from book by...." |
| III.  Responsibility of Borrowing Libraries | |
| A. | None |
| B. | When requesting more than one article from the same serial title, it is beneficial to lenders for the borrower to use the same lender string on each request. |
| C. | None |
| D. | None |

E.               The "due date" as established by the lender should be interpreted as the date the borrower should return the material to the lender, i.e., place in transit to lender. On OCLC requests, any "due date" information in the Lending Notes field should take precedence over "due date" in the fixed field.

Renewal requests should not be encouraged. When a renewal is requested, the borrower should request permission of the lender prior to the original "due date."

Borrowers should respect lenders' restrictions on a loan such as "in library use only" or "no photocopying permitted."

Borrowers should state on original requests whether or not substitutions in the format of materials will be acceptable, e.g., photocopy for hard-copy, microform for original, etc.

F.               None

G.              None

IV. Responsibility of Lending Libraries

A.               The lender should not make a substitution in the format of material requested without the agreement of the borrower. If the borrower makes no statement on the original request as to substitutions, lenders may assume any format is acceptable.

Lenders are encouraged to consider the variability of transit times for materials and to be as liberal as possible in setting due dates, keeping in mind the due date will be the date the borrower places the material in transit.

Libraries who do not loan materials via the OCLC ILL Subsystem should have their symbol placed on the OCLC non-supplier table so their symbol cannot be placed into a lender string. This would in no way limit them from loaning via ALA form or methods other than OCLC.

B.               AMIGOS members are encouraged to enter their lending policies into the "OCLC Name-Address Directory."

C.              None

D.              None

E.              None

V. Expenses

A.                    Proper wrapping of materials for shipment by both
                      borrowers and lender cannot be overemphasized.

B.                    All AMIGOS members are encouraged not to charge each
                      other. AMIGOS signatories to this Code may charge
                      non-signatories who charge them.

                      *Non-suppliers are defined as those libraries who borrow
                      materials but do not loan materials.*

                      The lender retains the right to limit the number of pages
                      that will be copied for any one request. Lenders have the
                      discretion to determine the charges in excess of 50 pages,
                      e.g., to charge for 56 pages or only for 6 over the 50.
                      Lenders willing to photocopy more than 50 pages should
                      receive agreement from the borrower for these charges.

C.                    None

VI. Violation of the Code    None

# Interlibrary Loan Code for Libraries in the State of Connecticut
(Reprinted with permission.)

I. Definition

An interlibrary loan is a transaction in which library material, or a copy of the material, is made available by one library to another upon request.

II. Purpose

The purpose of this code is to facilitate interlibrary loan transactions in Connecticut.

III. Scope

Under the terms of this agreement it is permissible to request any type of material on interlibrary loan except those specifically excluded by a library's interlibrary loan lending policy.

IV. General Responsibilities

1. Every library should have an interlibrary loan policy. Updated policy statements should be maintained online and/or in published directories. They should be in a standardized form.

2. All staff responsible for performing interlibrary loan transactions should be completely familiar with the operation of automated interlibrary loan systems in use at their library.

V. Responsibilities of Borrowing Libraries

1. Every library has an obligation to publicize its interlibrary loan service so that its users are aware of it.

2. It is the borrowing library's responsibility to provide the proper bibliographic citations.

   a. Materials requested must be described as completely and accurately as possible following accepted bibliographic practice.
   b. When the borrowing library has access to the holdings of the lending library it should provide complete and accurate bibliographic information as it appears in the database.
   c. Sources of verification should be given for all items verified in standard bibliographic tools. When the item requested cannot be verified, the statement "cannot verify" should be indicated, along with the user's source of reference and a list of bibliographic sources searched.
   d. Every request must include the specific date beyond which the material will not be accepted by the user. If the user indicates that there is no time limit, this information must be included.

3. Placement of requests

   a. The most efficient placement of an interlibrary loan request is directly from the borrowing library to the lending library.

   b. The borrowing library should get the patron request into the ILL system within two days of receiving it.

   c. The preferred method for transmitting interlibrary loan requests is electronic.

   d. Whenever possible, interlibrary loan requests should be filled in-state. Libraries should search whatever statewide databases they have available to them.

   e. Requests should be placed first with libraries on the same C-car route or within the same region, then to other libraries in Connecticut, then outside the state.

4. Interlibrary loan is always a transaction between libraries. Individuals going to a public library outside their community to borrow materials should do this through Connecticard, not through ILL.

5. There should be uniform ILL periods throughout the state. Standard loan periods to the borrowing patron will be four weeks.

6. A loan may be renewed unless a hold is outstanding.

7. The borrowing library must instruct the user to return loans to the borrowing library, not to the lending library or to another library.

8. The borrowing library is responsible for compliance with the copyright law (Title 17, U.S. Code) and its accompanying guidelines, and should inform its users of the applicable portions of the law. An indication of compliance must be provided with all copy requests.

9. The borrowing library is responsible for materials from the time they leave the lending library until they are returned to that library.

10. The borrowing library should be prepared to assume any costs charged by the lending library. If charges are more than nominal, the lending library will inform the requesting library and obtain authorization to proceed with the transaction. Borrowing libraries should attempt to anticipate charges and authorize them on the initial request.

11. The borrowing library should adhere to any restrictions placed by the lending library on the use of the materials borrowed.

12. The borrowing library should initiate notification of the patron within twenty-four hours of the completion of the ILL transaction.

13. If the request was made through a third party, the borrowing library should provide that party with any required notice of receipt and return.

VI.  Responsibilities of the Lending Library

1.  The decision to lend materials is at the discretion of the lending library.

2.  Lending libraries should process requests within two working days, or cancel requests and notify the borrowing library within two working days.

3.  If the borrowing library has made a good faith effort to provide complete bibliographic verification, the lending library will make every attempt to fulfill the request.

4.  Whenever possible, the lending library should provide the borrowing library with a reason why it is unable to fill a request.

# International Interlibrary Loan Code

## International Lending*: Principles and Guidelines for Procedure (1978)—Major Revision 1987.

*'Lending' is held to include the sending of photographic and
other reproductions in place of the original.
(Reprinted with permission from the International Federation
of Library Associations and Institutions.)

The mutual use of individual collections is a necessary element of international cooperation by libraries. Just as no library can be self-sufficient in meeting all the information needs of its clientele, so no country can be self-sufficient. If the library service of a country is to be effective methods must be devised to obtain access to material held in other collections in other countries. International lending has as its aim the supply by one country to another, in the surest and fastest way, of documents that are not available in the country where they are needed.

The following guidelines, agreed by the Standing Committee of IFLA's Section on Interlending in 1978 and modified in 1987, represent a major revision of the Rules agreed by IFLA in 1954. While they have no mandatory force, and while every country must determine the ways in which it conducts interlending, the guidelines are strongly urged on individual countries and libraries as a basis for the conduct of international lending. They are preceded by a statement of Principles of international lending agreed in an earlier and slightly different version in 1976 by National Libraries and by the Standing Committee of IFLA's Section on Interlending, and are accompanied by a commentary which seeks to elucidate and amplify certain aspects of the guidelines.

## PRINCIPLES OF INTERNATIONAL LENDING

1.  Every country should accept responsibility for supplying to any other country, by loan or photocopy, copies of its own publications, certainly those published from the present date, and as far as possible retrospectively. This responsibility may be discharged in various ways, among which national loan/photocopy collections appear to have particular advantages.

2.  Each country should have a national centre or centres to coordinate international lending activity for both incoming and outgoing requests. Such centres should be closely linked with, if not part of, the national library where there is one.

3.  Each country should aim to develop an efficient national lending system, since national lending systems are the essential infrastructure of international lending.

4.  As far as possible, photocopies or microfilms should be supplied in the place of loans of original copies.

5. Fast methods should be used for supplying and returning items. Airmail should be used whenever possible.

6. All requests should be dealt with expeditiously, having regard to accuracy, at all points: the requesting library, any intermediary used and the source library.

7. Standard and simple procedures should be developed and adopted, particularly procedures for requesting items and for reclaiming any payment.

## GUIDELINES FOR PROCEDURE

1. General
   Each library should, within any nationally agreed policy, use the most efficient methods for identifying locations of wanted documents and transmitting requests.

   Commentary
   1. Speed of supply is extremely important to most users. Every effort should be made to follow routines which are simple and time-saving. International requests often take far longer to satisfy than those dealt with nationally so that should be modified where necessary procedure to reduce delays. All communications should be in clear and simple language and legible to avoid misunderstanding across linguistic barriers.

2. National Centre for International Lending

   2.1 Each country (or, in the case of federal countries, each state or province) should have a centre playing an active role in international lending. Its main functions are:

      a) to act as a centre for the receipt of requests from abroad and their transmission onward to libraries within its own country when direct access to collections is not possible or accepted;

      b) to act as a centre for the transmission of requests to foreign countries from libraries within its own country when direct access is not possible or not accepted;

      c) to provide where necessary bibliographical support and expertise to ensure that requests sent abroad reach the required standards;

      d) to gather statistical information from within its own country on international loan transactions and to send these figures regularly to the IFLA Office for International Lending.

2.2 Centres for international lending may, and should where possible, also perform the following functions:

a) to perform a coordinating role for national interlending;
b) act as the main national centre for the supervision and construction of union catalogues and their maintenance;
c) to have direct access to significant library collections in their own country;
d) to provide an information service on interlending;
e) to have responsibility for planning, developing and supervising an efficient national system of interlending where this function is not adequately performed by another agency.

Commentary

2. The nomination or establishment of national centres to carry out the functions mentioned in 2.1 and 2.2 is strongly recommended as the most efficient and effective means of carrying out these functions. In those countries where no such national centre has been nominated or established the following recommendations are made:

2.1a Published guides, as comprehensive as possible, should be provided to facilitate the direction of requests by other countries. All libraries within the country should make strenuous efforts to observe the same procedures for handling and when necessary circulating requests received from other countries.

2.1b In the case of loans of originals, individual libraries should accept responsibility for ensuring that no loanable copy of a required work exists in another library within the country before sending requests abroad. See 3.4 below.

2.1c The collection of statistics, which is vital for monitoring trends and efficiency, should still be carried out on a national basis.

2.1d Strong coordination is essential if the international requirements and responsibilities of a country without a national centre are to be fulfilled efficiently. A coordinating body may be in a position to fulfil some of the functions of a national centre.

3. Procedure for Requesting

3.1 All requests using paper forms shall be on the forms authorized by IFLA, unless otherwise stipulated by the library to which requests are sent. Requests submitted by telex (TWX) or electronic mail shall conform to agreed standards.

3.2 To ensure that inadequate or inaccurate requests are not sent abroad the borrowing library shall verify, and where necessary complete, the bibliographic details of items requested to the best of its ability, giving the source of reference where possible. Where necessary or appropriate details shall be checked or completed by the national centre.

3.3 Requesting libraries should keep a record of all requests, each of which should have a serial number.

3.4 In the case of loans of originals, all reasonable efforts shall be made to ensure that no loanable copy is available in its own country before a request is sent abroad. Documents that are available in a country but are temporarily in use should only be requested on international loan in exceptional circumstances.

<u>Commentary</u>

3. *Requests for loans* should normally go through national centres, since otherwise it is very difficult to ensure that there is no other loanable copy in the country, and loans are expensive. It may be decided that it is easier, cheaper and faster to apply direct abroad (for example, when the only known location is outside the country); however, a record of all such requests should be sent to the national centre for information. *Requests for photocopies* may however in appropriate cases be made direct to foreign libraries, not necessarily in the country of publication.

3.1 Forms should wherever possible be completed in typescript.

3.2 Inadequate requests cause delays, and may have to be returned for further checking.

Where a request is inadequate because the requesting library has insufficient bibliographic resources to check it, it should be checked by the national centre or centres before it is despatched.

3.4 This is the responsibility of the appropriate national centre when no comprehensive record of national holdings is generally available.

3.5 Fast methods include airmail, telex, telefacsimile, direct computer transmission and electronic mail.

4. Procedure for Supplying

4.1 Every country has a special responsibility to supply its own national imprints on international loan. No country or library is under an obligation to supply a work that has been requested, but all reasonable efforts should be made to satisfy international requests.

4.2 Items shall be sent direct to the requesting library except where, for administrative reasons, it is specifically required that they should be sent to the national centre.

4.3 All documents lent should be clearly marked with the name of the owning library.

4.4 Packages containing items sent in response to requests shall be clearly marked: "INTERNATIONAL LOANS BETWEEN LIBRARIES."

4.5 No library receiving a request should normally retain it for longer than one week (two weeks in the case of difficult requests) before supplying the item or returning the request to the national centre or the requesting library.

4.6 When a request cannot be satisfied, the requesting library should be notified at once.

4.7 When the satisfaction of a request is likely to be seriously delayed, the requesting library should be notified at once.

Commentary

4.1 The responsibility of each country to supply its own national imprints is emphasized: without the acceptance of such a responsibility, both availability and speed of supply are seriously jeopardized. This responsibility is an essential element in Universal Availability of Publications.

4.4 Clear statements on the outside of packages are necessary to avoid problems with Customs.

4.5 Difficult requests include requests that require extensive bibliographic checking and requests that are satisfied by making copies of long documents (e.g. microfilms of books).

4.6 Failure to notify inability to supply or delays in supplying
&   causes further delays and uncertainty in the requesting library.
4.7 In countries with no national centre, fast procedures should be devised to transmit to other libraries requests that cannot be satisfied. If such procedures are not possible, the requests should be returned at once to the requesting library.

5. Conditions of Supply

5.1 Where photocopies are supplied, libraries supplying and receiving them must abide by any requirements necessary to satisfy relevant copyright regulations.

5.2 Original documents when received by the borrowing library shall be used in accordance with its normal regulations, unless the supplying library stipulates certain conditions.

5.3 Items should be sent by the fastest postal service available.

Commentary
5.3 It is recognized that in some cases the use of airmail, although desirable, may not be possible because the cost cannot be borne by either the borrowing or the supplying library. The use of fast methods of transmission is nevertheless very strongly urged, since slower methods may make libraries reluctant to lend and inconvenience the individual user.

6. Period of Loan

6.1 The loan period, which shall in all cases be specifically and clearly stated, shall normally be one month, excluding the time required for despatch and return of the documents. The supplying library may extend or curtail this time limit.

6.2 Application for extension of the loan period shall be made in time to reach the supplying library before the loan period has expired.

7. Procedure for Returning

7.1 Documents lent should be returned by the fastest postal service available. Packages shall be marked 'INTERNATIONAL LOANS BETWEEN LIBRARIES.'

7.2 Libraries returning documents shall observe any special stipulations by supplying libraries with regard to packaging, registration, etc.

7.3 Documents shall be returned to the supplying library except where return to the national centre is specifically stipulated.

Commentary
7.2 Special stipulations may relate to special packaging in the case of fragile documents or registration in the case of rare items.

8. Receipts

No receipts shall be provided either for the supply of an item or its return to the supplying library, unless specifically requested.

9. Responsibility for Loss or Damage

From the moment a library despatches an item to a requesting library until it returns, the requesting library shall normally be responsible for any loss or damage incurred, and pay the supplying library the full estimated cost of such loss or damage, including where requested any administrative costs involved.

Commentary

It is in the interests of all concerned to ensure that all items are adequately packaged. Claims from supplying libraries for loss or damage cannot be seriously entertained if packaging by them has been inadequate.

Supplying libraries are expected to help where necessary with postal inquiries in cases of loss or damage.

10. Payment

Accounting and payment procedures should be minimized. Payment shall be made or waived according to agreements between the two countries or libraries involved. Payment between national centres or individual libraries receiving and providing a similar number of satisfied requests should be waived. Payment may also be waived when the number of items supplied to a particular country or library is so small as not to justify the accounting procedures involved.

Commentary

Simplified methods of payment include:

a) prepaid systems, whereby national centres or libraries buy numbers of coupons in advance, and send an appropriate number of coupons with each request;

b) deposit accounts, whereby the supplying library holds a sum deposited by a requesting library and deducts amounts from it according to each item supplied;

c) flat-rate payments, whereby average rather than individual costs are recovered; or unit payments, whereby charges are made in a limited number of units. Either of these methods may be combined with pre-payment or deposit accounts.

Payment may be made by national centres, which may recover it from requesting libraries in their countries, or direct by requesting libraries, according to the system in operation in the requesting country. The requirements of the supplying library or country, which should be as simple and clear as possible, must in all cases be observed.

Different practices may be applied to loans and to photocopies or other reproductions sent in place of loans: for example, two countries, or a group of countries, may agree to waive charges for loans but not for photocopies.

11. Statistics

Libraries participating in international lending shall keep statistics of requests received from and sent to other countries, and those satisfied in each case. These statistics shall be sent each year to the national centre or national association for forwarding to the IFLA Office for International Lending.

Commentary
The statistics to be collected should include:

1. The total number of requests sent abroad and the total satisfied a) by loan, b) by photocopy.

2. The total number of requests received from abroad and the total satisfied a) by loan, b) by photocopy.

The above statistics should preferably be kept in rank order by country.

Where it is not possible to collect figures for satisfaction rates over all requests, they may be estimated from sample surveys.

A fuller statement of recommended statistics is given in *IFLA Journal*, vol. 3, no. 2, 1977, pp. 117-26: International Lending Statistics.

# Model National Interlibrary Lending Code

(Reprinted with permission.)

This model national code for interlibrary lending was drawn up in 1983 by the IFLA Office for International Lending for the IFLA Section on Interlending. It is recommended as a model for all countries that do not at present have a national code for interlibrary lending or that wish to revise existing codes.

A model national code clearly cannot take account of all variations in practice between countries. Provision has therefore been made for individual countries to include information specific to their country (see sections in square brackets).

It is important to understand the research and study that lies behind this code. The following documents are recommended:

  i. Line, MB (and others). *National interlending systems: a comparative study of existing systems and possible models.* Paris, Unesco, 1980. (PGI/78/WS/24 Rev.)
 ii. Line, M B and Vickers, S. Principles of national interlending systems. *Interlending Review*, 1978, vol. 6, no. 2, 50-53.

If the model code cannot be adapted to any particular country's needs, the following checklist may be used as a guide to the topics that a code should cover:

  i. definition of interlending.
 ii. a statement of any broad principles.
iii. any other national regulations, manuals, etc. that should be known.
 iv. verification of requests.
  v. location of required materials and/or channels to be used.
 vi. standard formats.
vii. transmission methods for requests.
viii. treatment of requests received.
 ix. delivery of requested material.
  x. loan periods, return of material, renewals.
 xi. responsibility for loss or damage.
xii. charges and payment procedures.
xiii. statistics.

## MODEL NATIONAL INTERLIBRARY LENDING CODE

### Scope

The object of this code is to improve efficiency by providing standard procedures for interlibrary lending ('interlending' for short). It does not preclude other agreements between local or subject-related groups of libraries, nor does it apply to international lending (which has its own code,* agreed by IFLA).

### Definition

Interlending is the process whereby one library obtains from another specified library material requested by its users and not available from its own stock. The requested material may be sent as a temporary loan or a copy may be supplied or transmitted instead.

### Principles

Interlending should be recognized as a vital element in making library materials available to users. Libraries are expected to acquire materials most likely to be required by their users but should also expect to borrow material from other libraries to meet legitimate demands by users for material that is not in stock. All libraries should publicize their interlending services to their users. In the interest of mutual support and the widest possible availability of published documents (which is in the public interest), libraries should be as liberal as possible in their interlending policies and should seek to develop and support a fast and efficient national system.

An awareness of the costs involved in servicing requests is important. Alternatives to interlending should be considered where economically justified, for example acquisition, personal visit to another library, another document on the same subject.

It is legitimate to request any kind of library material, but rare, fragile, or bulky items, or items that cannot be photocopied and are in high local demand, are less likely to be readily supplied. The supplying library has the ultimate right to decide whether to supply any requested item.

Requesting libraries should be aware of existing regulations and agreements on interlending. (*State here any specific codes, manuals, etc. that should be known.*) Supplying libraries should make available on request a statement of their interlending policy and charges.

---

*International Lending: Principles and Guidelines for Procedure* (1978), *IFLA Journal*, 1978, vol. 4, no. 4, 377-382.

*Requesting*

Requests made by users should be scrutinized and despatched by the requesting library as quickly as possible: within one working day for straightforward requests and up to three working days for requests with poor bibliographic details. Where the details given by the user are inadequate or suspect, the requesting library should make a reasonable effort to verify the information in whatever bibliographic tools it possesses; if unsuccessful, it should state the sources tried.

Details of the requested item should be adequate for its identification by the supplying library. The exact bibliographic details required may vary from one supplying library to another. A source of reference should be quoted wherever possible.

Decisions on where to send requests should depend principally on the likelihood of first-time success; reapplication or circulation of requests among libraries is a principal cause of delay and high costs. If possible, a small number of regular channels should be utilized consistently. Large numbers of requests should be sent only to those libraries that are willing to accept them. Location tools, whether printed or on-line, and union catalogue centres should be used as and where appropriate. [*State any specific location services that should be used.*]

Standard request forms or other standard formats should be used. [*State any standard forms or formats that should be used.*] Where a loan, photocopy, microfilm, etc. is specifically required, this should be stated on the request.

Where copyright restrictions may apply, a declaration should be made by the requesting library that it has conformed to them.

Requests should be despatched by fast transmission methods, for example by Telex or the fastest regular mail service. [*State any particular transmission method(s) that should be used.*]

*Supplying*

Libraries receiving requests should deal with them as expeditiously as possible. When a request cannot be satisfied or if there is likely to be a serious delay in supplying (more than two weeks), then either the requesting library should be notified immediately or, if there is a rota of locations, the request should be passed to the next location.

The supplying library should ensure that items supplied on loan are clearly marked with the name and address of the owning library, the data by which the loan is to be returned and any special conditions that apply to it. Loan periods should be adequate to allow for transmission in both directions as well as use by the borrower. [*State any standard loan period.*] Items supplied should be packaged carefully and addressed clearly, and despatched by fast postal or other delivery services.

## Receipt and Return

The borrowing library should take due care of material received on loan and respect any special conditions. Loans should be returned in time to arrive at the supplying library by the due date. Requests for renewals should be avoided if possible and in any case should be made well before the due date; where no response is received, the renewal may be assumed to have been granted.

Notification of receipt of an item on loan or of its return to the supplying library is not necessary, unless specifically requested.

The borrowing library is responsible for any loss or damage of material loaned to it, from the time of its despatch by the supplying library to its return there. However, supplying libraries should take the precaution of insuring any particularly valuable items before despatching them.

## Payment

Where the number of requests is low or the number of items supplied between libraries is roughly in balance (that is, where accounting costs would be higher than the charges levied), then inter-library payments should be waived. However, large net lenders may justifiably charge for providing interlending services. Payment procedures should be simple and efficient, for example by using flat-rate charges or by batch invoicing. Supplying libraries should make information on their payment procedures and current charges readily available to requesting libraries.

Charges made by supplying libraries should not normally be passed on by borrowing libraries to individual users, although a small standard charge may be made so as to deter frivolous requests.

## Statistics

All libraries should keep records of the number of requests sent to and received from other libraries, and the number satisfied in each case. Other basic statistics (which may be estimated by sample surveys if it is not possible to keep comprehensive figures) are the number satisfied by loan/photocopy/microform and where possible, estimates of the speed of supply. Where a national body exists to co-ordinate interlending statistics,* libraries should forward their statistics to it annually.

---

*The IFLA Section on Interlending has drawn up standard questionnaires for the collection of national lending statistics. Copies are available from the IFLA Office for International Lending, c/o British Library Lending Division, Boston Spa, Wetherby, West Yorkshire LS23 7BQ United Kingdom.

# Appendix B

## Sample Interlibrary Loan Agreements

### Reciprocal Borrowing Agreement

(Provided by Mississippi State University, Mitchell Memorial Library)

Dear Librarian,

We are interested in establishing a reciprocal borrowing agreement with your institution. If you are able to participate in such an arrangement, please indicate what areas can be reciprocal. We are willing to give all of our services free of charge.

Lend books at no cost _____
Supply photocopies at no cost_____

Thank you.

Sincerely,


Martha Irby
ILL Librarian


_____
Signature of agreement


_____
Institution


_____
OCLC symbol

### State Library Telefacsimile Network Agreement

# Arkansas State Library
One Capitol Mall • Little Rock, Arkansas 72201-1081

Office of Library Services and Development
Library Network Services                                      (501) 682-6052

*Letter of Agreement*
*Arkansas Telefacsimile Libraries' Protocols*

As a participating member of the Arkansas Telefacsimile Libraries Network, the

---

**Name of Library**

---

agrees to abide by the telefacsimile protocols approved by a majority vote of the network member libraries.

The participant agrees it shall abide by the telefacsimile protocols established by the network members until the participant notifies the Arkansas State Library that it no longer wishes to be part of the network.

---

| **Library Director** | Date |

---

| **Telefacsimile Supervisor** | Date |

# Arkansas State Library

One Capitol Mall • Little Rock, Arkansas 72201-1081

Office of Library Services and Development
Library Network Services                                    (501) 682-6052

### *Arkansas Telefacsimile Libraries' Protocols*

## PARTICIPATION IN TELEFACSIMILE NETWORK

It is expected that libraries which received LSCA subgrants to purchase telefacsimile equipment will automatically participate. Other Arkansas telefacsimile libraries are invited to be participating members of the network.

## ACCESS

Libraries should use established interlibrary loan channels before referring a request beyond local and regional resources.

## WHAT MAY BE REQUESTED

Requests for monographs and journal articles as well as subject requests may be submitted via FAX.

## LIMITS ON REQUESTED MATERIALS

Information supplied via FAX should be limited to 20 pages or less, unless there is an exceptional need. Items exceeding this number of pages should be sent by traditional mail or courier service.

If a requested item is not available or exceeds the page limit, the lending library should notify the borrowing library by FAX, OCLC or phone that they are unable to fill the request or that materials are being sent by mail.

## REQUEST CATEGORIES

There are four types of requests—

URGENT requests are of an emergency nature, such as medical or legal requests.

RUSH requests are for information needed quickly. The need for a requested item will be the determination of the *borrowing library*.

ROUTINE requests are standard interlibrary loan requests transmitted via FAX.

NON-priority requests are standard interlibrary loan business with no time constraints, requested via FAX or through normal interlibrary loan channels.

Reasonable response times for the lending library to respond with either the requested information or a status report are as follows:

URGENT - 1 hour     RUSH - 4 hours     ROUTINE - within 24 hours

NON-PRIORITY - Use normal interlibrary loan procedures

When there is an URGENT request, the borrowing library should contact the potential lending library by phone to inform the lender that an URGENT request is being sent.

## FORMAT FOR REQUESTING MATERIALS

All types of requests, whether ILL or Reference, should be sent on a standard A.L.A. Interlibrary Loan form, using established guidelines. Print the following information clearly at the top of the form:

> FAX
> Type of request (i.e. Subject, ILL, etc.)
> Priority designation

Pertinent information for filling the request should be included on the form, such as the following:

> Time and date of request transmission
> Time frame of expected response
> Verification of sources already checked
> Telefax number of requesting library
> Name and phone number of contact person

Bibliographic information should include the following:

Periodicals: Periodicals: Periodical title, volume and date. Author and title of article and pagination. A copyright compliance statement must also be included.

Books: Author, title, and publication date as well as ISBN if possible.

Subject Request: Supply as much specific information as possible, with a list of sources already consulted.

## CHARGES FOR MATERIALS

Participating libraries are not expected to charge a fee for telefacsimile transmissions for Arkansas requests.

Recovery costs for non-library related fax service are at the discretion of the fax library. Public libraries may not profit from recovery costs. A maximum recovery cost of $1.00 per page is recommended.

## ARKANSAS INTERLIBRARY LOAN REQUEST / TELEFACSIMLE TRANSMISSION

All telefacsimile requests should be made under the guidelines of the Arkansas Telefacsimile Libraries' Protocols

**Request Category:** (circle one ) URGENT [1 hour]    RUSH [4 hrs.]    ROUTINE [24 hrs.]
NON-PRIORITY [normal ILL-Fax or Mail]    REGULAR [for schools-48 hrs.]

**Type of Request:** [ ] LOAN; will pay fee _____ [ ] PHOTOCOPY; Max. cost of_____
[ ]_____

| Request no.: | Date: | Need before: | Notes: |
|---|---|---|---|

Call no.    [Lending library name & address]

**A
Request
[Modified]**

Patron information:
Book author; OR, Serial title, volume, issue, date, pages; OR, Audiovisual title:

Book title, edition, imprint, series; OR, Article author, title          This edition only [ ]

Verified in; AND/OR, Cited in:
ISBN, ISSN, LC card, or other bibliographic number:

[Borrowing library name & address]

Request complies with                    Authorization:_____
[ ] 108 (g)(2) Guidelines (CCG)
[ ] other provisions of copyright law (CCL)    Telephone _____

| LENDING LIBRARY REPORT: Date _____ | BORROWING LIBRARY RECORD: | |
|---|---|---|
| Date shipped _____ Shipped via _____ | | Number of pages sent: |
| Insured for $_____ Charges $_____ | Date received _____ Date returned: _____ | |
| DUE _____ [ ] Return insured | | Additional Comments: |
| Packing Requirements _____ | Returned via _____ Insured for $_____ | |
| RESTRICTIONS:[ ] Library use only; | | |
| [ ] Copying not permitted [ ] No renewals | Payment provided $ _____ | |
| [ ]_____ | | |
| NOT SENT BECAUSE: [ ] In use [ ] Lacking | RENEWALS: | |
| [ ] Not owned [ ] At bindery [ ] Cost exceeds limit | | |
| [ ] Non-circulating [ ] Not found as cited | Date requested _____ | |
| [ ] Not on shelf [ ] Poor Condition [ ] Lost | | |
| [ ] Lacks copyright compliance [ ] On order | New due date _____ | |
| [ ] Vol/issue not yet available [ ] On reserve | | |
| [ ] In process [ ] Rerequest on | Renewal denied _____ | |
| [ ] Hold placed | | |
| [ ] Estimated Cost of: Loan $ _____ | | |
| Photocopy $ _____ Microfilm/fiche $ _____ | | |
| [ ] Prepayment required | | |

### Arkansas Telefacsimile Libraries' Protocols
### School Library Amendments (Draft)

The amendments to the *Protocols* listed below were developed by the school library members of the telefacsimile network. A second *Letter of Agreement* for the amendment has been signed by all school library members who joined the network prior to September 1992.

### ACCESS [added specifications]

School library facsimile members may send interlibrary loan and/or reference requests directly to other school library facsimile members without first contacting local or regional academic, public or specials library network members.

To help the other school library network members, school calendars from each participating school library will be distributed at the beginning of each school year.

### LIMITS ON REQUESTED MATERIAL [added specifications]

School library facsimile members understand the five (5) copies per title per year limitation cited in the *CONTU Guidelines on Photocopying under Interlibrary Loan Arrangements* to the U.S. Copyright Laws. Members have also agreed that no more than two (2) articles per day per school should be requested. At the end of the school year, interlibrary request and loan logs will be sent to the Coordinator of Library Network Services at the Arkansas State Library.

### REQUEST CATEGORIES [added specifications]

A fifth categories will be used for school library borrowing and lending.

REGULAR requests are for standard interlibrary loan requests that should be answered by fax (if possible).

REGULAR—WITHIN 48 HOURS

### FORMAT FOR REQUESTING MATERIALS [edited]

All types of requests, whether ILL or Reference, should be sent on a standard A.L.A. Interlibrary Loan form, *or the modified school library form*, using established guidelines....

# Agreement Between Library and Regional Network: AMIGOS

*AMIGOS Selective User Agreement (Sample)*

This Agreement is to record the understanding between the AMIGOS BIBLIO-GRAPHIC COUNCIL, INC. (AMIGOS) and _____ (Library) regarding the terms and conditions on which AMIGOS will provide products and services for the _____ [Group Access Capability (GAC)] [Group Access Capability/Union List (GAC/UL)] Group.

1.  Obligations of Library as an AMIGOS Selective User.

    1.1  The Library shall use the OCLC PRISM ILL service and related files in accordance with standards and guidelines promulgated by AMIGOS and OCLC. The Library shall not download or otherwise copy any bibliographic records from the OCLC System.

    1.2  The Library shall observe the terms and conditions of licensing and other agreements required by OCLC for the use of specific products, services, and equipment obtained by the Library through purchase, loan, or lease.

    1.3  Neither the execution of this Agreement nor the Library's purchase from AMIGOS of OCLC equipment shall bestow upon the Library membership in AMIGOS or any of the rights and privileges of membership in AMIGOS.

    1.4  Upon receipt of a properly executed invoice, the Library shall pay for services rendered and products or equipment delivered. Invoices may originate from the Group Administrative Agent or from the AMIGOS office. Failure to pay within 120 days may result in suspension of all services.

2.  Services.

    2.1  AMIGOS shall provide the Library access to the OCLC Online System solely for the use of the OCLC PRISM ILL service. The terms and prices as defined in the attached *Schedule A: AMIGOS Fee Schedule* and any subsequent versions are hereby made a part of this Agreement.

    [2.2  When serving as the Group Training and Support Coordinator, AMIGOS shall provide to the Library information, training, and documentation determined by AMIGOS to be necessary for correct and efficient use of the OCLC PRISM ILL service and related files.]

[2.3 When serving as the Group Training and Support Coordinator, the Group Administrative Coordinator shall provide to the Library information, training, and documentation determined by AMIGOS to be necessary for correct and efficient use of the OCLC PRISM ILL service and related files.]

3. Warranties.

3.1 AMIGOS pledges that if for any justifiable cause it is unable to provide services, AMIGOS will return to the Library all funds received from the Library for the unused portion of the contracted services.

3.2 The Library agrees to indemnify and hold AMIGOS harmless from any claim arising out of a dispute that rights of anyone are violated or infringed upon by the Library's use of services and products provided under this Agreement.

3.3 THE PARTIES AGREE THAT THE GOODS OR SERVICES PURCHASED THROUGH AMIGOS INCLUDE ONLY SUCH WARRANTIES OF TITLE AND AGAINST INFRINGEMENT THAT AMIGOS MAY RECEIVE, AND MAY LAWFULLY ASSIGN TO LIBRARY, FROM THOSE ENTITIES WHICH SUPPLY PRODUCTS, DATA, OR INFORMATION TO AMIGOS. AMIGOS ITSELF MAKES NO WARRANTIES OF TITLE OR AGAINST INFRINGEMENT. AMIGOS MAKES NO WARRANTY, EXPRESS OR IMPLIED, INCLUDING ANY WARRANTY WITH REGARD TO THE FITNESS FOR A PARTICULAR PURPOSE OR MERCHANTABILITY OF ANY SERVICE OR PRODUCT PROVIDED PURSUANT TO THIS AGREEMENT.

4. Termination of Services.

4.1 This Agreement may be terminated on 90 day written notice by either party. The agreement may also be terminated by the Library with a 30 day written notice after receipt of an AMIGOS price adjustment.

4.2 If a governmental body is appropriating funds for the Library and does not allocate funds needed to make payments beyond the Library's then current fiscal period, the Library may terminate the Agreement on 30 day written notice by citing the appropriation change.

4.3 Following 30 day written notification that the Library has failed to observe contractual obligations as specified in Paragraphs 1.1-1.4, AMIGOS may suspend services for the period in which the Library is in violation. Upon review of the Library violation of said contractual obligations, the AMIGOS Board of

Trustees may terminate Library services immediately, notwithstanding Paragraph 4.1.

4.4 Suspension of services or termination of this Agreement shall not relieve the Library of the obligation to pay fees, assessments, or other charges, if any, theretofore accrued and unpaid.

5. Other.

5.1 This Agreement shall take effect upon the latest date of execution by duly authorized representative of AMIGOS and Library. The Agreement shall e automatically renewed each July, following receipt and acceptance of the AMIGOS *Schedule A: AMIGOS Fee Schedule* revision, subject to termination provisions of Section 4.

5.2 This Agreement shall be governed by, subject to, and construed in accordance with the laws of the State of Texas.

CONCURRENCE:

_____          _____

For (Library)                                    Sharon E. Johnson
                                                       For AMIGOS Bibliographic
                                                       Council, Inc.

                                                       Director of Business Services


_____          _____

Title                                              Title


_____          _____

Date                                              Date

# State Multitype Interlibrary Loan Network Agreement

## *Letter of Agreement*
## *Iowa Interlibrary Loan Program*

To encourage and support multitype resource sharing through interlibrary loan, the State Library of Iowa is offering a net lender reimbursement program to Iowa libraries.

The _____ Library agrees to participate in the Iowa Interlibrary Loan Program from October 1, 1989, through June 30, 1990, in accord with the guidelines listed below. The State Library of Iowa agrees to provide net lender compensation to the participating libraries in accord with the terms of the guidelines below.

## GUIDELINES

1. This program is based on reciprocity, the *sharing* of resources. Each participating library must be willing to lend materials to other Iowa libraries. To facilitate this, each library must contribute MARC records of its holdings to the state database, the Iowa Locator.

2. Reimbursement will be for the number of *net* lending transactions, that is, the total number of items loaned to other Iowa libraries during the period of this agreement *less* the total number of items received from other Iowa libraries.

3. The lending library will assess no interlibrary loan charge for either the borrowing library or the end user. Prohibited interlibrary loan charges (assessed by either the lending library or the borrowing library) would include service charges, use charges, telecommunications charges, postage, etc. However, charges for damaged or lost materials are not consider interlibrary loan charges.

4. The lending library will follow its own policy regarding the charge to the borrowing library for lost or damaged materials. The borrowing library, in accord with its own policy, will collect this amount from the responsible patron. The State Library will not provide reimbursement for materials lost or damaged through interlibrary loan.

5. Only items loaned to *Iowa libraries* are eligible for this reimbursement program. Eligible libraries are public libraries (including the State Library), college and university libraries, community college and area school libraries, elementary and secondary school media centers, and AEA media centers. Only items borrowed from Iowa libraries are counted in the calculation of the net lending total.

6. During this initial year, special libraries are not eligible to participate in this program. This means that items loaned to special libraries (business libraries, hospital libraries, law libraries, governmental agency libraries, etc.) cannot be included in the calculation of a net lending total.

7. Any type of library material can be included in the count of interlibrary loan transactions (books, periodicals, photocopies of library materials sent by mail, copies of library materials sent by telefax, audio tapes, video tapes, films, etc.). A copy of an article or a copy of a number of pages from one book would be counted as one interlibrary loan transaction. Each lending library will follow its own policies regarding the lending of nonprint materials and noncirculating materials.

8. Requests for interlibrary loans can be placed in any convenient manner acceptable to the lending library (ICAN, OCLC, other electronic mail programs, fax, telephone calls, mail, etc.). Lending libraries will count all lending transactions equally regardless of how they received the request. When sending requests, libraries will follow the appropriate, existing protocol for ICAN, OCLC, the Regional Libraries, or any other special agreement.

9. Requesting libraries may send interlibrary loan requests via fax but will request only materials from known locations (e.g., periodicals included in a union list of serials). If there are several known locations, the following protocol will be observed:

a) Send request first to the known library location in same community.

b) Send request to library of same type (e.g., public library to public library) considering:

  1) Geographic proximity (normally closest library first)

  2) Size of library (normally smallest library first in order to distribute the lending responsibility).

c) Send request to other types of libraries, again considering geographic proximity and size of library.

10. The State Library's reimbursement of net lending must be used to *supplement*, not *replace* local funding support, or the library will not be eligible for net lending reimbursement. This applies to all types of libraries participating in the agreement.

11. The State Library's reimbursement of net lending will not replace state funds distributed through the Iowa Regional Library System. The public libraries that are regional resource centers (including the distributed resource center libraries in the Central Region) are not eligible for this program.

12. AEA Media Centers already are funded to provide service to schools. Thus, an AEA media center's total number of items loaned cannot include items sent to teachers or to school media centers. Items that an AEA media center sends to public libraries or academic libraries are eligible for net lender reimbursement.

13. Participating libraries will report monthly statistics and make claims for payment in accord with directions and deadlines established by the State Library. Lending libraries will send to the State Library verification of loans (e.g., copies of ALA request forms). The detailed statistics available through the ICAN and OCLC programs are sufficient verification for these transactions.

14. When the State Library receives the final statistics for the period of time covered by this agreement, the total funds available for this program will be divided by the total number of net lending transactions to determine the precise rate of reimbursement. Thus, please note that reimbursement will occur after July 1, 1990.


_____Library          State Library of Iowa


_____Federal ID
                Employer Number


_____Signature

_____
_____Title            Shirley George,
                                                 State Librarian of Iowa

# Appendix C
## Interlibrary Loan Job Descriptions

The following are actual interlibrary loan job descriptions from universities, public libraries, and specialized organizations. They encompass all levels of interlibrary loan, from the interlibrary loan librarian to the librarian assistant, and from the professional to the paraprofessional. Because these are real job descriptions, readers should be aware that they are specific to the organization of origin and not generally representative of all positions carrying that same title.

### Professional: University Library

*Mississippi State University*
*Mitchell Memorial Library*
*Public Services*

**Job Title:** Interlibrary Loan Librarian

**Job Description:**

General Description: Interlibrary loans are transactions in which material is loaned by one library to another library for the use of an individual borrower. Interlibrary loan service supplements the library's resources by making available, through direct loans for a short period of time, materials located in other libraries. Interlibrary loan is available to anyone on campus.

Duties/Responsibilities: The duties and responsibilities of the Interlibrary Loan Librarian are to work effectively with campus patrons to verify, locate, and obtain the material these patrons need. This office also checks, gathers, and either lends or photocopies any type of library materials needed for the purpose of research for any patron.

#### I. Administrative
Train, supervise, and coordinate interlibrary loan students. Keep up to date in the field by reading professional journals. Organize and coordinate all aspects of the interlibrary loan services.

#### II. Reference
Provide assistance to patrons needing help in locating correct references. Provide assistance to patrons away from the campus who have no library experience. Be able to use ULS, NST, and other tools. Be able to use indexes such as *Biological Abstracts, Engineering Index*, and so on. Provide general reference services on any floor. Be familiar with reference tools in all reference areas.

223

### III. Instruction

Be able to use the CRT terminal. Train and supervise students in the use of the CRT. Keep complete and accurate records of the transactions sent through the OCLC system. Be able to use the CLSI terminal. Train and supervise students in the use of the CLSI terminal. Train and supervise students in CLCAT and CIRCONLINE. Be able to use the Xerox fax machine. Keep complete and accurate records of transactions sent and received on the fax machine.

### IV. Miscellaneous/Other

Keep records of invoices sent and received, carefully sending the money collected to the circulation department for deposit. Provide service to the agricultural researchers in the state. Send monthly bill to the regional library. Keep complete and accurate records of these requests. Help cover the schedule for public services. Help with seminars, tours, and orientations concerning interlibrary loan. Provide general service to anyone needing assistance.

## Professional: Public Library

### *Jefferson County Public Library*
### *Lakewood, Colorado*

**Job Title:** Head, Circulation/Reciprocal Services

Purpose: The incumbent performs professional work in managing circulation services and interlibrary loan services.

Essential Duties/Responsibilities (Listed in Descending Order of Importance):

1. Directs and coordinates the circulation and reserve system, including investigating and solving problems with the system and patrons, writing updates, and explanation of changes in system procedures and acting as the resource person to branch personnel; acts as the final resource to resolve patron complaints and problems.

2. Supervises operation of Central Overdues department, including assuring effective communication with patrons in resolving problems, analyzing procedures and initiating changes for improvement.

3. Supervises centralized Interlibrary Loan department.

4. Plans, coordinates, and conducts appropriate circulation, on-line catalog and reserves system training for new and substitute employees.

5. Acts as a liaison with Technical Services to identify and solve circulation and reserve problems. Participates in committee work with outside groups relating to circulation and Interlibrary Loan issues.

6. Performs related work as required.

Supervision: Directly supervises clerical and professional staff. Works under the general supervision of associate director of Public Services.

Education: Master's degree in Library Science

Certification: None

Experience: Three years of professional library experience.

Desired Qualifications: Some experience with computerized databases and in supervision.

## Paraprofessional: University Library

*Floyd College, University System of Georgia*

**Job Title:** Library Assistant III/For Circulation

Nature of Work: This is specialized sub-professional and supervisory library work performed in a functional unit of a university system library.

Employees of this class apply a knowledge of modern library methods and techniques in performance of varied library work and sub-professional library duties of considerable complexity, including use of on-line computer equipment. Work requires a familiarity with standard library organization and routines which may be gained through considerable experience in library work or through special training in library science. Employee exercises some discretion and judgment in performing, and in supervising lower-level assistants in performing routine sub-professional tasks, although advice and assistance are readily available from professional or paraprofessional personnel. Routine tasks, once learned, are ordinarily performed without direct supervision. Work may be subject to periodic checks but is primarily reviewed through conferences and observation of results.

Illustrative Examples of Work: Supervises a complex public service function, such as a circulation desk and reserve book section. Trains, assigns, and supervises student assistants. Operates computer terminal for on-line catalog and patron databases. Creates records in database for reserve items if necessary. Edits existing item records for reserve status and barcode. Enters and edits patron records. Assists readers in making effective use of library facilities. Performs routine reference functions. Performs library orientation sessions as requested. Supervises library routines at circulation desk, including preparation of cash deposits and maintenance of cash drawer. Maintains and assimilates library circulation desk, including preparation of cash deposits and maintenance of cash drawer. Maintains and assimilates library circulation statistics. Checks materials in and out at circulation desk. Is responsible for overall maintenance of circulation files. Supervises shelving of returned materials. Supervises maintenance of stack order and neatness. Prepares and sends out overdue notices for materials not returned on time. Sends out fine due notices when a charge is owed. Prepares and sends to admissions and records office an updated holds list of students delinquent with books or fines. Sends clearances for students who have cleared their delinquency records. Processes materials going on course reserve and coming off course reserve. At the end of each academic year compiles list of items long overdue, sends list to appropriate faculty, determines replacement costs. Serves as library's telephone receptionist in absence of secretary. Sends out notices for personal reserve.

Desirable Knowledge, Abilities, and Skills: Knowledge of the principles, methods, and materials of library science in relation to circulation, bibliography, reference, and library computer facilities. Some knowledge of one or more foreign languages. Ability to perform varied library work with speed and accuracy. Ability to establish and maintain effective working relationships with library patrons, faculty members, and subordinate employees. Ability to deal tactfully and courteously with others. Ability to use a typewriter, audio-visual equipment, microfilm equipment, copy machines, and peripheral devices used by computer-based library systems.

## *The American University, Washington, D.C.*

**Classification Title:** Reference Assistant

**Functional Title:** ILL (borrower)

**Department:** Reference

**Reports To (Title):** Head of Reference

**Position Summary:** Provide interlibrary loan assistance to the university community, the Washington Research Library Consortium (WRLC), and other libraries. Maintain accurate records of all interlibrary loan transactions. Assist with other reference activities and projects.

**Principal Duties and Responsibilities:**

Borrow library materials for eligible members of the university community. Using the OCLC, ALADDIN, reference sources, and consortium loan systems; verify; locate; request; and return materials in accordance with library and WRLC standards. (50%)

Maintain accurate records of all interlibrary loan transactions. Summarize interlibrary loan statistics. Supervise student assistants. Accept and return payments for interlibrary loan transactions. (30%)

Maintain current awareness of all ILL computer systems and the lending process. Serve as reference receptionist. (10%)

Other duties as assigned. (10%)

**Titles of Positions Directly Supervised:** Shelving Assistants

**Number of Individual Positions:** 2 WkSt

**Total Number of Full-Time Equivalents:** 0.67

**Total Number of FTE Employees Directly Supervised:** 0.67

Describe the typical methods and level of communication used to perform the job. (Verbal, written, form letters, modification of form letters, etc.): Verbal and written. Responsible for providing accurate responses to questions concerning the reference department, interlibrary loan system, and the university library in general.

What type of decisions are made? What type of decisions must be referred to others before action may be taken? Decisions made within preestablished policies and procedures.

**Special Education/Experience or Other Requirements:**

**Minimum number of years/months experience required:** 1-2 years related experience in library environment.

**Minimum level of education required:** 2 years college.

**Knowledge of machines (word processor, computers, etc.) required:** PC, Mainframe

**Typing speed required:** _____

**Other Requirements:** Familiarity with WordPerfect, ALADDIN, CD-ROM, PAIS, OCLC, or the like.

## Paraprofessional: Public Library

### *Topeka Public Library*

**Job Title:** Interlibrary Loan Assistant

**Division/Unit:** Public Service-Adult Services

**Reports To:** Adult Services Unit Manager

**Purpose of Position:** To provide information and materials to the public in the most efficient manner possible, and to assist the interlibrary loan librarian.

**Responsibilities (General):** Fill in at other public service desks as needed. Plan displays of materials and/or assist with programming in the unit. Assist patrons in the use of CD-ROM products, indexes, and microfilms. Other duties as assigned.

**Responsibilities (Special):** Assists the interlibrary loan librarian with duties (provides the full range of interlibrary loan functions). Works at the reference desk, as needed.

**Educational Requirements:** College degree or previous experience with interlibrary loan.

**Preferred Skills/Experience:** Service-oriented attitude. Basic computer knowledge. Ability to work well with the public and fellow workers, and maintain a positive attitude about work. Previous experience in a public library.

# Paraprofessional: Special

*Montana Historical Society, Library and Archives Program*

**Job Title:** Library Technician II

**Department:** Department of Education-Montana Historical Society

**Division:** Library and Archives

**Section:** Library

**Job Description:** The Montana Historical Society Library is charged by statute with acquiring, preserving, organizing, and making accessible to the public published material in all formats pertinent to the study of the history of Montana, the surrounding region, and in selected subjects, the Trans-Mississippi West. The Library also provides reference support to other programs in the Society, participates in Society-wide projects, and assists researchers in use of materials. It is an official depository for state publications.

**Duties and Responsibilities:** This position is the ranking paraprofessional in the library, with primary responsibility for a variety of library tasks and quasi-professional duties in other tasks.

1. Performs descriptive cataloging of library materials in various formats, following standardized practices and entering into automated systems.

2. Acts as preservation librarian, identifying and evaluating library materials requiring preservation. Determines and performs in-house treatments using appropriate conservation materials and procedures. Arranges for and monitors quality of preservation microfilming and preservation photocopying with commercial firms. Determines and monitors types of binding and rebinding procedures used, including preparing/supervising materials for commercial bindery, answering public inquiries regarding preservation of library materials, and keeping statistics.

3. Acts as serials librarian, responsible for identifying and recommending appropriate new serials titles. Obtains complimentary or exchange arrangements where appropriate, performing or supervising check-in and application of classification, identifying and claiming lost or unsent issues, handling invoices, monitoring expenditures, corresponding with publishers and subscription service agents, and keeping statistics.

4. Acts as newspaper librarian, responsible for identifying new state newspapers and obtaining complimentary subscriptions, overseeing completion of microfilming of runs of Montana newspapers, including preparing/supervising preparation of newspapers for filming, reviewing film for quality, tabulating expenditures.

5. Acts as interlibrary loan librarian, responsible for reviewing and acting in timely fashion upon requests from other libraries, dealing with loaning and borrowing institutions by mail and phone, and keeping statistics.

6. Acts as assistant administrator for library microcomputer system, serving as principal back-up to technical services librarian, able to understand, operate, and train new staff in all software, to obtain proper assistance for software and hardware problems, and perform preliminary troubleshooting.

7. Assists in reference as necessary, including instructing of patrons in library policy, in use of library and archives catalogs, indexes, special files, and specialized equipment, retrieving material for patron use, answering inquiries that do not require extensive search or extensive personal knowledge of Montana history.

8. Assists technical services librarian as directed in management of library section and Library and Archives program administration records, devising setting up files, weeding, transferring inactive records, etc.

9. Performs clerical tasks such as reshelving materials, writing purchases orders, etc., as necessary.

10. Performs special projects within section as assigned by technical services librarian and/or within program as assigned by program manager.

**Supervision Exercised:** Library Clerk II

Nature of Supervision: Trains and exercises lead worker supervision over the library clerk in certain of that position's duties which are part of the larger overall tasks for which this position is responsible. Trains and supervises volunteers working on projects related to the position's tasks.

Equipment or Machinery Used: Microcomputer, electric typewriter, photocopy machine, microform reader/printers, microfiche reader, conservation equipment (bookpress, fume hood, pH meter, hygrothermograph, etc.).

Knowledge, Skills, and Abilities: Considerable knowledge of library theory and procedures, especially cataloging techniques, classification systems, loan procedures, and knowledge of and skill in basic book and paper preservation techniques. Ability to use and explain library tools and services, to supervise work of others, to deal courteously with the public and the staff, to communicate lucidly and politely in person and by mail with a variety of recipients, to follow general instructions, interpret procedures, and recommend improved procedures, to exercise independent judgment while distinguishing problems which should be called to the attention of the supervisor, to deal with computer system operations and use a word processing program.

Education and Experience: Graduation from a college or university with a Bachelor's degree in a general field, preferably but not limited to American history. Completion of formal, basic library courses or continuing education training in serials control, automation, cataloging, and conservation work. Three years of experience in library work, with at least one at the level of Library Technician II.

# Appendix D
## Interlibrary Loan Professional Library Annotated Bibliography

### Bibliographies

Allen, G. G., and K. Deubert. *Guide to the Availability of Theses II: Non-University Institutions*. New York: Saur, 1984.
Supplements *Guide to the Availability of Theses*. Contains entries from institutions around the world.

*British National Bibliography*. London: British Library, 1950-present.
A national bibliography based upon books deposited in the Copyright Receipt Office of the British Library.

*Chemical Abstracts Service Source Index (CASSI)*.
A part of the Chemical Abstracts Service Information System. Directs users to literature in the field of chemistry, biology, engineering and physical science. Entries include the International Standard Serial Number (ISSN) or International Standard Book Number (ISBN). Contains bibliographic data and library holdings information, as well as title abbreviations.

*Dissertation Abstracts International*. Ann Arbor, Mich.: University Microfilms, 1938.
Contains abstracts of American and European doctoral dissertations submitted by cooperating Universities. Microfilm copies of the dissertations may be purchased from University Microfilms.

Downs, Robert Bingham. *American Library Resources: A Bibliographic Guide*. Chicago: American Library Association, 1951.
Contains general descriptions of the holdings of several thousand libraries in a region or in a subject field.

Evans, Charles. *American Bibliography*. Chicago: The Author, 1903-1959.
Contains books, periodicals, and pamphlets printed in the United States from the beginning of printing (1639) through 1800.

International Federation of Library Associations and Institutions Staff, ed. *Guide to the Availability of Theses*. New York: Saur, 1985.
Provides availability, either through interlibrary loan or photocopying, of theses and dissertations for institutions all over the world.

*National Union Catalog*. Washington, D.C.: U.S. Library of Congress, 1948.
Though discontinued, the catalog provides excellent bibliographical and location data for older publications. It is a record of publications held by the Library of Congress and 1,100 other libraries.

*National Union Catalog, Pre-1956 Imprints*. London: Mansell, 1968-1980.
Supersedes the basic Library of Congress *Catalog of Books* and supplements. Contains holdings of the major research libraries of the United States and Canada.

*NUC: Audiovisual Material*. Washington, D.C.: U.S. Library of Congress, 1983.
Similar in arrangement to *NUC: Books*.

*NUC: Books*. Washington, D.C.: U.S. Library of Congress, 1983.
A microfiche version of the *National Union Catalog*. The index entries contain sufficient information for bibliographic verification. They include publisher, date, and LC class number.

*NUC: Cartographic Materials*. Washington, D.C.: U.S. Library of Congress, 1983-present.
Similar to arrangement to *NUC: Books*.

*Online Business Sourcebook*. United Kingdom: Headland Press, 1991.
Describes and evaluates business databases of all types. The primary focus is on the United Kingdom and Europe, although some American material is included. Organized by business topic and by country.

Sabin, Joseph. *Bibliotheca Americana: A Dictionary of Books Relating to America, from Its Discovery to the Present Time*. New York: Bibliographical Society of America, 1928-1936.
Full bibliographic information is given, including in many cases holding libraries.

Shaw, Ralph Robert, and Richard H. Shoemaker. *American Bibliography: A Preliminary Checklist for 1801-1819*. New York: Scarecrow Press, 1958-1966.
Designed to fill the gap between the Evans's *American Bibliography* and Roorbach's *Bibliotheca Americana*.

Shoemaker, Richard H. *Checklist of American Imprints for 1820-1929*. Metuchen, N.J.: Scarecrow Press, 1964-1971.
Gives complete information on titles listed, including location of copies.

U.S. Library of Congress. *A Catalog of Books Represented by Library of Congress Printed Cards, Issued to July 31, 1942*. Ann Arbor, Mich.: Edwards, 1948.
A verification tool for early American imprints.

Winchell, Constance Mabel. *Locating Books for Interlibrary Loan, with a Bibliography of Printed Aids Which Show Location of Books in American Libraries.* New York: Wilson, 1930.

Part 1 contains a discussion of standards and reference methods to be followed in locating books to be borrowed. Part 2 contains approximately 800 printed works indicating location of books in American Libraries.

## Catalogs and Collections

Ash, Lee, and William G. Miller, comps. *Subject Collections.* 7th ed. New York: Bowker, 1993.

A guide to special collections and subject emphases as reported by libraries and museums in the United States and Canada.

*Books in English.* London: Blaise Com Service, 1970- .

A bimonthly list of English language books cataloged by the Library of Congress for the British Library. In scope, it is similar to the *Cumulative Book Index.* It is produced by the British Library from combined MARC and UKMARC databases.

British Museum. Department of Printed Books. *General Catalogue of Printed Books.* London: Trustees, 1959-1966.

Contains a complete record of the printed books in the British Library from the fifteenth century in all languages except oriental.

Paris. Bibliotheque Nationale. *Catalogue General Des Livres Imprimes: Auteurs.* Paris: Imprimerie Nationale, 1900-1981.

In addition to comprehensive coverage of French publications, the catalog is strong in other Romance-language and classical materials.

## Directories

*Action for Libraries.* Denver, Colo.: Bibliographical Center for Research, 1975- .

Lists fax numbers of libraries in the Rocky Mountain region of the United States.

Barwick, Margaret M., comp. and ed. *A Guide to Centres of International Lending and Copying.* 4th ed. Boston Spa: British Library, 1990.

Includes a brief summary of the interlending systems in each country. Contains restrictions, charges, loan periods, and so on.

Canada. National Library, comp. *Interlibrary Loan Directory*, 5th ed. Ottawa: Canadian Library Association, 1989- .

Information given for each library includes name and address, messaging and delivery services, and interlibrary loan policy information. Also includes UTLAS library codes.

*Directory of FAX Numbers in New England Libraries.* Newton, Mass.: NELINET, 1990.

Lists the fax numbers of libraries in the New England region of the United States.

*The Directory of Telefacsimile Sites in North American Libraries.* 6th ed. Bethlehem, Pa.: CBR Consulting Services, 1991.

The title indicates coverage.

Morris, Leslie R., and Sandra C. Morris. *Interlibrary Loan Policies Directory.* 4th ed. New York: Neal-Schuman, 1991.

Provides interlibrary lending policies of more than 800 U.S. libraries arranged by state and then by library name. Also contains an index of library names. Includes information on loans and photocopying of books, periodicals, microforms, government publications, dissertations and theses, audiovisual materials, and computer software.

*The Official Facsimile Users Directory.* 2d ed. New York: FDP Associations, 1987.

Contains listings for non-library organizations such as businesses, associations, and government organizations. Published semiannually.

## Government Publications

U.S. Superintendent of Documents. *Monthly Catalog of United States Government Publications.* Washington, D.C.: Government Printing Office, 1985-present.
A bibliography of publications issued by all branches of the government.

## Handbooks

Boucher, Virginia. *Interlibrary Loan Practices Handbook.* Chicago: American Library Association, 1984.

Describes the procedures mentioned in interlibrary loan codes so they may be followed by inexperienced personnel. Updates the *Interlibrary Loan Procedures Manual* by S. K. Thomson published in 1970.

Canadian Library Association. Information Services Section. *Interlibrary Loan Procedures Manual*. Ottowa: The Association, 1971.
Describes the standard procedures for completion of an interlibrary loan transaction.

Cornish, Graham P. *Model Handbook for Interlending and Copying*. Boston Spa: IFLA, 1988.
Outlines the steps necessary for completion of an interlibrary loan transaction, emphasizing decisions that must be made at each step. It also includes the 1987 revision of the international interlibrary loan code "International Lending: Principles and Guidelines for Procedure."

Fishman, Daniel, and Elliot King. *The Book of Fax: An Impartial Guide to Buying and Using Facsimile Machines*. 2d ed. Chapel Hill, N.C.: Ventana Press, 1990.
Discusses features of the equipment and management of the technology. Also contains information on linking fax with personal computers.

Futas, Elizabeth. *The Library Forms Illustrated Handbook*. New York: Neal-Schuman, 1984.
Expert Commentary offers guidance on form design and use.

*International Loan Services and Union Catalogues*. 2d ed. Edited by Valentin Wehefritz. Frankfurt am Main: Klostermann, 1980.
Issued under the guidance of IFLA, the manual updates the earlier edition and reprints the rules for international lending adopted by IFLA in 1978.

Miller, Jerome. *Applying the New Copyright Law: A Guide for Educators and Librarians*. Chicago: American Library Association, 1979.
Contains clear and concise information on the copyright issue.

U.S. Library of Congress. Copyright Office. *Highlights of the U.S. Adherence to the Berne Convention*. Washington, D.C.: U.S. Library of Congress, 1989 (Circular no. 93).
Summarizes the changes brought about in U.S. copyright laws when the United States became a member of the Berne Convention for the Protection of Literary and Artistic works (March 1, 1989).

## Periodicals and Serials

Association of Research Libraries. Office of Scientific and Academic Publishers. *Directory of Electronic Journals, Newsletters, and Scholarly Discussions Lists*. Ann Okerson, ed. Washington, D.C.: The Association, 1991.
Includes more than 30 journals, 1,000 scholarly lists, and 60 newsletters in paperback book form or in electronic text. The book contains instructions to gain access to the resources available through BITNET and Internet.

Bjorner, Susan, ed. *Newspapers Online*. Needham Heights, Mass.: BiblioData, 1992.
A directory of more than 125 regional and national daily newspapers published in North America and available in fuel text on-line. Contains a newsmakers section and index and a geographic index to get the searcher to the appropriate newspaper.

Brigham, Clarence S. *History and Bibliography of American Newspaper, 1690-1820*. Worcester, Mass.: American Antiquarian Society, 1947.
Arranged alphabetically by state and town, it lists and gives historical notes for 2,120 newspapers, indicating location of files.

*Directory of Periodicals Online*. Toronto: Infor Globe, 1989.
Lists periodicals, journals, newspapers and newsletters that are indexed, abstracted, or available in full text in primarily English-language commercial on-line databases worldwide.

*Fulltext Sources Online*. Edited by Ruth M. Orenstein. Neekham Heights, Mass.: BiblioData, 1992.
Directory listing more than 3,000 journals, magazines, newspapers, newsletters, and newswires found in full text on-line. Includes names of databases, dates of coverage, lag times, and the degree of coverage. Contains a geographic index and a subject index.

*Gale Directory of Publications and Broadcast Media*. Detroit: Gale Research, 1993.
Published annually to provide ready access in a geographic arrangement to basic information about newspapers, magazines, journals, and other U.S. and Canadian publications.

*Gale International Directory of Publications*. Detroit: Gale Research, 1988.
A companion volume to the *Gale Directory of Publications*, it provides international, country-by-country, coverage of thousands of newspapers, magazines, journals, and other periodicals published in more than 100 countries.

Gregory, Winifred, ed. *American Newspapers, 1821-1936: A Union List of Files Available in the United States and Canada*. New York: Wilson, 1937.
Lists the exact holdings of newspapers in libraries, courthouses, newspaper offices, and private collections.

*New Serial Titles*. Washington, D.C.: U.S. Library of Congress, 1953.
A union list of serials held by libraries in the United States and Canada. A continuation of the *Union List of Serials*.

*Serial Sources for the BIOSIS Data Base.* Philadelphia: BIOSIS. Published annually.
Published annually for the identification of serials contributing to *Biological Abstracts, Biological Abstracts/RRM (Reports, Reviews, Meetings).* In addition to the traditional journal literature of biology, periodically published conferences, congresses and symposia, and review annuals, it includes title abbreviations, title changes, and suspended titles. It is not a location tool.

*Ulrich's International Periodicals Directory.* New York: Bowker, 1993.
A classified guide to current domestic and foreign periodicals. Contains complete bibliographical information, including ISSN for easier searching.

*Union List of Serials in Libraries of the United States and Canada.* New York: Wilson, 1965.
Used as a location tool for hundreds of American and Canadian libraries.

*United States Newspaper Program (USNP) National Union List.* 3d ed. Dublin, Ohio: OCLC, 1989.
This microfiche-based reference tool contains locations for thousands of U.S. newspaper titles published during the last three centuries.

U.S. Library of Congress. Catalog Publication Division. *Newspapers in Microform: United States, 1948-1983.* Washington, D.C.: Library of Congress, 1984.
Lists titles reported by libraries and commercial firms. Arranged by state and city with a title index. Historical notes are also given.

U.S. Library of Congress. Periodical Division. *Check List of American 18th Century Newspapers in the Library of Congress.* Washington, D.C.: Government Printing Office, 1936.
Arranged by state and town. For each newspaper, it gives historical notes and Library of Congress files.

Wynar, Lubomyr Roman, and Anna T. Wynar. *Newspapers and Periodicals in the United States.* 2d ed. Littleton, Colo.: Libraries Unlimited, 1976.
Arranged alphabetically under ethnic press. A location tool for English and foreign language publications.

# Bibliography

Abramson, Elliott M. "How Much Copying Under Copyright? Contradictions, Paradoxes, Inconsistencies." *Temple Law Review* 61 (1988):133-96.

"ACRL Survey Identifies Five Major Problems." *American Libraries* 22 (January 1991):108.

Adams, Roy. *Communication and Delivery Systems for Librarians.* Brookfield, Vt.: Gower, 1990.

Alabama Public Library Service. *ALIN Manual: The Alabama Public Library Service Interlibrary Loan Manual,* 2d ed. Montgomery: Alabama Public Library Service, 1990. (ERIC Document 325 133)

Alaska State Department of Education. Division of State Libraries. *Interlibrary Loan, the Key to Resource Sharing: A Manual of Procedures and Protocols.* Juneau, Alaska: Division of State Libraries, 1989. (ERIC Document 311 935)

Anand, Havelin. "Interlibrary Loan and Document Delivery Using Telefacsimile Transmission: Part II, Telefacsimile Project." *The Electronic Library* 5 (April 1987):100-107.

Arkansas Library Association. "Interlibrary Loan Code for the State of Arkansas." *Arkansas Librarian* 23 (1976):23-26.

Arms, Caroline, ed. *Campus Strategies for Libraries and Electronic Information.* Burlington, Mass.: Digital Press, 1990.

Ashley, F. W. "Interlibrary Loan from the Viewpoint of the Lending Library." In *Selected Articles on Interlibrary Loans,* edited by James A. McMillan, 53-56. New York: Wilson, 1928.

Avram, Henrietta D. "Current Issues in Networking." *Journal of Academic Librarianship* 12 (September 1986):205-9.

———. "U.S. Library of Congress Networking Activities." *UNESCO Bulletin for Libraries* 32 (March-April 1978):71-80.

Bailey, Carl. "Photocopiers vs. Copyright: Round Two." *Wilson Library Bulletin* 57 (October 1982):144.

Baker, Shirley K. "The Efficacy of Interlibrary Loan: A Study of Response Time for Interlibrary Loans Submitted by Mail, TWX, and an Automated System." In *Options for the 80's: Proceedings of the Second National Conference of the Association of College and Research Libraries,* edited by Michael D. Kathman and Virgil F. Massman, 259-64. Greenwich, Conn.: JAI Press, 1982.

Barringer, Sallie H., and Paul Fresch. "Free Online Search Days and Interlibrary Loan." *College and Research Libraries News* 50 (February 1989):142-43.

Beck, R. J. "Interlibrary Loan Code for Idaho." *Idaho Librarian* 20 (July 1968):98-102.

Becker, Joseph, ed. *Proceedings of the Conference on Interlibrary Communications and Information Networks.* Chicago: ALA, 1971.

Belanger, David. "Interlibrary Loan Via Electronic Mail: Improving the Process." *Wilson Library Bulletin* 63 (March 1989):62-63.

Bell, J. A., and S. C. Speer. "Bibliographic Verification for Interlibrary Loan: Is It Necessary?" *College and Research Libraries* 49 (November 1988):494-500.

*Berne Convention for the Protection of Literary and Artistic Works.* 99th Congress, 2d Session, Senate Treaty Document. Washington, D.C.: United States Government Printing Office, 1986.

Berry, John. "Interlibrary Loan and the Network." *Library Journal* 103 (April 15, 1978):795.

Bishop, David. "The Open Systems Interconnection: An Introduction." *Resource Sharing and Information Networks* 7 (1991):5-14.

Bishop, William Warner. "Interlibrary Loans." In *The Library Without the Walls.* New York: Wilson, 1927.

Bjorner, Susan N. "Full-Text Document Delivery Online—It Makes Sense." *Online* 14 (September 1990):109-12.

Bobay, Julie, Ed Stockey, and Mary Pagliero Popp. "Library Services for Remote Users with Linkway." *Reference Services Review* 18 (1990):53-57.

Boss, Richard W., and Hal Espo. "The Use of Telefacsimile in Libraries." *Library Hi Tech* 5 (Spring 1987):33-42.

Boss, Richard W., and Judy McQueen. *Document Delivery in the United States: A Report to the Council on Library Resources by Information Systems Consultants, Inc.* Washington, D.C.: Council on Library Resources, 1983. (ERIC Document 244 626)

Boucher, Virginia. "Consultants for Interlibrary Loan." In *Information Brokers and Reference Services,* edited by Robin Kinder and Bill Katz, 233-38. New York: Haworth Press, 1988.

Bowker, Richard R. "Editorial." *Library Journal* 35 (March 1910):101.

Boyer, K. J. "Interlibrary Loans in College and University Libraries." *Library Quarterly* 2 (April 1932):113-34.

Brandfonbrener, Eric D. "Fair Use and University Photocopying: *Addison-Wesley Publishing Co. v. New York University.*" *Copyright Law Symposium* 36 (1989):33-84.

Britten, William A. "BITNET and the Internet: Scholarly Networks for Librarians." *College and Research Libraries News* 51 (February 1990):103-7.

Brown, Charles H. "Interlibrary Loans: An Unsolved Problem." *Library Journal* 57 (November 1932):887-89.

Budd, J. "Interlibrary Loan Service: A Study of Turnaround Time." *RQ* 26 (January 1986):75-80.

Busching, Jamie. "*Shaw v. Lindheim*: The Ninth Circuits' Attempt to Equalize the Odds in Copyright Infringement." *Loyola Entertainment Law Journal* 11 (1991):67-99.

Byers, T. J. "Fax Boards for Fast Times." *PC World* 8 (January 1990):118-29.

Canales, Herbert G., and Karen K. Nichols. "Purchases on Demand for the South Texas Library System." *Texas Libraries* 43 (Fall 1981):113-18.

Carlson, William. "Mobilization of Existing Library Resources." *Library Quarterly* 16 (October 1946):272-95.

Casorso, Tracy. "Research Materials: Now Only Keystrokes Away." *College and Research Libraries News* 53 (February 1992):128.

Chamberlin, Elizabeth G. "An Interlibrary Loan Form for Small Libraries." *Library Journal* 75 (December 1950):21-31.

Chang, Amy. "A Database Management System for Interlibrary Loan." *Information Technology and Libraries* 9 (June 1990):136.

Chepesiuk, Ron. "The Dawn of European Economic Unity: What It Means for Libraries." *American Libraries* 23 (March 1992):212-15.

Clark, Philip M. *Microcomputer Spreadsheet Models for Libraries*. Chicago: ALA, 1985.

Cline, Gloria S. "The High Price of Interlibrary Loan Service." *RQ* 27 (Fall 1987):80-86.

Colbert, Antoinette W. "Document Delivery." *Online* 11 (January 1987):121-22.

_____. "Document Delivery." *Online* 10 (May 1986):91.

Colson, John C. "International Interlibrary Loans Since World War II." *Library Journal* 32 (October 1962):259-69.

"Computer Notes." *Chronicle of Higher Education* 37 (July 10, 1991):A16.

Condit, Lester. "Bibliography in Its Prenatal Existence." *Library Quarterly* 7 (October 1937):567.

Copler, Judith A. "Researching Remote Users—Library Services Through a Systemwide Computing Network." In *The Off-Campus Library Services Conference Proceedings, Charleston, South Carolina, October 21-22, 1988*, edited by Barton M. Lessin, 79-85. Mount Pleasant, Mich.: Central Michigan University, 1988.

Corbin, John. *Find the Law in the Library: A Guide to Legal Research*. Chicago: ALA, 1989.

Corbin, Roberta A. "The Development of the National Research and Education Network." *Information Technology and Libraries* 10 (September 1991):212-20.

Cornish, Graham P. "Copyright Law and Document Supply: A Worldwide Review of Developments, 1986-1989." *Interlending and Document Supply: The Journal of the British Library Lending Division* 17 (October 1989):117-23.

Cornish, W. R. "Moral Rights Under the 1988 Act." *EIPR: European Intellectual Property Review* 11 (December 1989):449-53.

Cossar, Bruce. "Interlibrary Loan Costs." *RQ* 12 (Spring 1973):243-46.

Coyne, Randall. "Rights of Reproduction and the Provision of Library Services." *University of Arkansas at Little Rock Law Journal* 13 (Spring 1991):485-516.

Crews. Kenneth Donald. *Copyright Policies at American Research Universities: Balancing Information Needs and Legal Limits.* Los Angeles: University of California, 1990.

Currie, W. Scott. *LANs Explained: A Guide to Local Area Networks.* New York: Halsted Press, 1988.

David, Charles W. "Remarks upon Interlibrary Loans Mid-20th Century Style." *College and Research Libraries* 10 (October 1949):429-33.

Dean, Nita. "The New Jersey State Library Provides ILL Access." *OCLC Newsletter* (July-August 1987):13.

DeGennaro, Richard. "Copyright Resource Sharing and Hard Times: A View from the Field." *American Libraries* 8 (1977):430-35.

DeJohn, W. "Use of Electronic Mail for ILL." *Information Technology and Libraries* 1 (1982):48-51.

"DELCAT Goes Statewide." *Wilson Library Bulletin* 63 (April 1989):10.

"Detroit Urges Use of Teletypewriters." *Library Journal* 52 (August 1951):1190.

Dingle-Cliff, Susan, and Charles H. David. "Comparison of Recent Acquisitions and OCLC Find Rates for Three Canadian Special Libraries." *Journal of the American Society for Information Science* 32 (January 1981):65-69.

*Directory of Online Databases.* Santa Monica, Calif.: Cuadra Associates, 1979- .

"Discussion on Library Coordination." *ALA Bulletin* 3 (September 1909):156.

Dodson, Ann T., Paul P. Philbin, and Kunj B. Rastogi. "Electronic Interlibrary Loan in the OCLC Library: A Study of Its Effectiveness." *Special Libraries* 73 (January 1982):12-29.

Dougherty, Richard M. "The Evaluation of Campus Library Document Delivery Service." *College and Research Libraries* 34 (January 1973):29-39.

_____. "Research Libraries in an International Setting: Requirements for Expanded Resource Sharing." *College and Research Libraries* 46 (September 1985):383-89.

_____. "To Meet the Crisis in Journal Costs, Universities Must Reassert Their Role in Scholarly Publishing." *Chronicle of Higher Education* 33 (April 12, 1989):A52.

Downs, Robert B., ed. *Union Catalogs in the United States.* Chicago: ALA, 1942.

Drake, Miriam A. "From Crystal Ball to Electronic Library." *Online* 14 (January 1990):6-8.

Dratler, Jay. "To Copy or Not to Copy: The Educator's Dilemma." *Journal of Law and Education* 19 (Winter 1990):1-49.

Drott, M. C., and B. C. Griffith. "Interlibrary Loans: Impact of the New Copyright Law." *American Society for Information Science Journal* 29 (September 1978):259.

Duggan, Maryann. "Legal and Contractual Aspects of Interlibrary and Information Service Operations." In *Proceedings of the Conference on Interlibrary Communications and Information Networks*, edited by Joseph Becker, 219-22. Chicago: ALA, 1971.

Dunaway, Robert W., and Michael A. Dillon. "*B.V. Engineering v. University of California, Los Angeles*: A License to Steal?" *Santa Clara Computer and High-Technology Law Journal* 5 (1989):349-61.

Dutcher, Gale A. "DOCLINE: A National Automated Interlibrary Loan Request Routing and Referral System." *Information Technology and Libraries* 8 (December 1989):359-70.

Eaton, Nancy L., Linda Brew MacDonald, and Mara R. Saule. *CD-ROM and Other Optical Information Systems: Implementation Issues for Libraries.* Phoenix, Ariz.: Oryx Press, 1989.

Eichhorn, Sara. "The Making of MELDOC." *College and Research Libraries News* 51 (May 1990):441-43.

Emling, J. W., J. R. Harris, and H. J. McMains. "Library Communications." In *Libraries and Automation, Proceedings*, edited by Barbara Evans Markuson, 203-19. Washington, D.C.: United States Government Printing Office, 1964.

Ensign, David. "Copyright Considerations for Telefacsimile Transmission of Documents in Interlibrary Loan Transactions." *Law Library Journal* 81 (1989):805-12.

Evans, Janet. "Using dBase III to Create a Photocopy Invoicing System." *Library Software Review* 5 (September-October 1986):263-74.

Farr, Marianne, and Barry Brown. "Explosive ILL Growth at the University of Montana: A Case Study." *Journal of Interlibrary Loan and Information Supply* 2 (1991):41-54.

Flanders, Bruce. "Barbarians at the Gate." *American Libraries* 22 (July-August 1991):668-69.

_____. "Dedicated Line." *American Libraries* 23 (January 1992):90.

_____. "Dedicated Line." *American Libraries* 23 (February 1992):174.

_____. "Interlibrary Loan in Kansas: A Low Cost Alternative to OCLC." *Wilson Library Bulletin* 61 (March 1987):31-34.

_____. "NREN: The Big Issues Aren't Technical." *American Libraries* 22 (June 1991):572-74.

_____. "OCLC Telecom Network Complete." *American Libraries* 23 (March 1992):242.

*Florida Library Information Network Statistical Report, July 1991-June 1992 (FY 92)*. Tallahassee: State Library of Florida, 1992.

Gates, Jean Key. *Introduction to Librarianship*, 2d ed. New York: McGraw-Hill, 1976, 53-71.

Gaughan, Tom. "The Corporate Culture of OCLC." *American Libraries* 22 (October 1991):894-96.

Genaway, David C. "Microcomputers as Interfaces to Bibliographic Utilities (OCLC, RLIN, etc.)." *Online* 7 (May 1983):21-27.

Genaway, David C., and Edward B. Stanford. "Quasi-Departmental Libraries." *College and Research Libraries* 38 (May 1977):187-94.

Giaccai, Susanna. "FLAN: Virtual Inter-linking Using Floppy Disks as a Local Area Network." *Electronic Library* 7 (June 1989):160-62.

Gillikin, David P. "Document Delivery from Full-Text Online Files: A Pilot Project." *Online* 14 (May 1990):27-31.

Gillock, Oliver P., Jr., and Roger H. McDonough. "Spreading State Library Riches for Peanuts." *Wilson Library Bulletin* (December 1970): 354-57.

Givens, Beth. "Montana's Use of Microcomputers for Interlibrary Loan Communications." *Information Technology and Libraries* 1 (September 1982):260-64.

Goehlert, Robert. "Periodical Use in an Academic Library: A Study of Economists and Political Scientists." *Special Libraries* 69 (February 1978):51-60.

Goldhor, Herbert. "An Evaluation of the Illinois Interlibrary Loan Network (ILLINET)" *Illinois Libraries* 61 (1979):13-18.

Gorin, R. S., and R. A. Kanen. *Florida Library Information Network Project: A Comparative Study of OCLC, TWX, U.S. Mail and Closed-Circuit Teletype.* Tallahassee: Florida State University, 1981. (ERIC Document 211 076)

Gorin, Robert. "Special Report: OCLC Users Appraise ILL Subsystem." *Library Journal* 105 (April 1, 1980):767-69.

Gould, Charles H. "Coordination, or Method in Cooperation." *ALA Bulletin* 3 (September 1909):122-28.

_____. "Regional Libraries." *Library Journal* 33 (June 1908):218-19.

Gralnek, Gaelle Helene. "The Forest for the Trees: Why States Should Not Be Immune from Suit for Copyright Infringement." *Arizona State Law Journal* 20 (1988):821-39.

Gravit, Francis W. "A Proposed Interlibrary Loan System in the Seventeenth Century." *Library Quarterly* 16 (October 1946):331-34.

Grazier, Robert T. "Cooperation Among Libraries of Different Types." *Library Quarterly* 16 (October 1946): 331-42.

Green, Samual. "Address of the President of the American Library Association at the San Francisco Conference." *Library Journal* 16 (1891):C5-6.

_____. "Inter-library Loans in Reference Work." *Library Journal* 23 (1898):567-68.

_____. "The Lending of Books to One Another by Libraries." *Library Journal* 1 (September 1876):15-16.

Greene, Robert J. "LENDS: An Approach to the Centralization/Decentralization Dilemma." *College and Research Libraries* 36 (May 1975):201-7.

Hacker, Harold S. "Implementing Network Plans in New York State: Jurisdictional Considerations in the Design of Library Networks." In *Proceedings of the Conference on Interlibrary Communications and Information Networks*, edited by Joseph Becker, 223-47. Chicago: ALA, 1971.

Hamaker, Chuck. "Costs of Scientific Journals Increase at Double the Rate of Research Costs." *ARL: A Bimonthly Newsletter of Research Library Issues and Actions* 153 (November 7, 1990):1-2.

Harry, Ruth, and Harold Astvold. "Interlibrary Loan." *College and Research Libraries* 8 (April 1947):157-60.

_____. "Interlibrary Loan Service and National Research." *College and Research Libraries* 10 (April 1949):145-50.

Hessel, Alfred. *A History of Libraries.* Translated with supplementary material by Reuben Peiss. New Brunswick, N.J.: Scarecrow Press, 1955.

Hewitt, Joe A. "The Impact of OCLC." *American Libraries* 7 (May 1976):268-75.

Holske, Alan. "On Meeting Interlibrary Loan Costs." *College and Research Libraries* 7 (January 1946):74-77.

Hutchins, Margaret. *Introduction to Reference Work.* Chicago: ALA, 1944.

Imroth, B. "The Role of the School Library Media Program in a Multitype Library Network." Unpublished dissertation, University of Pittsburgh, 1980.

"Interlibrary Loan Code for Georgia Libraries, 1981." *Georgia Librarian* 18 (November-December 1981):16-17.

"Interlibrary Loan Code for the Libraries of Mississippi, a Draft." *Mississippi Libraries* 14 (Winter 1980):178-82.

"Interlibrary Loan Code for New Mexico and the Channels for Interlibrary Lending in New Mexico." *New Mexico Libraries* 2 (Spring 1969):21-30.

"Inter-library Loans." *Library Journal* 23 (February 1893):61.

"Inter-library Loans." *Library Journal* 23 (March 1898):104.

"Interlibrary Loan Guidelines: Results of a Study of Wisconsin Referral Patterns." *Wisconsin Library Bulletin* 76 (July-August 1980):147-52, 189.

"International Interlibrary Loan." *ALA Bulletin* 34 (February 1940):99-100.

"Intrasystem ILL Cost-Effective for Pasadena-Based Co-op System." *Library Journal* 108 (November 1, 1983):2002-4.

Jackson, Mary E. "Library to Library." *Wilson Library Bulletin* 63 (February 1989):78-79.

_____. "Library to Library." *Wilson Library Bulletin* 63 (October 1989):143.

_____. "Library to Library." *Wilson Library Bulletin* 65 (April 1991):84-87.

_____. "Library to Library." *Wilson Library Bulletin* 66 (April 1992):86-88.

Jennerich, Elaine Zaremba, and Edward J. Jennerich. *The Reference Interview as a Creative Art.* Littleton, Colo.: Libraries Unlimited, 1987.

Jewitt, Charles C. *Report of the Assistant Secretary in Charge of the Smithsonian Institution for the Year 1850.* Senate Miscellaneous Documents no. 1, 31st Cong., Special Session, March 1850, 28-41.

John Crerar Library. *1895-1944: An Historical Report Prepared Under the Authority of the Board of Directors by the Librarian* (J. Christian Bay, Librarian). Chicago: Board of Directors by the Librarian, 1945.

Kaser, David. "Whither Interlibrary Loan?" *College and Research Libraries* 33 (September 1972):398-402.

Katz, Ruth M. "Trends in the Development of State Networks." *Advances in Library Automation and Networking: A Research Annual* 1, edited by Joe A. Hewitt, 169-88. Greenwich, Conn.: JAI Press, 1987.

Katz, William A. *Introduction to Reference Work, V. II: Reference Services and Reference Processes*, 3d ed. New York: McGraw-Hill, 1978.

Kaya, B., and A. Hurlebaus. "Comparison of United Parcel Service and United States Postal Service Delivery Speed and Cost for Interlibrary Loan." *Bulletin of the Medical Library Association* 66 (1978):345-46.

Keder, Jan. "Using the Campus Network for Interlibrary Loan and Book Orders." *Library Software Review* 8 (September-October 1989):250-51.

Kelsey, Ann L., and John M. Cohn. "The Impact of Automation on Interlibrary Loan: One College Library's Experience." *The Journal of Academic Librarianship* 13 (July 1987):163-66.

Kemp, Deborah. "Preemption of State Law by Copyright Law." *Computer/Law Journal* 9 (1989):375-90.

Kennedy, S. "The Role of Commercial Document Delivery Services in Interlibrary Loan." *Interlending and Document Supply* 15 (1987):67-73.

Kenny, Brigitte L. "Network Services for Interlibrary Loan." In *Proceedings of the Conference on Interlibrary Communications and Information Networks*, edited by Joseph Becker, 121-31. Chicago: ALA, 1971.

Kilgour, Frederick G. "Objectives and Activities of the Ohio College Library Center." In *Indiana Seminar on Information Networks*, edited by Donald P. Hammer and Gary C. Lelvis, 34. West Lafayette, Ind.: Purdue University Libraries, 1972.

Kilpatrick, Thomas L., David A. Brossart, and Raymond G. Einig. "A Photocopy Invoicing Application Using R:Base for DOS." *Library Software Review* 8 (May-June 1989):143-47.

Kimbro, Ernestine. "Interlibrary Loan Funding: Some Recommendations." *PNLA Quarterly* 51 (1987):23.

Kleiner, Jane P. "The Louisiana Rapid Communication Network: A System for Improved Interlibrary Loan Service." *LLA Bulletin* 33 (1971):103-8.

Koopman, Karl H. "Thoughts on Interlibrary Loan." *College and Research Libraries* 8 (April 1947):157-60.

Kwan, Millie. "Monitoring 5-5 CONTU Compliance Using ILLFILE and dBase III." *OCLC Micro* 5 (June 1989):13-15.

LaGuardia, Cheryl, and Connie V. Dowell. "The Structure of Resource Sharing in Academic Research Libraries." *RQ* 30 (Spring 1991):370-76.

Lane, William C. "A Central Bureau of Information and Loan Collection for College Libraries." *Library Journal* 33 (November 1908):429-33.

Levin, Carol, and Jim Nolte. "ILLFILE, ILLSORT, and ILLCOUNT Automate OCLC ILL Record Keeping." *OCLC Micro* 4 (April 1988):9-11, 26.

"Liberal Interloan Code Adopted by AMIGOS." *Library Journal* 105 (November 1980):2256-57.

Lindberg, Dennis L. "Why Automation? Getting Information Technology Off-Campus." In *The Off-Campus Library Services Conference Proceedings, Reno, Nevada, October 23-24, 1986*, edited by B. M. Lessin, 194-99. Mount Pleasant, Mich.: Central Michigan University Press, 1986.

Line, Maurice B. "National Interlending Systems: Existing Systems and Possible Models." *Interlending Review* 7(2) (1979):42-46.

Linsley, Laurie S. "Academic Libraries in an Interlibrary Loan Network." *College and Research Libraries* 43 (1982):292-99.

Lipscomb, Jeane Otten. "The WLN Interlibrary Loan Subsystem: Progress Report." *PNLA Quarterly* 51 (1987):17-18.

Little, Arthur. *A Comparative Evaluation of Alternative Systems for the Provision of Access to Periodical Literature.* Washington, D.C.: National Commission on Libraries and Information Science, 1979.

Lyle, Guy R. *The Administration of the College Library.* Chicago: ALA, 1944.

_____. *The Administration of the College Library*, 3d ed. New York: Wilson, 1961.

_____. *The Administration of the College Library*, 4th ed. New York: Wilson, 1974.

Mack, James D. "Teletype Speeds Interlibrary Loans and References." *Library Journal* 83 (May 1, 1958):1325-29.

Magarrel, J. "Fees for Interlibrary Loans Spread: Scholars Fear Work Will Suffer." *Chronicle of Higher Education* 27 (October 19, 1983):1.

Markuson, Barbara E. "Issues in National Library Network Development: An Overview." In *Key Issues in the Networking Field Today, Proceedings of the Library of Congress Network Advisory Committee Meeting, May 6-8, 1985,* 9-32. Network Planning Paper no. 12. Washington, D.C.: Library of Congress, 1985.

Marshall, N. "Copyright—Major Challenges Ahead." *Wilson Library Bulletin* 57 (February 1983):481-84.

Marshall, Nancy H., and Ronald P. Naylar. "Interlibrary Loan Issues." *RQ* 17 (Fall 1977):59-64.

Martin, Susan K. *Library Networks, 1986-87: Libraries in Partnership.* White Plains, N.Y.: Knowledge Industry, 1986.

_____. "Library Networks: Trends and Issues." *Journal of Library Administration* 8(2) (Summer 1987):27-33.

_____. "Technology and Cooperation: The Behaviors of Networking." *Library Journal* 112 (1987):42-44.

McAninch, Sandra, Bradley D. Carrington, and Barbara S. Hale. "Online to the Nation's Library: Kentucky's Experience with the Library of Congress Information System." *Online* 14 (November 1990):70-74.

McCallum, Sally H. "The Linked Systems Project: Implications for Library Automation and Networking." In *Advances in Library Automation and Networking, A Research Annual,* edited by Joe A. Newitt, 1. Greenwich, Conn.: JAI Press, 1987.

_____. "Standards and Linked Online Information Systems." *LRTS* 34(3) (July 1990):360-66.

McDonald, D. D., and C. G. Bush. *Libraries, Publishers, and Photocopying: Final Report of Surveys Conducted for the United States Copyright Office.* Rockville, Md.: King Research, 1982.

McKirdy, Pamela Reeks. "Copyright Issues for Microcomputer Collections." In *The Library Microcomputer Environment: Management Issues,* edited by Sheila S. Intner and Jane Anne Hannigan, 96-123. Phoenix, Ariz.: Oryx Press, 1988.

McMillan, James A. *Selected Articles on Interlibrary Loans.* New York: Wilson, 1928.

Melinet, Carl H. *The Administration of Interlibrary Loans in American Libraries.* Syracuse, N.Y.: Syracuse University, 1949.

Memaguax, E. A. "Effectiveness of Automated Interlibrary Loan." In *Library Effectiveness: A State-of-the-Art,* 161-71. Chicago: ALA, 1980.

"MIDLNET Goes Interstate with ILL Program." *Library Journal* 106 (December 1, 1981):2274.

Miele, Anthony W. "The Illinois State Library Microfilm Automated Catalogs (IMAC)." In *Microforms and Library Catalogs: A Reader,* edited by Albert J. Diaz. Westport, Conn.: Microform Review, 1977.

Mika, Joseph J., and Bruce A. Shuman. "Legal Issues Affecting Libraries and Librarians." *American Libraries* 19 (February 1988):108-12.

Miller, Connie, and Patricia Tegler. "An Analysis of Interlibrary Loan and Commercial Document Supply Performance." *Library Quarterly* 58 (October 1988):352.

Miller, Jerome K. *Applying the New Copyright Law: A Guide for Educators and Librarians.* Chicago: ALA, 1979.

Miller, Ron. "Network Organization—A Case Study of the Five Associated University Libraries (FAUL)." In *Proceedings of the Conference on Interlibrary Communications and Information Networks,* edited by Joseph Becker, 266-76. Chicago: ALA, 1971.

Moore, Cathy. "Do-It-Yourself Automation: Interloan Bulletin Boards." *Library Journal* 112 (November 1, 1987):66-68.

Moran, Michael L. "Insuring Interlibrary Loans." *RQ* 22 (Summer 1982):395-99.

Naude, Gabriel. *Advice on Establishing a Library.* Los Angeles: University of California Press, 1950.

Nelson Associates. *Interlibrary Loan in New York State.* New York: Nelson, 1969.

"Netting E-Journals." *American Libraries* 22 (November 1991):980.

"New Rules for International Loan." *UNESCO Bulletin for Libraries* 14 (January 1955):5-6.

Nitecki, D. "Document Delivery and the Rise of the Automated Midwife." *Resource Sharing and Information Networks* 1 (1984):83-101.

Nitecki, Danuta A. "Interlibrary Services: A Report on a Study for Measuring User Awareness and Satisfaction." *Tennessee Librarian* 28 (Summer 1976):85-94.

_____. "Online Interlibrary Services: An Informal Comparison of Five Systems." *RQ* 21 (Fall 1981):7-14.

Norman, Ronald V. "The Texas State Library Communication Network Today." *Texas Libraries* 33 (1971):42-46.

Nyquist, Corinne. "Interlibrary Loan and the ALA/SRRT Guidelines." *Journal of Interlibrary Loan and Information Supply* 1 (1990):45-46.

Oakley, Madeline Cohen. "The New Copyright Law: Implications for Libraries." *Cornell University Libraries Bulletin* 202 (October-December 1976):5.

Okerson, Ann. "With Feathers: Effects of Copyright and Ownership on Scholarly Publishing." *College and Research Libraries* 52 (September 1991):425-38.

Oklahoma Library Association. "Interlibrary Loan Code for the State of Oklahoma." *Oklahoma Librarian* 26 (July 1976):19-21.

O'Leary, Mick. "Local Online: The Genie Is Out of the Bottle, Part 1." *Online* 14 (January 1990):15-18.

_____. "Local Online: The Genie Is Out of the Bottle, Part 2." *Online* 14 (March 1990):27-33.

"Online." *The Chronicle of Higher Education* 38 (September 4, 1991):A26.

"Online." *The Chronicle of Higher Education* 38 (October 16, 1991):A25.

Ononogbo, Raphael U. "Performing Interlibrary Loans with Libraries in South Africa." *Journal of Interlibrary Loan and Information Supply* 2 (1991):13-19.

Owens, Major R. "The State Government and Libraries." *Library Journal* 101 (January 1, 1976):22.

Palmer, Foster M. "Interlibrary Loan Form—A Five Year Report." *Library Journal* 81 (October 1956):2167-69.

Palmour, Vernon E., et al. *A Study of the Characteristics, Costs, and Magnitude of Interlibrary Loans in Academic Libraries.* Westport, Conn.: Greenwood Press, 1972.

Parker, Wyman W. "The Network Concept: CONVAL." *Connecticut Libraries* 12 (1970):11-12.

Penick, Patricia H. "Ownership of Copyright." In *Modern Copyright Fundamentals: Key Writings on Technological and Other Issues,* edited by Ben H. Weil and Barbara Friedman Polansky, 67-71. Medford, N.J.: Learned Information, 1989.

"Photocopying Stores Agree to Pay Publishers Nearly $1.9 Million to End Copyright Case." *Chronicle of Higher Education* 38 (October 23, 1991):A13-15.

Porterfield, Genevieve. "Staffing of Interlibrary Loan Service." *College and Research Libraries* 26 (July 1965):318-20.

Prentiss, S. Gilbert. "The Evolution of the Library System (New York)." *Library Quarterly* 39 (January 1969):78-89.

Prescott, Peter. "The Origins of Copyright: A Debunking View." *EIPR: European Intellectual Property Review* 11 (December 1989):453-56.

"Projet de Revision du Reglement du Pret International." *Libri* 4 (1954):167-70.

Regan, Muriel. "Library Consulting: Challenge, Autonomy, and Risk." In *Information Brokers and Reference Services*, edited by Robin Kinder and Bill Katz, 217-29. New York: Haworth Press, 1988.

Reintjes, J. Francis. "Application of Modern Technologies to Interlibrary Resource Sharing Networks." *Journal of the American Society for Information Science* 35 (January 1984):45-52.

Reser, David W., and Anita P. Schuneman. "The Academic Library Job Market: A Content Analysis Comparing Public and Technical Services." *College and Research Libraries* 53 (January 1992):55.

Richards, David. "The Research Libraries Group." In *Campus Strategies for Libraries and Electronic Information*, edited by Caroline Arms, 57-75. Bedford, Mass.: Digital Press, 1990.

Richardson, Ernest C. "Co-operation in Lending Among College and Reference Libraries." *Library Journal* 24 (1899):C32-36.

_____. "Presidential Address." *Library Journal* 30 (1905):C6.

Rindfull, Robert. "Information Delivery and Fax Technology." *Online* 14 (July 1990):98-101.

Rogers, Sharon J., and Charlene S. Hurt. "How Scholarly Communication Should Work in the 21st Century." *Chronicle of Higher Education* 35 (October 18, 1989):A56.

Rouse, W., and S. Rouse. *Management of Library Networks: Policy Analysis, Implementation and Control.* New York: Wiley, 1980.

Rouse, William B., and Sandra H. Rouse. "Assessing the Impact of Computer Technology on the Performance of Interlibrary Loan Networks." *Journal of the American Society for Information Science* 28 (March 1977):79-88.

Russell, Dorothy W. "Interlibrary Loan in a Network Environment: The Good and the Bad News." *Special Libraries* 73 (January 1982):1-26.

Russell, Harold. "The Interlibrary Loan Code." *ALA Bulletin* 33 (1939):321-25.

Rutstein, Joel S. "National and Local Resource Sharing: Issues in Cooperative Collection Development." *Collection Management* 7(2) (Summer 1985):1-6.

Saffady, William. *Introduction to Automation for Librarians*, 2d ed. Chicago: ALA, 1989.

Sanford, Daniel, Jr. *Inter-Institutional Agreements in Higher Education: An Analysis of the Documents Relating to Inter-Institutional Agreements with Special Reference to Coordination.* New York: Columbia University Teachers College, 1934.

Schilling, Charles W. *A Study of the Interlibrary Loan Activity of the National Library of Medicine for the Fiscal Year 1967.* Washington, D.C.: National Library of Medicine, 1968.

Schmidt, Steven J. "PC/Fax Boards." *Journal of Interlibrary Loan and Information Supply* 2 (1991):7.

"Sidebar: Revision of the Massachusetts Automated Resource Sharing Plan." *Library Hi Tech* 6 (1988):35-36.

Smith, Dennis E., and Clifford A. Lynch. "An Overview of Document Delivery Systems at the University of California." *Journal of Interlibrary Loan and Information Supply* 2 (1991):21-32.

Smith, Dianna Lynne. *The Magnitude and Characteristics of Interlibrary Loan Involving Public, Academic, and Special Libraries in Tennessee.* Urbana: University of Illinois, 1976.

Sobel, Lionel S. "The Framework of International Copyright." *Cardozo Arts and Entertainment Law Journal* 8 (1989):1-27.

Southeastern/Atlantic Regional Medical Library Services. *Document Delivery Policy, Region 2.* Baltimore, Md.: Southeastern/Atlantic Region Medical Library Services, 1989. (ERIC Document 324 015)

"Spectra FAX Introduces Special Request Fax Information Retrieval Service." *IDP Report* 10 (October 6, 1989):9.

Statford, Jean Slemmons. "OCLC and RLIN: The Comparisons Studied." *College and Research Libraries* 45 (2) (March 1984):123-27.

Stevens, R. E., and D. L. Smith. "Interlibrary Loan in Tennessee." *Southeastern Librarian* 27 (1977):175-80.

Stevens, Rolland. "Other Answers to ILL Problems." *American Libraries* 10 (November 1979):582.

Stevenson, Marsha. "Design Options for an On-Campus Document Delivery Program." *College and Research Libraries News* 51 (May 1990):437-40.

Stoller, Michael E. "Electronic Journals in the Humanities: A Survey and Critique." *Library Trends* 40 (Spring 1992):647-66.

Stump, R. M. "The Iowa Library Information Teletype Exchange (I-LITE)." *Iowa Library Quarterly* 21 (October 1970):142-45.

"Summary of Nelson Associates' Second Study of the NYSILL Network." *Bookmark* 28 (May 1969):239-47.

Swank, R. C. *Interlibrary Cooperation Under Title III of the Library Services and Construction Act*. Sacramento: California State Library, 1967.

Swartz, Roderick G. "The Multitype Library Cooperative Response to User Needs." In *Multitype Library Cooperation*, edited by Beth A. Hamilton and William B. Ernst, Jr., 11-18. New York: Bowkers, 1977.

Sweetland, James H., and Darlene E. Weingand. "Interlibrary Loan Transaction Fees in a Major Research Library: They Don't Stop the Borrowers." *Library and Information Science Research* 12 (January-March 1990):87-101.

Swisher, Robert, Kathleen L. Spitzer, Barbara Spriestersbach, Tim Markus, and Jerry M. Burris. "Telecommunications for School Library Media Centers." *School Library Media Quarterly* 19 (Spring 1991):153-60.

Taler, I., and P. Klapper. "Automated and Manual ILL: Time Effectiveness and Success Rate." *Information Technology and Libraries* 1 (1982):277-80.

Taylor, David C. "Concerning the 1968 ILL Code." *RQ* 8 (Spring 1969):195-96.

Tenopir, Carol. "Article Delivery Solutions." *Library Journal* 115 (June 1990):91-92.

Thayer, Candace W., and Kathryn P. Ray. "A Local Network for Sharing Resources and Technical Support: BACS/PHILNET." *Bulletin of the Medical Library Association* 76 (October 1988):343-45.

Thompson, Dorothea M. "The Correct Users of Library Data Bases Can Improve Interlibrary Loan Efficiency." *Journal of Academic Librarianship* 6 (May 1980):83-86.

Thomson, Sarah Katherine. *General Interlibrary Loan Services in Major Academic Libraries in the United States*. New York: Columbia University, 1967.

Trevvett, Melissa D. "Characteristics of Interlibrary Loan Requests at the Library of Congress." *College and Research Libraries* 40 (January 1979):36-43.

Trudell, Libby, and James Wolper. "Interlibrary Loan in New England." *College and Research Libraries* 39 (September 1978):365-71.

Turock, Betty J. "Organization Factors in Multitype Library Networking: A National Test of the Model." *Library and Information Science Research* 8 (1986):117-54.

_____. "Performance Factors in Multitype Library Networking." *Resource Sharing and Information Networks* 3(1) (1985-1986):15-38.

Uridge, Margaret D. "Labor Saving Form Aids Interlibrary Loan." *Library Journal* 76 (June 1951):1010-11.

"U.S. and Mexican Libraries Test Interlibrary Loan Program." *Library Journal* 114 (November 1989):28.

Van House, N. "California Libraries and Networking: Report of a Survey." Belmont, Calif.: Peninsula Library System, 1985.

Waldhart, T. J. "Performance Evaluation of Interlibrary Loan in the United States: A Review of Research." *Library and Information Science Research* 7 (1985):313-31.

Waldhart, Thomas J. "The Growth of Interlibrary Loan Among ARL University Libraries." *Journal of Academic Librarianship* 10 (September 1984):204-8.

Walters, Edward M. "The Issues and Needs of Local Library Consortium." *Journal of Library Administration* 5 (Fall-Winter 1984):15-28.

Wareham, N. *The Report on Library Cooperation, 1984*, 5th ed. Chicago: ALA, 1984.

Watson, E. P. "Interlibrary Loan Code for Louisiana College and University Libraries." *Louisiana Library Association Bulletin* 26 (Summer 1963):69-70.

Weaver, C. G. "Electronic Document Delivery: Directing Interlibrary Loan Traffic Through Multiple Electronic Networks." *Bulletin of the Medical Library Association* 72 (1984):187-92.

Weaver-Meyers, Pat. *Interlibrary Loans in Academic and Research Libraries: Workload and Staffing*. Washington, D.C.: ACRL, 1989. (ERIC Document 317 208)

Weber, David C., and Frederick C. Lynden. "Survey of Interlibrary Cooperation." In *Proceedings of the Conference on Interlibrary Communications and Information Networks*, edited by Joseph Becker, 69-81. Chicago: ALA, 1971.

Werking, Richard Hume. "Automation in College Libraries." *College and Research Libraries* 52 (March 1991):117-23.

Wessling, Julie E. "Benefits from Automated ILL Borrowing Records: Use of ILLRKS in an Academic Library." *RQ* 29 (Winter 1989):209-18.

"Western Michigan TWX Serves Extension Students." *Library Journal* 93 (November 15, 1968):4234.

Whitcomb, Laurie. "OCLC's Epic System Offers a New Way to Search the OCLC Database." *Online* 14 (January 1990):45-50.

White, Carl M. "Services to Scholars." *Library Trends* 3 (1954):151.

White, Herbert S. *Librarians and the Awakening from Innocence*. Boston: G. K. Hall, 1989.

"Willful Copyright Infringement: In Search of a Standard." *Washington Law Review* 65 (October 1990):903-20.

Williams, Edwin E., and Ruth V. Noble. *Preliminary Memoranda: Conference on International Cultural, Educational, and Scientific Exchanges, Princeton University, November 25-26, 1946.* Chicago: ALA, 1947.

Williams, Gordon. "Interlibrary Loan Service in the United States." In *Essays on Information and Libraries*, edited by Keith Barr and Maurice Line, 204-5. Hamden, Conn.: Linnet Books, 1975.

Wilson, David L. "Libraries." *Chronicle of Higher Education* 38 (October 23, 1991):A21.

_____. "Researchers Get Direct Access to Huge Data Base." *Chronicle of Higher Education* 38 (October 9, 1991):A24-28.

Wilson, Louis R., and Maurice F. Tauber. *The University Library.* Chicago: University of Chicago Press, 1945.

Wilson, Louis Round, and Maurice F. Tauber. *The University Library*, 2d ed. New York: Columbia University Press, 1956.

Wilson, M. P. "How to Set Up a Telefacsimile Network—The Pennsylvania Libraries' Experience." *Online* 12 (May 1988):15-25.

Winchell, Constance M. *Locating Books for Interlibrary Loans.* New York: Wilson, 1930.

Wood, James L. *A Review of the Availability of Primary Scientific and Technical Documents Within the United States.* Washington, D.C.: Chemical Abstracts Service, 1969.

Wormann, Curt D. "Aspects of International Library Cooperation—Historical and Contemporary." *Library Quarterly* 38 (October 1968):347.

Wyoming Library Association. "State Interlibrary Loan Code." *Wyoming Library Roundup* 29 (March 1974):12-15.

Yen, Alfred C. "When Authors Won't Sell: Parody, Fair Use, and Efficiency in Copyright Law." *University of Colorado Law Review* 62 (1991):79-108.

# Index